DELTA FOUR

Australian Riflemen in Vietnam

GARY McKAY

ALLEN & UNWIN

First published 1996
This edition published in 1998 by
Allen & Unwin
9 Atchison Street
St Leonards NSW 1590
Australia
Phone: (61 2) 8425 0100
Fax: (61 2) 9906 2218
E-mail: frontdesk@allen-unwin.com.au
Web: http://www.allen-unwin.com.au

National Library of Australia
Cataloguing-in-Publication entry:

McKay, Gary.
   Delta Four: Australian riflemen in Vietnam.

   Includes index.
   ISBN 1 86448 905 7.

   1. Australia. Army. Royal Australian Regiment. Battalion,
   4th. 2. Vietnamese Conflict, 1961–1975—Personal
   narratives, Australian. 3. Vietnamese Conflict, 1961–1975—
   Veterans—Australia. 4. Vietnamese Conflict, 1961–1975—
   Veterans—Australia—Interviews. I. Title.

959.7043394

Typeset in Bembo and Garamond by DOCUPRO, Sydney
Printed by Australian Print Group, Maryborough, Vic.

10 9 8 7 6 5 4 3 2 1

CONTENTS

MAPS AND ILLUSTRATIONS

MAPS

ILLUSTRATIONS

THE INFANTEERS

They came from sun-tanned Aussie stock
of our cities and plains so wide
and left their souls in Vietnam
and only their families cried.
We may never see their kind again
in these delinquent years
as those young Aussies of city and bush
the brave young infanteers.
'Twas they who heard the nation's call
and they who volunteered
to leave our shores by ship and plane
and only their families cheered.
'Twas they who followed up the call
their ANZAC fathers made,
and fought the wily Viet Cong
with rifle and grenade.
But now the swinging Sixties
hippies' days are dead,
when brave young men through Asia's jungles
forced their way ahead.
By forests dim and jungle vine
towards the unknown quest,
to fight at last the elusive Cong
from within his hidden nest.
To you who fought the Asian war
your country had decreed,
we think of you in silence now,
you, who fought for God and creed.
To you who fought the Viet Cong
within your youthful years
the blood and soul of our nation's life
the brave young infanteers.

PETER SWEET
CHRISTMAS 1992
9 PLATOON, CHARLIE COMPANY, 8 RAR

This poem was written by Peter Sweet, a National Serviceman who served with Charlie Company, 8 RAR in South Vietnam in 1969–70. It was written as a Christmas gift for his mother and was intended to be for all infanteers who went to Vietnam and not for just those who were left behind as, in Peter Sweet's own words, 'all infanteers left a small part of themselves in Vietnam'.

PROLOGUE

BEFORE THIS STORY OF AUSTRALIAN RIFLEMEN can be told, it is necessary to retrace those steps that led us into the Vietnam War and understand how we as a nation became involved and what our involvement was. This is only a brief potted history and serious students of the war should delve more deeply to fully understand the entire breadth of the Australian involvement.

Australian forces were on operations in South Vietnam for the decade from 1962. It was the last occasion our land forces have been committed to active service (apart from the air defence gunners aboard H.M. ships in the Gulf War of 1991 and a battalion group in Somalia in 1993), and like all other wars we have fought, this conflict was not of Australia's making. But, unlike any of the previous conflicts in which Australians fought, the Vietnam War so divided Australia that it was not until 1987, some 15 years after the last troops returned, were the soldiers finally welcomed home. And only in October 1992 was a memorial to that conflict built and dedicated.

Australian operations were essentially low level and set at battalion level, or company group and sometimes platoon level. On a number of occasions our forces engaged Viet Cong and North Vietnamese Regular troops in major contacts, but the Long Tan and Coral–Balmoral style battles were relatively infrequent.

In the fifties and sixties the fighting in Indo-China was not of much interest to most Australians. The fighting in Vietnam was seen by the majority of people as an internal struggle for power. The background to our involvement can be traced to the late fifties when the 'Domino Theory' was developed as the central tenet of western political thinking and communism became Public Enemy Number One. The purges of communists and their sympathisers in the United States by Senator Joe McCarthy was widely reported and accepted by most Australians. Indeed, a similar public campaign, but with a more general thrust, driven by some immensely influential personalities such as R.G. Menzies, Arthur Fadden, Archbishop Mannix and B.A. Santamaria, occurred in this country. Our national leaders held very strong concerns about world-wide communist expansion and when South Korea was invaded, there was a prompt Australian offer to contribute to the relieving United Nations force. The perceived threat from communist expansion to regional security saw the formation of the South East Asia Treaty Organisation (SEATO) in Manila in 1954. Australia was a foundation member and, under the terms of the treaty, agreed to come to the defence of any threatened member nation.

The First Indo-China War ended in 1954, after the humiliating defeat of the French at Dien Bien Phu. At the subsequent peace talks in Geneva, France and the Viet Minh agreed to a demilitarised zone (DMZ) at the Seventeenth Parallel (separating the north from the south) to be supervised by an International Commission. In due course, there would be national elections to unify the country.

Accordingly, the communists took control of the industrialised north while the rural south continued to be ruled, in absentia, by the French puppet Emperor Bao Dai with Ngo Dinh Diem as Premier. The SEATO Nations also offered protocol status to South Vietnam, Cambodia and Laos, which meant they would be defended by the Treaty Nations should any of them be threatened. The offer was accepted.

After a referendum in 1955, Emperor Bao Dai was deposed and the Republic of South Vietnam was established with Diem as the first President. He immediately rejected the concept of national elections, arguing that the poll would not be free in the communist north where the population was larger by three to four million and so would automatically outweigh the vote of the fledgling Republic in the south. His stand was supported by President Eisenhower with a massive injection of US aid, including military advisers.

The Republic began to develop into a reasonably prosperous and peaceful state. North Vietnam, realising that reunification would not be achieved through elections, decided to force the overthrow of the Saigon government through an insurgent campaign, and re-activated the Viet Minh units in the south.

By 1959, the Second Indo-China War—or Vietnam War—had begun in earnest. The local guerillas, now known as Viet Cong, were receiving substantial support from the North Vietnamese Army, the NVA. Unable to cope with the growing insurgency, the Republic requested assistance under the terms of the SEATO Treaty. The response of the United States was predictably swift and Australia followed suit soon after.

Recent relevations from Government papers released under the 'thirty year' rule indicate that the Menzies government was extremely keen to get involved in Vietnam in order to gain regional security support from the United States. In May of 1962, the deployment of a team of 30 military advisers—the Australian Army Training Team Vietnam or AATTV as it came to be known—was announced. This was the beginning of over 10 years of Australian commitment to the conflict.

CHRONOLOGY OF THE WAR

The Vietnam War can be broken into a number of clearly defined phases:
     1962–1967
     1968

1969–1972, and
Post 1972.

I have singled out 1968 for special consideration because of
various events that made it a watershed in the conflict.

The war 1962–1967

In January 1962 the US military presence consisted of 2394
advisers with a one star commander. On 8 February that year
Headquarters Military Assistance Command Vietnam (MACV)
was established in Saigon. By the end of 1962 the US Forces
in country had swelled to over 11 000, and by the end of
1964 personnel from New Zealand, Korea, the Philippines,
Spain, Taiwan and Thailand had joined Australian and American troops.

November 1963 to January 1964 saw major political
upheavals in both Vietnam and the US. In Saigon a military
coup resulted in the assassination of President Diem and
General Duong Van Minh came to power. This began a
period of political instability in South Vietnam which saw
eight governments in 20 months. In America, John F. Ken-
nedy was assassinated in Dallas on 22 November 1963. Lyndon
Baines Johnson became the new President.

On 2 August 1964, the US destroyers *Maddox* and *C.
Turner Joy* were attacked by North Vietnamese patrol boats
while operating in the Gulf of Tonkin. The American ships
had no trouble in defending themselves but the attack had
lasting consequences. Two days later the US Navy carried out
retaliatory air strikes into North Vietnam and then, on 7
August, Congress passed the Tonkin Gulf Resolution that gave
the President unlimited powers to authorise any action to repel
armed attacks against US Forces. Even more importantly, it
authorised the President to take any steps necessary to assist
any nation requesting aid under the SEATO Treaty, in defence
of its freedom. In short, it provided the President with a *carte
blanche* to fight the war as he saw fit.

After a series of guerilla attacks on US facilities, on 2 March
1965 President Johnson approved the aerial bombardment of

North Vietnam. Six days later, the first US combat troops arrived at Da Nang. By March 1966 anti-government and anti-American rioting had erupted in South Vietnam resulting in General Nguyen Van Thieu being elected President.

The war—1968

In January, following the death in the previous month of Harold Holt, John Gray Gorton was appointed Prime Minister of Australia. It was in this year that the anti-war movement gained momentum and strength under the guidance of the very anti-war Labor Party.

On 30 January 1968, the North Vietnamese Army and Viet Cong launched their Tet or New Year Offensive country wide. Whilst the operation was defeated, North Vietnam gained substantial political mileage. The television coverage of the offensive suddenly brought home to the American and Australian peoples that the war was not going as well as the politicians and the military had claimed. This gave enormous impetus to the anti-war lobby.

The third significant event of that year was the election of Richard Nixon as US President. He came to power with a mandate to withdraw US troops from Vietnam.

The war—1969–1972

On 25 January 1969, in accordance with President Nixon's election promise, formal truce negotiations opened in Paris. Though in January the American strength in Vietnam reached its peak of 542 400 personnel, the American wind-down was already in train. On 8 June, Nixon announced the withdrawal of the first 25 000 combat personnel. The following month his 'Guam' doctrine paved the way for the 'Vietnamisation' of the war and the gradual shift of US ground forces to defensive operations in coastal areas. However, in March 1970, US and South Vietnamese forces attacked communist bases in Cambodia. This action inflamed the anti-war lobby and, in December, Congress repealed the Tonkin Gulf Resolution. Thus, all future policy decisions on the war had to be presented to the Congress.

1971 saw the South Vietnamese take the war into Laos. Whilst this operation did not include US advisers, it was supported by the US Air Force. On 1 July the withdrawal of US advisers from South Vietnamese units began. This is also the year on which this book is centred. Delta Company, Fourth Battalion, the Royal Australian Regiment (4 RAR) served in South Vietnam from April 1971 until Delta Four was withdrawn in March 1972. By August 1972 the last US ground combat troops had departed, leaving only 43 500 airmen and support personnel.

The war—post 1972

After a 17-year struggle, the end for the Republic came quickly. On 23 January 1973 a cease fire agreement between the US and the North Vietnamese was concluded in Paris and within two months the last American military forces had departed. Only one year later the final North Vietnamese offensive opened in the Central Highlands. In April, President Thieu resigned and General Minh became Head of State. Two days later the North Vietnamese entered Saigon. Within three years SEATO, too, had passed into history.

THE AUSTRALIAN BUILD UP—1962–1967

Australian Army Training Team Vietnam (AATTV)

In May 1962, the Menzies government announced the deployment to Vietnam of a small group of officers, warrant officers and sergeants.

The training team formed part of the US advisory system and came under the operational control of the US Military Assistance Advisory Group, later expanded into Military Assistance Command Vietnam ·(MACV). Initially the Australian role was training only and the advisers were not permitted to accompany the South Vietnamese on operations. After consultation with the US, and President Johnson's appeal to 'other flags', Menzies announced in June 1964 that Australia's role would extend to advising field units. To support the team, a

RAAF transport flight with six Caribou aircraft was deployed to Vung Tau airfield in August of that year. The flight expanded to become 35 Squadron in June 1966 and remained operational until February 1972.

Within three years, AATTV had more than trebled in size to 100 all ranks. Members of the team were now deployed with each battalion of the two South Vietnamese Divisions in I Corps area and elements were serving with the US Special Forces, the Vietnamese Territorials, the CIA, as province and district advisers and in Vietnamese Army and Ranger Training centres. On 29 April 1965 the Australian government announced the deployment of an infantry battalion to Vietnam and with it, a headquarters to command the total Australian force. Headquarters Australian Force Vietnam opened in Saigon on 5 May.

This book is about the men of one of the rifle companies of 4 RAR on their second tour of duty in South Vietnam. 4 RAR was raised at Woodside in South Australia on 1 February 1964 and was on operational service in Malaysia and Borneo only 18 months after being raised. In June 1968 it was deployed to South Vietnam where it served until 19 May 1969. It was fortunate for 4 RAR that many of the men who were experienced in jungle fighting in Borneo and Malaysia stayed on to be deployed on the first tour to Vietnam.

The Battalion returned to Australia from active service in December 1969, re-deployed to its new home in Lavarack Barracks in Townsville to join 2 RAR as part of the 3rd Task Force. 4 RAR was deployed in late April 1971 to replace 2 RAR. The Battalion, less Delta Four, returned to Townsville in December 1971 and Delta Company followed in March 1972.

Indo-China.

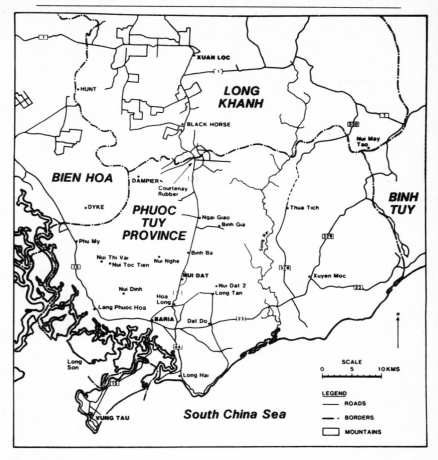

Phuoc Tuy Province.

PREFACE

When I told the Australian War Memorial (AWM) Grants Committee that I wanted to follow up from my first book *In Good Company* with a project to research the ethos of the Australian infantryman in battle, I could sense some scepticism. After all there are many books about the fortunes and misfortunes of Australian Diggers. But, what I wanted to explore was why does the Australian soldier do those things that have so uniquely placed him in a position of admiration and high status by fellow warriors?

I wanted to delve into the ethos of the Australian rifleman. Having been an infantryman myself for some 27 years, I had a pretty good feel for the nature of the beast, but typically I suppose I had never done much more than scratch the surface for fear of being thought of as some kind of Athenian by my fellow grunts.

The world of the Australian Digger is definitely a culture. It has been established for almost a hundred years and has been placed into the crucible of battle many times and forged in the toughest of environments. I intend to expose that culture to the reader and to give some insight into what the men of Delta Four think about all of those aspects, tangible and otherwise, that shape and define their culture as infantrymen. Note that I say 'he' in this book because it deals only with the experiences of a select group of men—the riflemen of Delta Four—and I am going to avoid the use of the expression 'he/she' for ease of reading.

I interviewed a number of men who made up the basic element of a rifle company in Vietnam in 1971–72. They were the men of Delta Company, the Fourth Battalion of The Royal Australian Regiment. With the aid of a John Treloar Research Grant from the Australian War Memorial, I have been able to visit a cross section of men who made up Delta Four, some 20 all told or about one fifth of the company. They range in rank from the Officer Commanding, a major, through every rank in the company to the lowest—the private soldier.

Because about 50 per cent of the Diggers were National Servicemen they have been represented in about the same proportion. I also interviewed people who supported Delta Four on their operations but were not actually posted to the rifle company. In addition, I travelled back to Vietnam in 1993 with some of the men and we spoke to the former enemy to determine what they thought of our Diggers as warriors.

Delta Four has been born out of an Oral History project for the AWM. The product of that project is not just an oral history but a method of passing on those things essential to an infantryman's survival in battle. Each of the chapters will reveal the various facets of the training, the jobs, the relationships, the fears, dangers, courage, *esprit de corps*, morale and leadership that bind these men together in the unreal and deadly world of combat. The elements of training a rifleman are much like building blocks, and what I hope I have done is to show what it is that binds those bricks together when the enemy, the terrain, the weather are all trying to pull them apart. All of the subjects in this book have graciously allowed their transcripts to be archived with the AWM and they are available for researchers, who may wish to explore their thoughts more deeply.

Naturally, I am deeply indebted to every single one of the men for allowing me to intrude into their lives after such an absence and in some cases stir up memories that many wanted to lay to rest. I must also thank the staff at the AWM for their assistance in the initial stages of the project, especially Bill Brassell, Bill Fogarty, Anne-Marie Conde and Dr Peter Stanley who gave me the initial push. I must also thank my wife, Gay, who despite battling severe cancer during these last few years, has helped me enormously with the transcripts and once again suffered as I have banged away on my keyboard late into the nights after work. She has been an inspiration to me and I hope and pray she survives to see this book come into print. To my publisher John Iremonger who I am so happy to see back in the Allen & Unwin fold who guided me and encouraged me and gave me the latitude to delay my work when my wife was undergoing chemotherapy and surgery, I offer my deep thanks. I must also thank Ian Bowring who took over the military stable from John Iremonger toward the end of this three and half year project and guided it to its successful conclusion. And finally but not least, to my editors, Jo Jarrah and Julia Collingwood, for turning my words into prose and shaping my manuscript into this book, I also extend my gratitude. This book would not have been possible without the assistance of the Australian War Memorial John Treloar Research Grant.

1

TRAINING, TRAINING AND MORE BLOODY TRAINING

I know every company that has been to Vietnam probably thought they were in the best company—I have really got no doubt that ours was. I think it would have been very few if any companies went to Vietnam better trained, better prepared or a tighter unit than our company.[1]

WALLY BURFORD
LANCE CORPORAL, 12 PLATOON

FROM MOTHS TO BUTTERFLIES

From the moment a man enlists into the Army he undergoes a metamorphosis from civilian to soldier through a process known as 'training'. Training is designed to teach the soldier that he is now a member of a team and that everything he does from now on is for a cause far greater than his own desires.

In effect, the training at places like the Recruit Training Battalion at Kapooka deliberately aims to 'break' the individual down from an independent thinking person into a tool that the Army can use. The Army wants to re-shape and re-mould him into what it requires and demands. One National Serviceman,

Wally Burford, who experienced the charms of recruit training at Puckapunyal in Victoria said of it:

> It was that bloody bleak over there. I wasn't the sort of person to get homesick, but by gee, I think everyone in the hut was homesick for the first couple of weeks there. Just the 'busy-ness' of it all. I think in retrospect it was a very good idea. They never gave you two minutes to think about anything else other than the Army for the first four weeks. Running from place to place, needles, medicals, mental tests and the whole shooting match. I think it set the trend for my time in the Army in that you got used to handle exhaustion.[2]

The Army wants a person who will respond immediately and without question to orders, exercise self discipline and do exactly what they are told. But at the same time the Army also wants its soldiers to show initiative and to use the grey matter between their ears when required to do so. It does not want automatons. The Australian experience in battle shows that the Digger is generously imbued with this characteristic and it is encouraged throughout the soldier's training.

According to Private Dean Cooke, a Regular soldier and rifleman, to be later a section second-in-command (2IC), the aim was 'to find out who is suitable and who is not. It's no good going on further if you can't get through the pre-grade stages.'[3] It was probably a good thing the initial training was tough and uncompromising because there were two types of soldiers who had to be melded into a homogenous group.

THE MELTING POT—REGULAR ARMY AND NATIONAL SERVICEMEN

The training for the individuals who made up Delta Four was extremely varied. The officers came from three different training backgrounds: one was trained in the United Kingdom under the British officer training system, three were trained at the Officer Cadet School, Portsea in Victoria and one (the author) was trained as a National Service Officer at the Officer Training Unit, Scheyville in New South Wales.

The senior non-commissioned officers (warrant officer, staff sergeant and sergeants) all progressed through their careers by attending and passing promotion courses that dealt specifically with the essence of their trade—namely infantry soldiering. Each step was assessed and their suitability to command men was always questioned.

For the junior non-commissioned officers (corporals and lance corporals), it was a different kettle of fish. Some of the junior NCOs had been through many years of soldiering and some had been on previous campaigns such as in Borneo or a previous tour of duty in South Vietnam as a Private soldier. About half of the junior NCOs in Delta Four were National Servicemen and had very limited experience. They did, however, have the benefit of being trained directly by the battalion as Initial Employment Trainees (IETs). They received their Infantry Corps Training in the Fourth Battalion, the Royal Australian Regiment (4 RAR) rather than at the Infantry Centre at Ingleburn or the Third Training Battalion at Singleton in New South Wales. This meant that the soldiers were assessed for their leadership abilities by many of the NCOs of the battalion with whom they would later work closely.

The conscripted National Servicemen who joined 4 RAR and Delta Four were usually twenty years old. There were some soldiers who had deferred their two-year call-up, consequently they were usually a couple of years older than their Regular Army counterparts and had often seen a bit more of the world. When it came to promoting Diggers into positions of junior leadership, it was more often based on ability to lead than pure infantry basic skills. Therefore, it was not uncommon to see National Servicemen in command positions despite their relatively junior time in the Army.

The Regular soldier who was allotted to the Infantry Corps after his recruit training at Kapooka was usually between 17 and 19 years old and had finished a minimum of three years at high school. More often than not he came from a lower to middle-income bracket and he was usually from the city. The Regular soldier had to sign on for a minimum of three or six years service. He could not leave before that time unless he was dishonourably or administratively discharged or released from his obligation on medical grounds.

There was little animosity between the two groups of 4 RAR. There was always a lot of chiacking between the two but there was very little to differentiate them, especially in basic infantry skills. The Company Quarter Master Sergeant (CQMS), Bob Hann, said:

> I thought they were tremendous. That is it purely and simply. I don't know whether the soldiers we had were typical of National Servicemen or not. I don't know whether our company was typical, but by Christ we had some fine young National Servicemen in our company.
>
> They were more mature. I suppose because the Regular Army soldier tended to join the Army when he was 17 or about his mid-twenties. Not many of them come in at 20 and it seemed to me that was a pretty good age. We had a few dunder heads amongst them I suppose but I always tried to look at the National Servicemen we had and the comparable Regular Army soldier and there is no comparison. The National Serviceman was a stand out in my book.[4]

One of the company commanders of Delta Four, Major Jerry Taylor, had also served with many soldiers during his regimental career and he believed that National Service offered more than numbers to the rapidly expanding standing Army that was committed to several theatres throughout South-East Asia at the time:

> I hope Australia knows the debt of gratitude it owes to its National Servicemen of the Vietnam years. In my view they were some of the finest young men that it's been my privilege to encounter in all my years of soldiering. And a credit, too, to the system which trained them. I only ever came across two who really objected to it, and they didn't go to Vietnam anyway.
>
> By the time I arrived in Delta Company it consisted of 55 per cent Regular soldiers, and 45 per cent National Servicemen. It was essentially impossible to tell the difference between the two groups—they were all totally

professional. Apart from a bit of good natured leg pulling by one group of the other, relations between the two were always excellent. In my view National Servicemen achieved standards of professionalism that were just as high as their Regular counterparts. They were absolutely equal in physical courage.[5]

This maturity that is spoken of was confirmed by one of the Regular soldiers from 11 Platoon who went on to make the Army his career. Geoffrey 'Jethro' Hannah spent his tour of duty as a rifleman and section 2IC. He thought:

They were older and I can say now, they were more mature than us guys. They had civil employment for quite a while before they came into the Army. I found them to be snobbish at first because we were younger but they couldn't accept that we had been in the Army a little bit longer than them. But generally the National Serviceman to me was that you definitely needed their maturity to keep us younger blokes in line.[6]

TRAIN HARD—FIGHT EASY

The platoons of Delta Four went through minor-infantry-tactics training within their sections in the training area behind the battalion lines at Lavarack Barracks in Townsville. As they developed and honed those skills, they progressed to platoon training at the Mt Stuart Training Area where they could practice platoon formations, drills and manoeuvre at platoon level. This training was very much influenced by the young platoon commanders who were guided quite firmly by their platoon sergeants, all of whom had seen action on a previous tour of duty in South Vietnam. This trust placed in these young leaders was essential in building up the morale and confidence of the men who would later bear the brunt of close combat.

The real training for war began at the Jungle Training Centre (JTC), Canungra, situated in the Gold Coast Hinterland. All soldiers warned for active service and units of battalion size were required to attend training at the JTC. Most of the instructors at Canungra were Vietnam veterans. The other major preparation for deploying to Vietnam was the final training exercise which was usually held at Shoalwater Bay just north of Rockhampton. Here umpires were allotted to assess the performance of the platoons, companies and units for the benefit of the commanding officer and the Task Force commander who owned that particular battalion.

Canungra carried a well deserved reputation as a 'hard' place and where one would be driven to the extremes of physical and mental endurance. It was often quoted at Diggers 'that if they couldn't hack Canungra, they wouldn't be able to hack Vietnam'. The Battle Efficiency (BE) Course that ran for four weeks at JTC was the acid test at Canungra. The soldiers were put to the test in a series of exercises in the jungle around Canungra. The instructors, known as Directing Staff or DS, not only taught but assessed the performance of each individual and especially the leaders of the Diggers. The DS were merciless in their reports on leaders and the units who were put through their paces at JTC. The importance of this external assessment of the capabilities of the company and the actual training in the jungles around Canungra was seen by the Company Sergeant Major (CSM), Warrant Officer Class Two Noel Huish as invaluable:

> We knew that this is the sort of country that we were going to be into. But, more importantly, the instructional staff at JTC were all highly skilled and experienced in precisely the sort of thing we were about to become involved in, and their imparting knowledge was vital.[7]

As the Company Sergeant Major, Huish was in a position of not only being a trainer in the company but CSM, and he saw the assessment of the company by the DS at JTC as vital in preparing the company for jungle fighting:

> I was able to get an overview of just how good or bad we were and of course so were the JTC staff, and so their reports were vital to fix any little bloody errors that we still

had. Because on your own you could do it wrong a hundred times and not realise it. So, I think the assessment that we got was invaluable.[8]

But nothing in this world is totally perfect and one of the Delta Four platoon commanders, Second Lieutenant Kevin Byrne, was not totally enamoured with some of the DS, feeling that some should have been more carefully selected:

Some umpires I found absolutely useless. They were nit picking and they had, I guess, an abrasive attitude. Some umpires were quite good. I remember going on one exercise in particular, in fact it was an assessment exercise at Canungra and I had a tall gangling umpire called [Captain] Lochie McLean, and I thought, where did this guy spring from? But I learnt a hell of a lot from Lochie McLean as an umpire. Obviously he reported on me and assessed me but at the same time he taught me.[9]

Canungra became the 'Passing Out' stage of their training in the minds of many who went through the BE Course. They felt that once they had been through that phase of their preparation for going to Vietnam, they were virtually ready to go to war and only needed fine tuning. Second Lieutenant Kevin Bryne, commander of 10 Platoon, Delta Four continues:

I think the thing that was special about Canungra was that it had a variety of different types of training facilities at hand. It was intense, it was deliberately intense, and the other special thing about it was, Canungra was an independent assessment phase where the battalion and the company and the platoons went through altogether and there was a healthy competitiveness with your other companies, your brother platoons. Also, it was a tough environment and I think that was tremendous training, particularly the live firing range, the ambush ranges, that awful confidence course and obstacle course. At the end of it, I remember jumping on the Herc out at Amberley and flying back to Townsville and I felt as if I'd really earnt my bread and butter.[10]

Some commanding officers sacked their platoon and occasionally company commanders for their inability to perform when under pressure brought about by long hours, tough physical endurance and an ability to respond quickly and aggressively in the jungle. For some soldiers, Canungra was the trigger that alerted them that they were finally on their way to a war zone. One National Serviceman who became a reinforcement to Delta Company, Grahame Tooth, remembers the Jungle Training Centre in this way:

> Once you got to Canungra, I think it dawned on you that what you were training for—that you were going to Vietnam, or that there was a possibility of it, because everything was oriented around incidents that you would come across in Vietnam. They would have a little short course set up in the jungle, where you walked through and there was all different things like booby traps and a bloke hiding in a bunker. Another couple of blokes jumped out of a tree and so it was set up like a real life situation which you would find once you went to Vietnam. They had a trench-like system set up where you crawled along this trench and while you're crawling through, these blokes were firing live rounds over your head with an old Vickers machine gun, and of course with these live rounds flying over your head you're actually shitting yourself, but it gave you a real-life situation of being shot at.[11]

TRAINING FOR WAR

Many Diggers and their officers thought that Vietnam was never as hard as the training they did at Canungra or on the battalion exercises at High Range or Mt Spec in the tropical training areas north of Townsville. Each battalion exercise was designed to hone the skills necessary for conducting operations in Phuoc Tuy Province. Exercise GRANITE VALE at High Range north of Townsville was plain hard yakka in the heat and tropical savannah. When the battalion deployed on their last exercise THIRD STAB at Mt Spec it was more like Vietnam when 36 inches fell in 10 days. Mt Spec is hilly, thickly vegetated and tough terrain and was a demanding locale for training. One thing the hard training did do was to provide a bond and experience for the men of Delta Four to relate to when things got tough later in Vietnam, a view which is echoed by Private Wally Burford:

> I think the training in Townsville really prepared us for the job that we ended up having to do in Vietnam. Townsville itself I found a lot harder and the conditions a lot more harsh than they ever were in Vietnam. It made the physical side of Vietnam a lot easier. Our preparation was absolutely first class.[12]

The aim of his training at Canungra and on the battalion exercises was:

> To fight as part of a unit in Vietnam, as part of an infantry company in Vietnam. To be part of a team and I think most certainly that was accomplished.[13]

Belief in the efficacy of one's training is important in shaping the attitudes and behaviour of soldiers. If they have a strong belief that their training has fully prepared them for the task ahead, then they will probably react in the most positive manner when first confronted by real combat. It is essential also in developing that intangible feeling of *esprit de corps* which can be the cement that holds the rifle section, platoon and company together. Infantrymen must have confidence in themselves and their team if they hope to survive in combat. A veteran from the Borneo Confrontation and from Vietnam, Platoon Sergeant Daryl Jenkin felt:

> Anxious, probably, as I had spent three years in Asia before that. Not frightened. I don't think at any stage was I frightened. After the training you do, you tend to think that 'it won't happen to me'. It might be happening all around you and you still tend to think that nothing will happen to me—that happens to other people, not me.[14]

9

Recruit Grahame Tooth (*left*) photographed with another National Serviceman in their newly issued equipment at Kapooka in 1970. Australians were still wearing boots and gaiters in training units in the early 1970s and living in Second World War huts such as those behind Recruit Tooth. (*Photograph courtesy of Grahame Tooth*)

PERFECT PRACTICE MAKES PERFECT

For all that, training for training's sake is not enough. The training must be relevant and proper. Australian Rugby Union Coach Bob Dwyer said to me in 1984 that, 'Practice doesn't make perfect. Perfect practice makes perfect.'[15]

The men of Delta Four were required to train for operations in a Counter Revolutionary Warfare environment and in a tropical, jungle terrain. They were lucky. Canungra had given them the drills and techniques. They had been exposed to the tough terrain around Mt Spec—rugged, tropical ground on which to perfect their skills and test their limits of physical endurance. One wonders how other battalions coped, such as 3 RAR, who on their second tour of duty were deployed from South Australia in winter and arrived to fight in the jungle clad plains of Phuoc Tuy Province. The simple art of navigation is completely different in the jungle. There are no reference points, re-sections for navigation are next to impossible and it becomes a matter of counting paces and travelling on bearings. The longer one does it, practices it, lives it night and day, the better you become and the more confident you are about where you think you are. However, Second Lieutenant Graham Spinkston thought that the jungle training done by Delta Four was good but not long enough and that the troops were not conditioned enough. He cited:

> Exercises tended to be 10 days including one day getting there and one day getting back. I think we needed to spend three weeks solid in the jungle and get used to being tired, dirty and under the pressure that we had on operations; whereas you knew that you were there for 10 days and you could pace yourself for that and with a couple of days to go, you knew that the exercise was nearly over and there was a battalion attack or a cordon and search coming up and when that was finished, we were all going home. I don't think we had the length of training in one hit that we got on operations. The first operation was six weeks and that was a long drag and at the end of that the whole company was just about stuffed.[16]

REALISM IN TRAINING

The closer the training is to war, the better the soldiers will react when they are ultimately faced with their first contact with the enemy. Fighting in the jungle is about reflexes and the soldier needs to know as much about what it will be like and how he will be feeling when the time comes. It is a fact of life that one does not always win, and often in the sharp, violent and sudden clashes in close country no one really knows who won or lost the encounter except for the casualty count on each side. Consequently when platoons take casualties without having an enemy body to bury at the end of it all, they can be dismayed and lose confidence. One Private soldier, Bob Meehan thought that:

> All through training the enemy always died and we always came out on top. So, maybe in training, occasionally we should be killed so we know that we are not invincible. We all went over as if we were going to win it. So, maybe in hindsight we had a false impression of ourselves. Maybe

in training they should have killed us off, killed a few of us just to get the reality going. Thrown a bit of blood on us, a bit of red stuff.[17]

Meehan's attitude is not defeatist but quite realistic. Sooner or later soldiers will die in combat given enough exposure to it. For the average rifleman the chances of being killed were one in 16. The chances of being wounded were substantially greater, about one in five or six, especially with mine incidents. In Delta Four as it turned out, it was one in ten of being killed and one in 10 of being wounded. But statistics count for nought when the aim of the training is to prepare soldiers for that dramatic eventuality and the clash and clamour of close combat. The key to survival is drills and to be alert and ready for the unexpected.

FIELD FIRING

There are almost no occasions in jungle warfare and close combat for riflemen to take a well aimed shot at their enemy. More often than not, they are standing, moving or crawling along the jungle floor. For scouts, instinctive shooting is the key to surviving the initial moments of the contact. They must be able to fire instinctively and accurately at their target without taking the time to bring the weapon to the shoulder. For the remainder of the riflemen, it is about being able to engage targets in a close country environment; being able to shoot in the bush; being able to shoot and look through the foliage and successfully hit fleeting targets with some certainty. For all riflemen, regardless of what weapon they carry, must also know when not to fire. The practice of taking soldiers out to a rifle range and engaging Figure 11 targets on whistle blasts on a grassy mound is fine for initial skills training and to allow them to develop basic shooting, grouping and aiming skills. But, when those infantry soldiers are training for war they must be shooting in a field firing environment at every opportunity. This includes carrying their full basic load of ammunition to enable them to adjust their webbing, their bodies and their drills to the weight around their waists. Perfect practice makes perfect. The more a rifleman is familiar with shooting in, through and around vegetation, the better he will become. Field firing adds another dimension and greater reality to training. One of the section commanders in 11 Platoon, Corporal Warren Dowell saw its value in his own preparation:

> I would have liked to have seen more live-firing exercises and more calling in of artillery and that sort of thing. It was only once we got in country that my platoon commander actually started—probably because training restrictions were lifted off him—pushing us through doing dry DFs (artillery Defensive Fire tasks) and then live DFs. I am pretty sure that he was the only platoon commander that was doing that, and that is the sort of thing that section commanders have got to know.[18]

DRILLS

Fighting in the jungle against a guerilla enemy is all about speed of reaction—the quick and the dead. The reason for this is quite simple, the vegetation is thicker, the distance one can identify and recognise legitimate targets is shortened to distances of about 10 to 15 metres and the consequent time for reaction is down to several seconds—at most. The Company 2IC of Delta Four, Captain Peter Schuman, MC, was on his third tour of operational duty and he had previously fought in Borneo and South Vietnam. SAS trained, he values the following:

> It just depends who on the day does it fastest. Whether you do it or the enemy does it who wins the battle. It is as simple as that. Drills, drills and drills. If you have got the right drill at the start, you are off to a flying start.[19]

The drills must go hand in glove with basic skills to enable soldiers to fight in the jungle. Peter Schuman also firmly believes that:

Soldier skills must come first. You have got to be able to survive in the jungle. Look after your health, be silent, observant and be able to fire through jungle. *Through* jungle, just see a fleeting target and be able to fire through; don't worry about leaves and sticks and anything else that gets in the way—just go for what is at the end of the tunnel. And train every soldier to do that.[20]

STRESS

The infantryman is placed under enormous pressures both physical and mental on the battlefield. It is too late if his first encounter with these pressures are on his first patrol or contact in a war zone. Private Dean Cooke believes:

I think you need to be mentally prepared as well as physically prepared. I think one goes with the other and I think (our training) was conducive to those circumstances that we tended to be involved with in Vietnam.[21]

This initial exposure to stress during training was probably underdone. Many of the men of Delta Four thought their physical preparation was fine and in many cases they thought it was very good. Quite a few, however, thought that more emphasis should have been placed on the mental preparation for combat as explained by Section Commander, Corporal Warren Dowell:

I was probably as well-trained as I could be made, that is learning drills and what to do, but I don't think I was mentally prepared. You can do a lot of training with blanks and that sort of thing, but I wasn't really mentally prepared or mentally tough enough when I got there. We used to do a week out at High Range; two days break in Lavarack Barracks, and then we started to get four weeks out and a week in, but you knew that at the end of those four weeks or week you were going to come back to camp and have a couple of days in camp and get drunk and carry on. When you got in country (Vietnam) that break wasn't there as much, you were always 'in country' and I found the 12 months was a long time.[22]

The exposure to stress soon 'sorts the wheat from the chaff'. Delta Four had two company commanders, one who left after six weeks in country owing to illness. He was instrumental in training the company for Vietnam and he did it with ruthless efficiency as Dowell continues:

> Our Company Commander [Major F.J. Kudnig] was extremely tough on us physically and pushed us quite a bit, and I think it was this tough training that got us through a lot of trouble once we got into country and into contacts. We were very, very fit, which is a must for infantry soldiers. Physically he was tough on us and he pushed us to the limit as far as doing long route marches and nine-milers and that sort of thing.[23]

Dowell contends that the stress and pressure the group were placed under by Kudnig assisted them later on when they were in combat and especially when the company was under great stress on one particular occasion.

AGGRO

The infantrymen, often referred to as 'grunts', have a pretty nasty job to do and in jungle fighting it is often done at very close quarters. Consequently the name of the game is aggression—Diggers going forward, hard, fast and unrelentingly. It soon drives the enemy out of his hole and into the way of the soldiers' bullets. Instilling aggression is part and parcel of training. The company commander who replaced Major Franz Kudnig, Major Jerry Taylor, gave his thoughts on training for war in this way:

> My experience is that it is tied up with all the other elements of training of which physical fitness, physical toughness and emotional toughness play a very large part. I believe that people feel aggressive if they feel good about themselves

and about the unit that they work for, and one of the best ways to get people to feel good about themselves is by giving them a very high standard of physical fitness and toughness to achieve. I believe really that aggressiveness is one of the elements of success and that is achieved by the complete package of training, whether it is individual, physical unit training and if at the end of the day the individuals or the sub-units and the units feel good about themselves—then that is when they become good in battle and they are aggressive in battle.[24]

This chapter has tried to place the importance of training in perspective. The sections, platoon and the whole company are made up of individuals who together must combine to work and produce a result that, if not done correctly or in the best possible speed, could result in dire consequences for some or all of them. Training must be relevant and done properly. Hard, tough training prepares the Diggers for the battlefield and creates an environment which draws the men together and produces that initial camaraderie which will carry them into battle. The soldiers in a rifle company are like the bricks in a wall and their training is what initially holds them together.

2

THE STEAK AND KIDNEY

My mind was going back and thinking well here it is, I am actually going to war.[1]

GARRY HESKETT
PRIVATE

AFTER ALL THE WORK-UP EXERCISES, Canungra, assessed field exercises and interminable field firing exercises, the Fourth Battalion deployed to South Vietnam in May 1971. An advance party of 118 men departed by Qantas 707 several weeks before the main body and prepared for the arrival of the rest of the battalion who were to embark on the converted ex-Royal Navy aircraft carrier, the HMAS *Sydney*. Known colloquially to the soldiers as the 'Steak and Kidney', travelling to Vietnam on this troopship was far from being a pleasant experience. The poorly ventilated *Sydney* had been built for the cooler climes of the north Atlantic and when steaming at 14 knots through the muggy, tropical seas en-route to Vung Tau, the Diggers on board suffered.[2]

They found to their surprise that they would be sleeping in hammocks and packed in like sardines in the stuffy mess decks. The soldiers of Delta Four were finally on their way to war. Private Garry Heskett, who was a mortarman destined

to join Delta Four later in his tour, felt the first reality of
going to war:

> Apart from anything else on the ship, I remember the first
> night was the quietest night I ever spent on that ship. It
> was absolutely deathly silent. You could have dropped a pin
> as far as I was concerned; we all just lay there and I
> remember laying there, on the bunk and waiting for the
> Captain to come through and do his inspection or whatever
> it was at that time, and just looking around and it was
> deathly silent. People must have just been thinking. My
> mind was going back and thinking well here it is, I am
> actually going to war. So, what's it going to be like? All
> the things that could face you; the terrors; the fears.[3]

The old troop ship steamed leisurely through the sluggish
waters of the Coral Sea inside the Great Barrier Reef, through
the Torres Strait and into the Arafura Sea and then turned
north through the Indonesian archipelago between Borneo
and Java. All the while it was flanked by RAN destroyer
escorts who ensured that the *Sydney* would not come under
attack as had been threatened by the Indonesian President Mr
Suharto. It was rumoured that the *Sydney* was travelling at
such a slow speed because RAN submarines were escorting
it. The cynics in the group thought otherwise, they reckoned
it was because 14 knots was all that the old troop ship could
muster without the rivets shaking loose. In fact the ship was
travelling at best speed.

ON BOARD TRAINING

Life on board *Sydney* may have been boring for some but it
was far from idle. A training regime had been developed to
keep the soldier's skills at a peak, which was not easy given
the restricted room on board and the fact that the flight deck
was covered in cargo and vehicles destined for Asian ports
under the Colombo Aid Plan. The one main advantage of
travelling by sea was the acclimatisation that sailing through

Delta Four led by its first OC, Major Franz Kudnig, marching through Townsville before they embark on the HMAS *Sydney* and leave for war. (*Photograph courtesy of Bob Meehan*)

the equator and tropics gave to the men as they neared their destination. The journey also allowed those junior leaders to get closer to the men in their sections and platoons.

The Diggers were instructed in subjects such as first aid, current dispositions and actions in South Vietnam and in particular in Phuoc Tuy Province, and cultural and social aspects of the country. Lessons included revision of air and artillery fire support request procedures, posting sentries, the Rules of Engagement and radio telephone procedure. In addition, lectures were given on the various dress, weapons, equipment and characteristics of the Allied Forces that the men would be likely to meet in their area of operations (AO). To keep in practice, a shooting program was developed. Sections would line up facing astern and fire instinctively in a 'snap shoot' style at inflated latex balloons which were weighted with a small amount of water and dropped overboard off the rear of the flight deck.

Infantry battalions will always take the opportunity to have a go at each other and cast aspersions on each other's abilities as evidenced by a signal received from 3 RAR by 9 RAR on board HMAS *Sydney* when they were deploying to Vietnam in 1968 which included words to the effect, 'Your approach has been plotted by the trail of balloons you have left behind. Welcome to Vietnam. Please hurry.'[4]

ARRIVAL

After 10 days the coast of Vietnam came into hazy view and the ship anchored in Vung Tau harbour. Clearly visible was Cape St Jacques with a prominent ship wreck adorning its headland. Once the anchor chains rattled out and the ship was at rest, the soldiers began their final packing and preparation for disembarking, including a full rehearsal. For some, the last night on board was a little apprehensive and the evening dragged slowly by. The quiet of that last night was occasionally punctuated by the 'scare charges' the RAN personnel were dropping around the ship to discourage Viet Cong (VC) sappers from planting limpet mines onto the ship. Private 'Jethro' Hannah recalled:

I think in my case it was excitement in a lot of ways. I didn't know what to expect when I got there, but I think the excitement came because you had so much time cramped together with the rest of the men in your platoons and company that it was all you spoke about. Then, listening to the older fellows that had been to Vietnam calm you down and tell you what it is going to be like. I think it was more excitement than fear.[5]

Hannah's platoon sergeant was 26-year-old Daryl Jenkin who was about to embark on his third campaign, having served in Borneo and South Vietnam with Delta Four. Despite his previous combat experience and eight years infantry service, he found that returning to a combat zone could have its effects:

On the first tour I was a corporal and I was a bit younger then and probably a little more gung ho, the same as everybody else. The second time around I knew what we were going to be in for. As the platoon sergeant I knew the responsibilities that were about to happen and quite a bit of it was going to be on my head. So, probably anxious, not frightened. Anxious would be the word. But, I was quite confident that the platoon would do extremely well because it was a pretty good outfit all round.[6]

After breakfast the next morning, the Diggers assembled in their pre-arranged muster stations and awaited a call to assemble on the flight deck. As they came up the aircraft hangars onto the flight deck, they were assaulted by the clamorous roar of the US Army Chinook helicopters which would take them to their new home at the 1st Australian Task Force base at Nui Dat. None of the Diggers who were on their first tour of duty had seen or ridden in one of these incredibly noisy machines before. They were hustled on board and filed onto the lowered rear ramp and sat down on the webbing seats along each side of the aircraft. Black aircrew sergeants snatched their rifles out of their hands and inverted their weapons, muzzle down, as was the US Army custom when flying in aircraft.

As the Diggers from 4 RAR scrambled onto the huge choppers, the outgoing soldiers of 2 RAR who were on their way home yelled greetings and other licentious remarks including the fact that, 'No one had 365 days to go!' The fresh, clean shaven young Diggers of Delta Four eyed their veteran counterparts as they crossed each other's paths and the faces on the men told it all. The men from 2 RAR were grinning, happy and confident. The Diggers from 4 RAR were slightly apprehensive, watchful and wide-eyed. Private Dean Cooke, who was just 10 days over 19, reminisced:

> I think there was a sort of an air of excitement if you can say that. I often think of the pictures of the old Diggers— First World War and Second World War—going away all happy and that. I think it was pretty much the same. You're young, it's like an adventure in one sense. I have heard a lot of old First World War Diggers say that and I think I can relate to that because, it's a new experience, and even though it's war, in some sense it's almost unreal. It's not reality really, I suppose until you're actually involved in it. But, I think there was the excitement of it all, going to something different and really being part of a group that you're proud of.[7]

The huge American Army Chinooks quickly lifted the Diggers off the gently rolling deck of the *Sydney* and took them up to a height of about 1000 feet where each and every Digger twisted in his seat to catch a glimpse of the thick green jungle canopy that was passing below. The trip to Nui Dat would take about 20 minutes. The varying shades of green vegetation below were pock marked in a seemingly endless crazy pattern of shell and bomb crater holes half filled with water which reflected the blazing tropical dry season sun. Private Dean Cooke continues:

> First impression—that was interesting. A slight shudder of fear went through me. One thing that stuck in my mind was there was a negro guy in the back of the Chinook and we had never seen these, he had an under and over. The M16 with an M79 actually attached to it. I remember actually flying over the country reasonably low and all these crater holes and it put a bit of a shudder through me because the reality started coming home, you know you are in a war torn country. That was my first impression, that is still vivid in my mind. And then the landing at Eagle Farm.[8]

THE DAT

'Eagle Farm' was the helicopter landing zone inside the Nui Dat base that the battalions used when deploying to and from the various AOs. On arrival at the Task Force Base, the soldiers were met by their platoon and company guides and trucked off to their respective tent lines which were nestled in under the rubber trees about 100 metres inside the base perimeter. The tents were capable of sleeping four soldiers on army cots with each Digger afforded a grey steel wardrobe, a 'table, personnel' and a tubular steel chair. The floor boards were usually resting on upturned 105 mm howitzer cartridge cases which had been hammered into the soil of the Nui Dat rubber plantation. Blast walls of sandbags encased in corrugated roofing iron came up about a metre or so above the ground as blast and fragmentation protection. Outside every tent were fighting pits which would be occupied in case of ground attack on the base. Scattered amongst the company and platoon tent lines were aluminium huts, which were heavily louvred for ventilation and which housed stores and company offices. Most of the main administrative type buildings were aluminium sheds bolted onto concrete slabs. Each company area had a Diggers canteen, known colloquially as the 'boozer', and a combined officers and sergeants mess. Toilets were six-man deep trench latrines and showers were corrugated iron affairs with hot water—occasionally.

For some soldiers returning for their second tour of duty this was a time of *deja vu*. Major Jerry Taylor recalls:

> The worst thing about arriving back in Nui Dat was finding that not only was I back in the same lines that I had been three years before, but worse, I was in the same tent! My batman in Support Coy 2 RAR was Private Terry Vidler, and he had made all sorts of what I call 'Swedish' type furniture out of old ammo boxes to tart up the interior of the tent a bit. Most of it was still there. It was just like getting back to The Dat after a long R & R. It was very depressing. So I went straight to the Officers' Mess and got pissed.[9]

Most of the soldiers in Delta Four were now facing a completely different environment. As Private Grahame Tooth explains, this had its problems:

> You were taught in Australia everything has got to be done by the book, and when you went over there, half the rules were thrown to the shit house. Like live ammunition, we were carrying it around like nothing. In Australia it was locked away behind closed doors. I think, once people were there for a short period of time I found that they placed no value on anything. I think you just threw discretion to the wind really. You think well, shit, what's going to happen? I might be here today, I mightn't be here tomorrow, so you didn't have any value on life or anything like that. And I believe that was a major psychological problem.[10]

From now on the Battalion title would formally be 4 RAR/NZ. This was because 4 RAR was an ANZAC Battalion with only three rifle companies. The fourth rifle company was a company of New Zealanders who went by the title of V or Victor Company.

The Diggers were given a tour of the base in the back of trucks and then warned out for duties within the camp for the next couple of days. The Delta Four Diggers were taken down to their Company perimeter which faced east toward the distant rubber and battle field of Long Tan where Delta Company, 6 RAR had fought so valiantly five years earlier.[11] Along the perimeter, spaced about 100 metres apart, were elevated bunkers, heavily sandbagged and connected by telephone wire to an intricate system of command and area bunkers which would act as a Fire Support Coordination Centre if and when the base was ever attacked. The young Diggers found they were now on a fulltime war footing and there was no such thing as 'non-tac' or a non-tactical scenario, where security could slip and people could relax and not worry about being alert.

For the next few days the soldiers were briefed on matters of safety and various Standard Operating Procedures (SOP). One of the most memorable of these orientation briefings was

Private Kevin Benson (*right*) clowning around in his tent at Nui Dat with Private Bob Simms from 11 Platoon. (*Photograph courtesy of Kevin Benson*)

given by an American Army helicopter gunship pilot who had a chalk board detailing minimum safety distances for the various types of ordnance that he could deliver in support of unprotected troops. For the distance of 7.62 mm mini-gun fire was written, '25 meters from own troops'. He nonchalantly walked up to the board and amended it to read, '23 meters'. This was somewhat startling for his audience who had only ever seen mini-gun fire at well over 250 metres.

The people most affected by the employment of weaponry in the war zone were the gunners. The field artillery were responsible for ensuring quick, accurate and continuous indirect fire support to the ground troops and they had a huge adjustment to overcome. The Forward Observer of Delta Four was Lieutenant Greg Gilbert from 104 Battery, 12 Field Regiment, and he found his greatest challenge was in the procedures he now had to adopt:

> I think it has to be baptism by fire really when you go there, because certainly all the firing we did at Holsworthy and then on High Range in Townsville was all textbook-type shooting where you would sit on a hill and watch the fall of shot with binoculars. When you went to Vietnam the skills required were quite different and most of the time you didn't even see the shells landing. You had to learn

how to adjust artillery by sound rather than sight and being able to differentiate how far an artillery shell was away by the sound of the explosion.[12]

For the infantry platoon commanders, who would also be required to call for and adjust their supporting indirect fire on occasions, there was a sudden and awesome impact of what would be required of them. Mistakes in calling in fire in the past had been tragic and no one wanted a repeat of errors in calling in the devastating fire of the 105 mm high explosive shells. Greg Gilbert continues:

> In artillery shooting in Australia, you are usually at least two kilometres away from where the artillery was landing. Whereas the techniques of bracketing and all that sort of stuff that you did on the range in Australia you never did in Vietnam. You just keep on dropping them then until you got them as close as you could bear. When you got to Vietnam you generally had to add a thousand metres anyway because of the lack of accuracy in the maps and had to start off a thousand metres out to get your first round down, and then you could bring them back.[13]

As Gilbert stated, the accuracy of the maps and the fact that there was very little geographical terrain visible to conduct re-sections and relate map to ground meant an enormous responsibility on the junior leaders to ensure that they always knew exactly where they were on the ground. To fail in this seemingly simple chore could have disastrous effects.

Orientation was finished, the soldiers and their leaders had been fully briefed, kitted and spurred and after two weeks of in-country preparation the Diggers were unleashed on short 'shake down' operations or patrols to ensure that everything worked and all SOPs were functional.

The men of Delta Four were launched on their first operation code named IRON MAIDEN. This was what being a 'grunt' was all about. This was to be their bread and butter.

3

THE BREAD AND BUTTER

*For me I knew that if I didn't do my job for that half hour
or so, if it wasn't done correctly and something happened,
and someone got killed—I knew it would be on my
shoulders.*[1]

JETHRO HANNAH,
LANCE CORPORAL, 11 PLATOON

HOW DID OUR DIGGERS MANAGE against an enemy who knew
the jungle backwards and was more adept to living and moving
in it than his Australian counterpart? What enabled the Diggers
to survive counter revolutionary warfare and often have the
edge over their wily foe?

Infantry soldiering is often lampooned by other Corps as
the toil of men who do not have the brains for more complex
work. In fact nothing could be further from the truth. The
craft of the infantryman falls into two major areas: field craft,
the skill of practising one's trade in the bush; and battle craft,
the art of surviving in combat and giving the enemy every
opportunity to die for his country. Despite the Diggers facing
many problems, difficulties and challenges on patrol in South
Vietnam, they displayed these two crafts to a high degree of
success.

27

PATROLLING

The Australian infantry battalions operating in Vietnam opted for a policy of search and destroy or search and clear as techniques for uncovering the enemy camps, caches and strong points in the jungle. This tried and true method of saturating an area with patrols was learnt in the counter guerilla operations against the communist terrorists in Malaya. The fail-proof way to ensure that an area was clear of enemy was to physically pass over it on the ground. There are two main types of patrols, fighting and reconnaissance. The bulk of patrols in Vietnam were fighting patrols, which were designed to either fight for information or destroy the enemy. Even the Special Air Service Regiment (SASR) patrols from the rotated Sabre squadron—which was also based in Nui Dat—evolved from recon to hard hitting fighting patrols despite their small make up of only five or six men. The emphasis was to aggressively seek out and destroy the enemy.

Patrolling and tracking were skills passed down through the Infantry Corps when soldiers attended their Corps training at the Infantry Centre at Ingleburn in New South Wales. The method chosen to do that patrolling was to insert into an area by a variety of methods from helicopters, APCs or even trucks. The soldiers of Delta Four found that they soon got into a pattern of searching an area and when that was found to be clear they would then relocate to another area of operations (AO), usually by helicopter. The average rifle company patrol duration in 4 RAR was about three weeks, but as fate would have it, Delta Four usually spent six weeks out in the scrub, returned for about five to seven days and then went out on another six-week patrol.

Patrol preparation

A day or two before patrols would deploy, the Delta Four Company Commander would present his orders and concept for the next operation. The Orders Group usually consisted of the Company Second In Command, Captain Peter Schuman, MC; the three rifle platoon commanders, Second

28

Lieutenants Kevin Byrne, Gary McKay and Graham Spinkston commanding 10, 11 and 12 Platoon respectively; the artillery Forward Observer, Lieutenant Greg Gilbert; the Company Sergeant Major (CSM) WO2 Noel Huish; the Company Quarter Master Sergeant (CQMS) Bob Hann; and the CHQ radio operator in his tented office in Nui Dat. Here the OC would give his formal orders usually onto a map of the AO which might have an overprint of battalion and company boundaries marked upon it. For the platoon commanders the important boundaries were the ones that separated them from each other and who was likely to be on any other boundary. All eyes would scan the map for the distinct Intelligence Section red markings for previous contacts or likely enemy positions or sightings.

After the formal orders, which always followed the standard Army sequence of delivery, the company commander would usually run through how he saw the operation panning out and what he saw as likely courses of action if and when something may be found. The amount of fire support that would be available would be discussed and the likelihood of air support for air to ground attack and for other support would be detailed.

The platoon commanders would then return to their own tent lines and prepare their own orders to give to their section commanders. Any platoon commander with his head screwed on would ensure that he ran his orders past the most experienced man in the platoon—the platoon sergeant—before he issued them verbally to his corporals. I did this as a matter of course and it saved a few embarrassing moments when a detail was overlooked or steps, which meant little to me but a lot to the Diggers, were omitted. Consultation between the young platoon commander and his own 2IC, the platoon sergeant, is essential if the team is to work together. Platoon Sergeant Daryl Jenkin explains:

> I certainly think you should understudy the platoon commander and know what's happening in the platoon in case the platoon commander suddenly isn't there. I think that they both learn off each other. But something must be there

between the platoon commander and the platoon sergeant; and if it is not there, then that platoon can't possibly succeed. I think a lot of things you work out together.[2]

After the orders were presented to the section commanders, the corporals would clutch up their sections and proceed to filter down the information that referred specifically to them and the job they would have to do on the next operation. Many soldiers describe this passage of information as 'mushroom farming' or 'being fed on shit and kept in the dark'—to coin an oft used and heard phrase. Nobody likes to be kept in the dark, but unfortunately it happens because knowledge is power and assists the weaker leader to retain control. The down side of not informing soldiers can be disastrous as it affects individual and sometimes team performance. Private Dean Cooke was sometimes not impressed:

> Sometimes I would get the feeling you were kept like a mushroom I suppose. The corporals had their O Groups, they used to come back and tell us things . . . I think that's an important factor—information—knowing what's going on because it is your own little world and I think you need to know what's going on.[3]

Most Diggers wanted to know just a few basic facts. These revolved around when they would be going out bush, for how long, how far they would be walking and how many enemy were expected in the area. From that they could map out their personal administration concerning letters home, what to load in their back pack and when they would taste their next beer.

From a corporal's perspective, there were certain responsibilities that had to be met in order to get the best out of the section and to stay alive. Corporal Warren Dowell from 11 Platoon and later Company Headquarters Support Section, saw his role in the information flow in this manner:

> I think my main job was to keep the section sharp and alert at all times; to keep their minds occupied; to give them as much information as I could, so that they could maintain

their alertness and know what was going on. The link between the platoon commander, the section commander and the section is an information link. Not only must you carry out his commands but you have got to pass on what he is thinking and what he tells you to the soldiers. Because the better informed the soldiers are, the more they will maintain their alertness and do what has got to be done.[4]

Warren Dowell goes on to explain how he saw the role of his platoon and company leaders:

The platoon commander and company commander give guidance, but it is actually a section commander who has to interpret that order and actually say to the blokes that I want you to do this, this and this. Certainly it is a section commander at the forefront; on the Kokoda Track, Nui Le or on the streets of Somalia.[5]

Once the orders were passed down, the final preparations for deploying to the field would begin. Weapons would be tested and kits inspected to make sure the webbing and equipment the Diggers would carry or wear to the field was fully serviceable and didn't rattle. The Diggers would be fully loaded with their first line of ammunition, and rations would be issued.

Rehearsals for ambushes, contact drills and specific actions anticipated in the operation would then be rehearsed under the canopy of the rubber inside the base. Platoons would practise setting up banks of Claymore mines, insertion and withdrawal drills for ambushing, signals in ambush and a plethora of the many small but vital procedures for conducting complicated manoeuvres. Platoons were always contriving and adjusting their own special SOPs for drills such as harbouring and posting sentries which could then be activated without any more than a few hand signals or whispered words of command. Harbouring is the terminology for a platoon or larger group to go into all-round defence to protect itself from ground attack. It is a simple, well rehearsed drill to get the soldiers onto the ground quickly, quietly and safely.

Another procedure that was finely tuned by the platoons of Delta Four was 'track squatting'. This was a formation designed to take advantage of discovering an enemy sign on the track and being able to place the platoon astride the path with a minimum of fuss. Platoons would often track squat, if they found a track and wanted to see if any enemy would come bowling along it and it could be done by day or by night. The platoon's GPMG M60 machine guns would be sited firing along the track and if time allowed, the M18A1 high explosive Claymore mines would be placed in banks along the track leading into the track squat position. A bank of Claymores consisted of several mines linked together with detonating cord which gave an instantaneous initiation of all the mines with a devastating effect on anyone caught in their blast zone. This siting of guns and mines gave a double exposure to any enemy unfortunate enough to stumble into the waiting Diggers. Platoons could harbour at night in this formation relatively safely provided there were no easy access paths into the flanks of the track squat. The track squat was often preferred over a formal ambush which required lengthy preparation and usually depended on reliable information. Most ambushes conducted by Delta Four platoons extended over several days. A track squat should never last more than overnight as detailed reconnaissance is essential if one is to stay in the one place in the jungle for more than 12 hours.

Going in

The Company would insert into an area to be searched or cleared and then split off into platoon patrols and each platoon would be given a set of five or more grid squares, depending on the type of terrain therein, to search. After five days there would be a need to resupply and after 10 days the Company would reform, replenish and take new orders for the next 10 days. Every 10 days the men would change their jungle green clothes for fresh clothes that had come back from the laundry at Baria or Phuoc Le, the Provincial capital of Phuoc Tuy. Mail would come in and be hungrily devoured by the riflemen. The day of resupply was usually one of 'make and mend' as all the kit in the platoons was checked for repair and Diggers could write last minute letters to be taken out on the dirty laundry back load.

The senses

It must be understood that the majority of patrols that Delta Four conducted were on foot. Owing to the general nature of jungle terrain, the infantryman comes down to relying on sound, sight and smell. Movement of the soldiers through the jungle undergrowth had to be silent. For the men of Delta Four there was no hacking away with machetes at the vines and branches which impeded their way. It was a slow, methodical, noiseless passage where secateurs silently cut a path for the rest of the platoon to follow.

The need for silence was a prime reason for platoons or patrols travelling in single file. Anything other than that formation meant too much noise, difficulties with keeping the Diggers on the right track and direction, and a good chance of accidental clashes in the thick bush. Rarely did the Diggers move in anything larger than a platoon group.

All communications up and down the platoon formation were by field signal and if the platoon was halted no one spoke above a stage whisper. This meant that everything the men did from opening up his canteen and unfolding his aluminium mug for a brew to simply having a pee had to be done quietly. The aim of the game was to be able to hear the enemy before he heard you. Soldiers learnt to 'ghost walk', a method where the sides of the boot are placed down on the ground before the rest of the foot to make sure that a boot wouldn't be heavily placed on broken twigs or branches.

Equally, at night light was never used. White light can be seen for an extraordinarily long distance in jungle despite the thick vegetation and lights were not used unless in an absolute emergency such as saving someone's life.

Eyes like a cat

There is a technique of 'looking through the jungle' that infantryman must develop. The aim is to look at the gaps in

Private Wally Burford in war paint while patrolling in Phuoc Tuy Province. National Serviceman Burford became a section 2IC later in his tour. (*Photograph courtesy of Wally Burford*)

the foliage and scan at knee height and below, where the branches usually have less foliage because the sun cannot penetrate down to the jungle floor. This allows the men to see if anyone is standing or moving and it pays to drop down on to one's stomach to be able to actually look 'through' the bush.

As the riflemen were patrolling they each had a specific task depending on where they were positioned in the platoon. The scouts were obviously the eyes, ears and noses of the platoon as they were at the point or head of their formation. But, because Murphy's Law rules, the enemy will not often decide to bump into your patrol head on. Instead he will strike you from a flank, oblique angle or from the rear. That is why each and every soldier, in the words of Lance Corporal Wally Burford, were:

Literally just all eyes and ears trying to achieve that ultimate
goal of finding someone so we could initiate a contact.[6]

Every soldier was allocated an arc or responsibility on one
side or the other of the single file formation. It was then his
task to ensure that he scanned that arc to make sure that
anything he heard or saw in that arc was picked up. The
hardest thing about patrolling in the jungle was, according to
most of Delta Four, to be staying alert. Wally Burford continues:

As a rifleman, just to stay alert was the main thing. You
become a bit complacent after a while because you haven't
had a contact for a while, or you haven't come across enemy
sign. You tend to get in your own little nitty gritty world
and you start thinking about your next leave and all that
sort of business rather than the job at hand. So, the most
important thing is keeping switched on and continuing to
make sure you do stay alert. By staying alert you can save
yourself; and most certainly save other blokes in the platoon
as well.[7]

Light infantry?

Staying alert, as Wally Burford emphasises above, was no easy
matter. The weight the riflemen carried on their backs and in
their basic webbing was prodigious. It was extremely enervating and tiring, especially moving through the thick jungle
where one had to continually step over fallen logs and vines
on the jungle floor. Combined with the heat and humidity,
it made for hard work to stay alert and responsive.

The average rifleman in Delta Four carried about 30
kilograms of equipment on a normal patrol. This weight was
made up of his basic webbing which consisted of a waist belt
and yoke carrying his small arms ammunition of usually 100
rounds of 7.62 mm or 140 rounds of 5.56 mm ball ammunition. He carried two HE (high explosive) fragmentation
grenades, a smoke grenade or a CS gas canister. On his belt
he would have up to four water bottles and two mugs known
as cups canteen—one for cooking and drinking, the other for

shaving. He would have a machete or a bayonet and if his waist was large enough a bum pack for other equipment such as a torch, first aid kit, spare socks, rations and probably a waterproof poncho. Some Diggers carried knives for general purpose use if they didn't have a bayonet on their webbing, especially the machine gunners and signallers. Each platoon carried only one or two 'tools, entrenching' or lightweight folding shovels because the need to dig in when halted was fairly uncommon. The enemy mortar threat was negligible for Delta Four for most of their tour. Bravo Company from 4 RAR, however, had a nasty experience when Second Lieutenant Dan McDaniel's platoon was mortared with 60 mm mortars on one occasion and suffered heavy casualties—though none very serious.[8]

Enterprising soldiers would 'obtain' C4 plastic explosive (PE) from mates in Sapper units or the Assault Pioneers to use as a rapid means of heating their mugs for brews of tea or coffee. From experience I can verify that this is a sure fire way to heat a cup of coffee very quickly—provided you don't have the base of the aluminium mug too close to the flame of the brightly burning explosive or it will burn a hole through the mug in a matter of seconds! Another reason for using C4 or PE was because the issue hexamine tablets that came with the rations were bloody hard to light in the wet season when everything in your gear was usually soaked.

In their back pack, the Diggers carried the bulk of their rations, spare ammunition for the section machine gun, an M18A1 Claymore mine, his sleeping gear which was usually a mattress cover, a silk (a lightweight nylon sleeping bag liner), a mosquito net, a nylon hammock (if he had one) and spare ammo.

Some platoons supplemented their weaponry that was normal as in the case of my platoon which captured a US Army GPMG M60 from 274 Viet Cong Main Force Regiment and retained it for use in the platoon. This gun, which was eventually carried by a soldier called Ralph Niblett, became known as the 'floating gun'. It had no number two to help Ralph Niblett man the weapon and he travelled behind the lead section machine gun team. The tactics for employment were quite simple. On contact with the enemy, the lead section scouts would either initiate or return fire. The lead gun team would deploy to one side of the track and the floating gun would deploy to the opposite side. This would then give the lead section a very powerful fire base whilst the remainder of the section closed up and then dealt with the situation.

THE JOBS

The normal fully manned rifle platoon consisted of a head-quarters with an officer platoon commander (second lieutenant or lieutenant), a sergeant who was the second-in-command of the platoon, and two private soldiers who acted as radio operators and orderlies. There were three rifle sections, each commanded by a corporal called the section commander with a lance corporal as second-in-command. The rifle section was broken up into three groups: the scout (two scouts if you were lucky), gun (the section 2IC and No. 1 and No. 2 on the gun), and rifle group (usually four riflemen). The total rifle platoon complement was an officer and 33 men plus attachments such as stretcher bearers, engineer sappers for 'splinter teams' and mortar fire controller or forward observer parties—depending on the task the platoon was given. To get a feel for what a platoon on patrol actually did and how each of the men in Delta Four went about their day to day jobs, we will now look at each man's position from the front of the platoon heading toward the rear.

Scouts

As mentioned earlier, the point man, the rifleman whose job it was to be the eyes and ears of the platoon, came under a great deal of pressure to make sure he was the initiator in any contact and not have the initiative taken away from him. One soldier who spent a great deal of time as forward scout was 'Jethro' Hannah from 11 Platoon:

I think being the forward scout was, you knew that the rest
of the platoon or the section, depended on your ability to
listen, to see and to guide the rest of the section. That was
the hardest. So, therefore, you knew you had to do your
job. I believe that the most important part was to concentrate for that period of time, then rest when you could
later on.[9]

The strain placed on scouts in Vietnam was enormous. As
expressed by Jethro Hannah above and in the introduction to
this chapter, there was the heavy burden of life and death
responsibility. The scouts had to be alert, have quick reactions
and yet still abide by the Rules of Engagement.[10] The normal
manning in a rifle platoon is for two scouts who support and
cover each other whilst they are patrolling. However, once
in country, platoons became decimated with injured and sick
soldiers, soldiers required for perimeter duty in the Task Force
Base, and men scheduled for rest and recreation (R & R)
leave. This often meant that platoons had a strength of around
20 or 24 in the field and the obvious position to sacrifice was
the second scout.

Consequently, the scout was often on his own and it was
found that the maximum time a scout could endure leading
through the jungle was about 30 to 40 minutes. After that
time he tended to lose 'the edge'. Most of the platoons in
Delta Four rotated their scouts at around these durations. One
of the forward scouts from 12 Platoon, Regular soldier Private
Garry Sloane, thought that fatigue was both physical and
mental, and that time up front

. . . would be determined by the type of terrain that you
were going through. You were always taxing your mind
and looking everywhere and you were touching and feeling
and your concentration was pretty hyped up. As soon as
you did start to feel tired you wouldn't keep going—you
would get your number 2 and put him up there. I don't
think I ever spent a day where I wasn't glad that it was
over when you crawl into the hammock for the night. You
were the eyes and ears and everything, and you're on the

boil all the time. You just couldn't relax while you were patrolling.[11]

Despite the obvious danger some scouts loved being at the front of their platoons as Private Garry Sloane explains:

> We were always told that the three people that the enemy went for first were the scout, the gunner and the section commander. But I just liked being up the front because you knew what was going on. You get the first brief off the section commander once the orders come in over the radio. You could prepare yourself.[12]

There was great debate in Delta Four when the XM 203 grenade launcher (known as the 'under and over') first appeared on the scene around June or early July 1971.[13] Some thought that the weapon was best located with the scout because he could place canister (shot gun) into the general area of the contact and then use his rifle to place more accurate fire where it was required. Others thought that the under and over was best placed with the section 2IC who would act as a grenadier and use the HE rounds of the M79 portion to better effect because he was further back from the initial point of contact and could direct the fire of the GPMG M60 machine gun with the grenade launcher.[14] The canister or buck shot round was not that powerful owing to the size and composition of filling in the cartridge load. After firing it at plywood targets on the 'range' at Nui Dat most Diggers opted for Garry Sloane's solution:

> I used to use the buckshot rounds, but I would pull three or four apart and load the first round up and juice them up a bit. On the M16 side of it, I had 30 round magazines. The first one I had chocker block full of tracer and then the second one was just normal bullets. My thought there was that if the shit hit the fan, I would let the shotgun go first and scatter them and poke it above their heads and let the tracer go so the gun group could see where the rounds were going and by that time everyone would be in position

and they would be opening fire and I could just sit back and change mags and wait.[15]

In 11 Platoon the SOP was for the scout to carry an M16 rifle with 30 round magazines. The magazine loaded onto the rifle would be packed with a predominance of tracer bullets so that those attempting to identify the targets in the initial confusing burst of fire could be rapidly guided onto the enemy. The section commander carried the M203 for a while but most of the corporals abandoned it after they found that they had more important things to do in contact than act as a grenadier.

The section commander

Many veterans who served in the battalions will tell you that this is where the 'real war' was fought in Vietnam for the infantry. The vast majority of actions were minor clashes and skirmishes with platoon commanders only occasionally getting to 'drive' their platoons in contact. Corporal Warren Dowell saw his main responsibilities as

> . . . making sure that I kept the blokes informed and kept the blokes on their toes. Making them aware all the time of what was going on.[16]

There is a constant returning to the theme of security. It dominated all thinking and recollections of the veterans of Delta Four whenever they were asked what was the most important thing about patrolling in the jungle. Dowell continues and sums up the security issue:

> Over there you could go days without coming across sign or anything and yet you can—with the weight that you are carrying and being tired—tend to drop off. Once you have dropped off you have lost your security—and your safety.[17]

The machine gunner

Behind the section commander normally travelled the machine gun team. These two men served the GPMG M60 American belt fed, gas operated weapon. This gun could spit out 600 rounds per minute, but when used in normal rates of fire on Australian infantry patrols, it was usually fired in bursts of five to 10 rounds to conserve ammunition. The number one on the gun was the firer and responsible for ensuring that the gun was placed wherever the section commander wanted it. He had to carry this weighty gun and a fair proportion of its ammunition. The number two on the gun was there to assist in loading the ammunition into the weapon and to protect the number one when he was engaging targets. A good number two would also be spotting for his gunner so that fresh targets could be engaged rapidly without losing the momentum of the fire. The number two also carried the spare barrel for the M60 which was the first US Army machine gun to use a quick-detachable barrel which was air cooled and thus ran hot. His last task was to take over the gun if the number one was hit.

Most gun teams carried about 600 to 800 rounds between them and several members of the section would carry another 200–400 rounds. Some of the Kiwi (New Zealand) machine gun teams who were predominantly Maori soldiers and fairly strong and stocky, carried 1000 rounds between the gun team alone. Carrying the gun required a certain amount of stamina and dedication as it was a heavy beast weighing 10.4 kilograms clean. To lug it through the bush was difficult and very tiring and it required constant maintenance to keep the dirt and vegetation out of the working parts and off the disintegrating link belt ammunition. Because of its devastating effect, it was the first target in a contact if they intended to stay and make a fight of the clash. It was zeroed in by its distinctive 'dukka dukka dukka' thudding sound and the crash of the heavier 7.62 mm 'long' NATO bullets.

The gun usually stayed with one man during his tour of duty unless he was promoted or moved to another job within the platoon or company. Private Bob Meehan explains why he wanted to be a machine gunner:

> To me the main job is to keep yourself alive and keep your mates alive and that was to have the firepower. And to me the firepower was the GPMG M60. If you can't hit them you can always keep their heads down and that's why I wanted it. And we had a lot of camaraderie between the machine gunners and we had people like [Private D.J.] 'Vic' Morrow, or [Corporal P.L.] 'Dogs' Foley, and [Private T.B.] Trevor Gorringe. Machine gunners were always trying to outdo everybody else. Even when we had night shoots with the machine guns, we all worked in with each other to make sure that we were all on target. So, you know it's just the mateship, I don't know if the scouts ever had that mateship.[18]

I asked the machine gunners what was the most important thing about their job and they invariably replied much along the lines of Bob Meehan:

> Number one is know your weapon; know its capabilities; and one of the main things is to know exactly where your men are before you go into contact. Just being the fire power of the section and to be there when needed. So, if you're a forward scout and come under fire our job was to get as close as possible to give him support, so you either take the enemy out or give him time and keep the enemy's head down so he can withdraw or do his job whatever situation he's involved in.[19]

At night the gun is the focal point for section defence and is where the picket is located. The picket is a platoon sentry point and each platoon would normally have three sentry or picket points at night which were positioned just two or three metres forward of where the gun groups slept. Other members of the section would rotate through a double, staggered picket so that there was always a fresh man on the gun. Once the platoon was down to normal night routine there would be about seven people fully alert in the 32-man platoon. These were the six people manning the three machine guns on a staggered roster and the radio picket. This didn't always go as planned—especially in the deep, dark depths of tropical jungle as Meehan explains:

> You get dick heads when you are trying to sleep who get lost on their bloody way to the gun. When they're supposed to come and relieve the other fellows, they get lost, and the other fellow—he's half asleep so they wake you up to take over the gun so he can go and look for him. So, you're really not getting that rest, that's hard. In hindsight, it really didn't worry me. In those days you got pissed off a little bit but it was part of the job, it came with the territory I suppose.[20]

The pressure on the machine gunners was more relentless than on the forward scouts who would usually be rotated every half hour or so. The gunner was always carrying the gun and always under pressure to perform. As pointed out by Bob Meehan, even in ambush positions there's a little bit of extra pressure on the gunner, as they would be either the ambush initiators or back-up if the Claymore mines failed to fire. The gunners usually provided cut off fire to nail any fleeing enemy who escaped the initial burst of fire in the ambush and this sometimes meant being a little exposed to overshoots from over-exuberant members of the killing group firing outside of their designated arcs.

The section second-in-command

Command and control of the machine gun team was usually the domain of the section 2IC. The section commander usually directly commanded the rifle group of three to four riflemen including a grenadier carrying the 40 mm M79 grenade launcher during the assault. This light but very accurate weapon was carried by either the section 2IC or one of the riflemen. The weapon was usually slung over one shoulder across the body of the carrier which made it an embuggerance to get off when wearing a back pack, or even in the heat of battle with no pack. A Digger in 11 Platoon came up with the idea of fashioning a 'boot' for the weapon which carried the M79 'barrel-down'. The boot was sewn onto the side pocket of the large back pack and the weapon could then be rapidly extracted for use. Despite the officer commanding 11 Platoon issuing a directive that no-one was to carry a round up the spout of the colloquially named 'wombat gun', there was one amusing incident when Lance Corporal 'Snoopy' Pallant triggered a round when he caught his trigger in vines when he was moving through thick bush. Thankfully it merely thudded into soft dirt next to his ankle. 'Snoopy' was left with nothing but a red face and a huge reef up the backside from his boss.

The 2IC was responsible for the administration of his section. That basically meant ensuring that they were fed, watered, issued with whatever the platoon commander had decreed and when things needed replacing, he got it fixed. The 2ICs in the section worked closely with the platoon sergeant who co-ordinated the platoon's administration. The relationship between the section commander and his 2IC had to be close and not be a case of 'the bloke who looked after the bullets, beans and bandages'. As section commander, Corporal Warren Dowell says:

> He was definitely part of the command chain. He just wasn't in the section. He has to command the gun and be prepared to give orders to help his section commander fight the battle. We both relied on each other a lot and he was a very big part of the section, he can't just be a number, he is a leader just like the section commander.[21]

Dowell points out that he expected his 2IC to command the gun when they got into contact. This arrangement worked well because the gunner is usually firing and moving all the time to improve his position and orders for the gun are better relayed through the 2IC who can tell the gunner what his targets are and where he needs to be positioned and so on. This frees up the section commander to talk to his scouts and find out exactly what is going on and to plan free from the problems of co-ordinating the machine gun. Finally the section

2IC had to understudy the section commander so that he could take over the section at a moment's notice.

The riflemen

The basis of the platoon is built around the men who were initially riflemen and then after cross training and sometimes specialist courses the riflemen would graduate to other jobs within the platoon of rifle company. In effect the rifle group is the platoon nursery where new arrivals are put to see what skills they possess and what sort of character they have for further development within the platoon. Some would say that the rifleman's job was easy, others like Wally Burford would disagree and he saw his lot in a different light:

> I would come back to nights, pickets at nights without any shadow of a doubt. That to me was where everything came home. We were there during the wet, it was absolutely pissing pick handles at night. There was one night, I'll never forget it, we used to have a little comms cord which used to run from each hootchie out to the gun. I tripped over and lost the comms cord. So, I bloody walked around, kind of two steps left, two steps right for about two hours trying to find the comms cord. It was raining the whole time, in the end I started to get terrified that I might be in front of someone's hootchie; wake them up; frighten them; or might drift in front of the gun—even though I was pretty certain I was still pretty close to where it was I tripped over. So, I just had to sit there for the rest of the night—pissing pick handles on my own in the middle of the jungle.[22]

Such was the lot of the rifleman who would normally have his sleep interrupted for at least two hours every night to do gun picket and if the platoon was low in numbers it could mean longer stretches on the gun at night. With 12 hours of darkness being fairly consistent throughout the year it made for a general wearing down of the senses after six weeks straight in the bush. And, as has been already illustrated, the key to survival in the jungle against a guerilla enemy was security. The rifleman, therefore, was the basic building block in the platoon. If he didn't do his job, as lowly as it might have seemed to some, then everyone was at risk.

The riflemen worked hard, often forming the basis for the many work parties required for cutting landing zones for resupply helicopters, water parties and providing sentries when their platoons rested for longer than 15 minutes. They would always be the people called on for recce patrols, clearing patrols around the platoon or company harbour positions, clearing parties after contacts and ambushes, and burial parties for disposing of the dead enemy. These soldiers were never idle. Rifleman Dean Cooke sees the hardest part of being a rifleman as:

> Staying alert after a long patrol. Especially in the heat, you're sweating, it's hot. Especially when you get into rotten country, close country. You're struggling through the scrub and the heat and you tend to get pockets of it around you at times. Those things combined can just take that edge away and lose that alertness of that security.[23]

Each and every soldier is different and every individual will have a different perspective on soldiering. A National Serviceman, Kevin O'Halloran, who joined Delta Four as a reinforcement late in their tour and after most of the fighting had died down, saw a different sort of enemy—boredom. It has been said before that soldiering is 90 per cent boredom and 10 per cent absolute frightening chaos, but most occupations where men live on the edge are much the same. Firefighters train and get called into action much like infantrymen in a war zone, so boredom is nothing new. O'Halloran also agrees with several other men from Delta Four that sleep deprivation was his biggest hate:

> Lack of sleep was the most difficult. You became short and irritable with that. Night after night, I mean you used to virtually sleep with one ear open. Come picket duty time when the guy came to get you I always used to be able to hear him coming. I knew it was my turn. You couldn't get a good night's sleep.[24]

Rifleman Private Dean Cooke with an AK–47 Assault rifle his platoon captured in July 1971. All of the soldiers were given the experience of shooting the captured weapon to test its effect and accuracy. (*Photograph courtesy of Dean Cooke*)

There were other pressures on the riflemen as well. They were in a foreign country, the enemy often didn't wear a recognisable uniform and the soldiering itself was relentless and tough. To top it all off, very few soldiers spoke Vietnamese. All in all, it made for a fairly inhospitable environment. Kevin O'Halloran sums up his feelings this way:

> It was bloody hot, the mosquitoes, you were tired from lack of sleep, you were tired physically and you just had to keep going. That was the hardest thing—just to keep going. I suppose also, there was a lot of 'highs' in that, whilst I never got into contact personally, you were always out there, you were ready for it, there was a certain 'rush' there a couple of times. A big rush. I didn't like the joint, I never got to have conversations with many of the South Vietnamese at all. I didn't trust them. It was a totally foreign country to me and I just didn't like the place. I was glad to get out of it, I just never felt comfortable there. I suppose just being on the guard all the time there. That kept you going, but then the boredom set in—that was worse than anything, I suppose. Some days, as long as you had something to do you were all right, but if you were sitting down, you got bored easily.[25]

There should have been four riflemen in a rifle group but, as already pointed out, it was more often than not less than that establishment figure. I once had my total platoon strength drop to 21 men, which thus made the composition of three sections impossible. The solution was to make two large sections and carry extra firepower with another machine gun making a total of four in the modified platoon.

PLATOON HEADQUARTERS

The platoon commander is either a lieutenant or second lieutenant and is ultimately responsible for every man in his platoon. That responsibility extends to their training, their health, their morale and their welfare. He is the man who, as the saying goes, 'carries the can' when things go wrong. Conversely, he also gets the accolades when his platoon has a successful contact or ambush. The platoon commander is responsible for the platoon's navigation and its formation on the ground when travelling on foot. He is the one who decides what formations will be adopted, where machine guns will travel and what type of security measures are needed. It is obviously a demanding job but one which the platoon commanders of Delta Four relished. The Commander of 12 Platoon, Second Lieutenant Graham Spinkston, reflects on his job as a platoon commander:

> I had to make sure the platoon did what it was required to do in the sense of carrying out the instructions of the company commander. I think one of my roles was to keep the platoon informed of what was going on so that they knew what they were doing and why. I certainly was responsible for their welfare, to make sure that they were getting fed properly and had everything they needed as best we could. I was responsible for the way they operated, because it would have been very easy to say 'let's have a nice easy day today', but once you drop your standards, people start to get killed. Ultimately I think it was to keep them all alive—we were there to do a job but we would like to do it with as few casualties as possible. I think

maintaining the standards on long operations, because right up to the very last day of an operation you have got to keep on to the Diggers because you only need to make one mistake and you can lose people.[26]

Another platoon commander, Second Lieutenant Kevin Byrne of 10 Platoon, reminisced:

The most important part of my job was to deliver the goods. To lead my soldiers into battle, to do the best, to bring out the best in those soldiers in battle and bring them all home. That was my job. I personally thrived with the knowledge that these people expected me to produce and that drove me on to producing. And I must say that I loved my time as a platoon commander, loved it. Obviously, you know when you are climbing up a big hill with 80 pounds on your back and it's four o'clock in the afternoon and you had a company commander who said we're not going to stop until we get to the top and you knew it was eight hours away, and there's another false crest—I didn't like it. But they were only short periods of time. But the harder it was—the more I enjoyed it.[27]

The young platoon commanders who were in a war zone for the first time relied heavily on their platoon sergeants. Between them they had a wealth of experience. All had served in Vietnam previously and two had served in the Borneo campaign and in Malaya. All of them were long time members of the battalion and of Delta Four. Theoretically, the platoon sergeant's job is similar to that of the section 2IC. He is responsible for taking care of the administration of the platoon, while his leader gets on with the tactical aspects of 'fighting the battle'. Sergeant Daryl Jenkin was my platoon sergeant in Delta Four and he saw the role of the sergeant extending beyond just being the platoon administrator:

I think if you look at the platoon sergeant's role that's in the book it is probably the least thing that you do. It is administration, however, that is probably something that you just do. You don't really specifically train to do it. You just do it. It is something you learn from coming up through the ranks to make platoon sergeant. I think as a platoon sergeant you are 'jack of all trades'. You are everything. The morale of the platoon is certainly something that sits squarely with the platoon sergeant—probably more than the platoon commander in a lot of cases. If there are problems in the platoon, you probably get to know about it and have to sort it out as the platoon sergeant before it even goes to the platoon commander. Or any higher. I think if you can do that, it makes for a much better outfit all around. The platoon sergeant who thinks that he is only there for the administration has a problem. He just will never hold it together when times get tough.[28]

In the day-to-day tactical running of the platoon out on operations, the platoon sergeant is close at hand and has a wealth of experience on which the normally less experienced officer can draw. Daryl Jenkin continues:

A lot of things you work out together. As a platoon sergeant it was always good to be approached by a platoon commander and sit down and work something out together. That was always good. It is never so easy if somebody wants to dominate, and especially if you don't believe it is being done right. Then that can lead to problems, and I think that sitting down with section commanders is exactly the same thing. And section commanders sitting down with their section. It must go down the ladder. I am sure a company commander would at times ask advice from his platoon commanders.[29]

The important thing for the sergeants was to know everything about everyone in the platoon. All of the sergeants carried their own version of the platoon commander's notebook, which included shirt, trouser, boot and hat sizes so that replacement gear could be brought out to the field. It was also important that between the two of them, the platoon commander and his sergeant knew everything possible about their charges. From what courses they had completed to civilian qualifications, to even what their marital and financial state was. All of this information helped the platoon commander decide on who he would promote or place in a position of authority, who should attend subject courses for promotion and specialist courses. Many a time a radio message would come out to the platoon in the field asking who the platoon would be nominating for the next promotion course to be conducted in Nui Dat. Sergeant Daryl Jenkin saw his most important task in the 11 Platoon as:

> The welfare of everyone in the platoon. From generally knowing, as I did, most of their families; married ones, not that there were too many. Just knowing their background and their welfare. Knowing their moods. You might come across some Diggers who get a bit moody at things and you knew the times to just leave them alone rather than butt in. You must know your men extremely well. If you know your men well, I think half your problems are solved before they even happen.[30]

The Sigs

There were several soldiers whose job it was to carry the radio equipment, which was the lifeline of the platoon. In 1971 it was common practice for the rifle platoons to carry two ANPRC–25 set VHF radios. One was simply a back-up for the other but they were often used to monitor what was going on in the rest of the battalion or during a recce if it was being sent out further than usual. The radio was heavy, weighing some 7.6 kg. Spare dry cell batteries were required for when operating for more than 48 hours. The radio was carried in the normal Australian pattern pack, which meant that the radio operator often went without some of the small luxuries that other soldiers were able to squeeze into their kit. The batteries weighed about 0.68 kg and usually two were carried by the signaller or another member of platoon headquarters. In all the sig had some 10 kg of equipment along with his rifle, which was usually the lighter M16 Armalite, as well as his normal field equipment.

The most important 'weapon' in the platoon was the radio. It could call in more fire support and get you out of a jam quickly. It was essential, therefore, that it was manned by competent men who were not discards that the sections did not want. The men who manned the radio had to be alert, have initiative and be quick off the mark. They had to be able to answer a simple request with a short sharp answer that did not compromise the security of the platoon and yet still gave the information that was required. They needed to be able to listen to what the other two platoons were doing, in order to keep their boss informed about what else was going on in their AO. Consequently, they were always members of the Orders Group because they needed a feel for what was happening so they could answer questions from company headquarters without calling the platoon commander or the sergeant to the radio. They had to be able to give a brief and accurate situation report (Sitrep) in a contact, so that the platoon commander could get on with fighting the battle. They needed to be able to encode and decode short messages accurately. A sense of humour was very important because it was the sort of job where you got stuffed around a lot and usually not by someone in your own call sign.

The Diggers responsible for being communicators were trained by the battalion and called regimental signallers as opposed to Corps of Signals operators who manned the Task Force command and administration radios in Nui Dat. These hard working Diggers had another role and that was as orderlies in platoon headquarters. They carried messages by hand to section commanders or acted as runners (doing much the same job) when radio communications were not possible or not wanted. Orderlies were sometimes called batmen, that is the radio operators could be relied upon to have a hot brew ready for the boss when he came back from an orders group or a recce, and would get his food ready for him if he was busy preparing orders for the platoon. It was also a common practice that the next promotable private soldier be assigned to platoon headquarters to see how the platoon operated from a macro level and to see how things all fitted together. Lugging the radio around was a thankless task and not an easy one.

The operator would always be moving around to get better communication, or following the platoon commander around to ensure he was never far from the radio in case a message came through.

The second radio was usually held with the platoon sergeant (and a second radio operator) in case the first radio was damaged. The radio could then be used to alert the platoon sergeant or call the rear of the platoon. The second radio was carried by the second orderly who travelled with the platoon sergeant toward the rear of the patrol. It meant that the platoon could react quickly when moving in single file in the jungle as the column could be over 100 metres long if the vegetation was not too thick. The radio had to be manned at night and this task usually fell to platoon head-quarters. This meant that radio shift would be about two hours long and not too much of a strain on the people from headquarters. Some platoons fell into the dangerous trap of placing their radio on the machine gun picket. This is fraught with danger, as the radio can crackle into life and that sort of noise on the perimeter could be deadly to the person holding the handset to his ear. One cannot possibly concentrate on two things at once at night.

COMPANY HEADQUARTERS

The three rifle platoons and support section were all com-manded by company headquarters. Delta Four had two different company commanders during their tour of duty. Major Franz Kudnig was Company Commander before the tour during the training and preparation phase and for about eight weeks into the tour. He was replaced by Major Jeremy (Jerry) Taylor who had previously commanded Administration Company in 4 RAR. Because Major Jerry Taylor was the Company Commander for the greater part of Delta Four's tour, he was chosen to represent the views from the top of the hierarchal tree in the rifle company.

Company Headquarters (CHQ) comprised the Officer Commanding or OC, Major Jerry Taylor; the Company 2IC,

Captain Peter Schuman, MC; the Company Sergeant Major
(CSM) Warrant Officer Class Two Noel Huish; the Company
Quarter Master Sergeant (CQMS) Staff Sergeant Bob Hann
and about 12 Other Ranks who were clerks, pay repre-
sentatives, storemen, a detachment of cooks led by Sergeant
Joe Ryan, a medic attached from the medical platoon Corporal
Mick O'Sullivan (later to win a Military Medal) and from 4
Field Regiment the Forward Observer Party led by Lieutenant
Greg Gilbert, RAA. The attachments and their roles are dealt
with in the chapter entitled 'The Allies'. Consequently, CHQ
could be as big as a platoon if other attachments were thrown
in from the Corps of Engineers in the form of mini or splinter
teams and liaison officers or the addition of 'Bushmen Scouts'
who were Hoi Chanhs or ex-Viet Cong who had decided to
fight with the Allied Forces.

The officer commanding

The role of the officer commanding is most akin to a platoon
commander but on a much larger scale. He is responsible for
over 120 men who are deployed into the field. As in most
organisations, which have a chain of command and responsibility, it comes down to the fact that the company will closely
project and perform in a style and manner which resembles
its leader. Major Jerry Taylor saw his role in this way:

> Without doubt, I thought the biggest contribution I could
> make was to create an atmosphere in which everyone in
> the company worked willingly and well towards a common
> goal—which was success in battle.[31]

The platoon commanders are not only led by their company commander, but they are also guided, instructed, cajoled
and admonished. All of the platoon commanders looked upon
Jerry Taylor as a role model and one who they could turn to
for inspiration and guidance. Taylor, on the other hand, was
itching to get a run as a rifle company commander and escape
the relative boredom of being Base Defence Commander for

the Battalion Rear Party in Nui Dat. Jerry Taylor saw his tasks as:

> To create an atmosphere in which everyone saw their primary task as aggressively seeking out the enemy; to create an atmosphere in which the platoons could operate with a high degree of freedom of decision and action within the plan that I had laid down; and to manoeuvre the company in such a way that it would concentrate rapidly—say within 30 minutes—whenever the enemy was located; and that once concentrated, our aim would be to generate maximum violence at every point of contact.[32]

There are some very important points mentioned in that last comment from Taylor and they are worth discussing. The first was the 'atmosphere of aggressively seeking out the enemy'. For success in jungle operations, this is a most important trait that needs to be encouraged and developed. Fighting patrols—which were by far the predominant types of patrols deployed by 4 RAR—must have that 'killer' nature about them. It is no good going out on six-week patrols and pussy footing around and not using every means at your disposal to hunt down the enemy.

The second point Jerry Taylor makes is on the freedom of action he wished to extend to his platoon commanders. His predecessor did not do that and virtually told the platoons where and how they should search, and often, very often, set unachievable distances to be patrolled every day, with the consequent lack of proper searching and lack of security as the platoons desperately tried to meet objectives in time and space beyond their capabilities. This rigid and dictatorial approach caused much heartache and angst in the platoons and the platoon commanders felt mistrusted to do their job. When Jerry Taylor gave latitude and responsibility for searching and ambushing to his platoon commanders, results in the form of contacts came almost immediately. A different attitude pervaded the company and platoons became more aggressive and cunning as they followed their own leads and were able to adapt to varying situations within their own area of operations.

The last point that Taylor makes was indeed fortunate, for it saved the lives of many in 11 Platoon in late September 1971 when they came across a North Vietnamese Army regimental ambush and were badly outnumbered. As Taylor manoeuvred his platoons to support 11 Platoon, he was able to give support to the beleaguered infantrymen. On another occasion after 11 Platoon had made contact with a North Vietnamese platoon strength group, the enemy found themselves bouncing off 10 and 12 Platoon who were being manoeuvred to act as cut offs in an attempt to flush the enemy out of base camps or fortified positions.

For rifle company commanders in Vietnam, where their platoons were often thousands of metres apart, they had to rely on good communications and an understanding of how the young officers in the platoons would react or conduct themselves when confronted with difficult decisions. It was almost command by remote control. In Delta Four there would be nightly radio conferences commonly called 'prayers', where each platoon commander in turn would give a situation report on what his platoon had done and found during the day. After that, the company commander would ask what the next day's intentions were for each of the platoons. As this was often done in coded transmissions there would be a delay whilst the company commander deciphered what the platoons would be planning and either come back with an affirmative reply or discuss the plan to fit in with a bigger picture of which the platoons would not normally have been aware. Once battle is joined it is even harder, as confusion tends to be the predominant feature of contact in close country. Jerry Taylor describes some of the difficulties:

> For the company commander—the difficulties are being able to judge the dimensions of the battlefield accurately in order to allot troops to task; marking the Forward Line of Own Troops (FLOT) accurately; controlling manoeuvre; securing the flanks of the attack; and deciding where to locate himself to best influence the battle, which you must realise can be

taking place in a 360 degree arc; and finally orchestrating the use of supporting agencies in relation to the manoeuvre of the company.[33]

The company second-in-command

The company 2IC, Captain Peter Schuman, MC, was on his second tour of Vietnam having completed his first as a troop leader with the Special Air Service Regiment's (SASR) Number 3 Squadron in Vietnam. Schuman was amiable, approachable and knowledgeable, especially on matters pertaining to closing with and killing the enemy. The platoon commanders hung off every word he said and soaked up his vast array of handy hints when patrolling against the Viet Cong. As a company 2IC he often had to stay behind in Nui Dat and administer the company while they were out 'in the weeds'. He spent many weeks frustrated at not being able to join the company outside the wire. The administration of Delta Four was something that each and every soldier spoke very highly of and they fully appreciated what was done for them behind the scenes and out of the limelight. Peter Schuman saw his principal job as being:

> The health and welfare of the troops. Leave the tactics in battle and the leadership bit to the OC. He was the guy that had to train and give them confidence that he was the leader. I had to keep the guys well-equipped, shod, healthy, and get them their mail.[34]

The company sergeant major

Warrant Officer Class Two Noel Huish, who was also on his second tour with 4 RAR, used to rotate with Peter Schuman to be the battle 2IC for the company when it was on operations. As the senior non-commissioned officer in the company, a lot of responsibility fell on the CSM as the role model and disciplinarian for the soldiers:

> To a certain degree it's the role of mentor to the company as a whole. And that's not just the CSM, it's all of the experienced members of the company. You're right, there

were the usual admin tasks and the CSM is predominantly an admin man.[35]

The 'admin' or administration for the company was a plethora of tasks which generally appear mundane but were important to the soldiers—especially their mail. However, life for the admin man can get very exciting once battle breaks out as he is responsible for evacuating casualties and resupplying and redistributing ammunition in order that soldiers do not run out of opportunities to engage targets. As Schuman explains:

> Sometimes I couldn't protect myself because of resupplies and the nature of the work Company Headquarters was doing, at times you were just a mobile office in the field. I can tell you honestly, I don't think I fired my rifle on the whole tour. But a lot of guys around me protected me and fired their rifles and died. Not for the Company Headquarters. It was just part of the deal of soldiering. But I just had an office with five telephones. There was the Forward Observer net, the admin net, the ground-to-air, battalion command and the company internal net. So, I just walked along like a junior executive of a company with five telephones around me and five telephone operators, some highly prized staff, and just ran things from back of the firing line.[36]

A DAY IN THE LIFE OF A GRUNT

To understand what the infantrymen of Delta Four actually did—day to day as part of their 'bread and butter'—it is worthwhile to follow them through their daily routine and take the occasional side step to look at the types of activities that they had to conduct and execute.

The patrol is platoon strength and it is just before first light, probably around 0530 hours and the men on gun picket will have woken the section 2IC, who in turn will be gently shaking those men in their respective sections from their sleep. The riflemen drag on their boots, basic webbing and, if erected, drop their hootchies onto the ground—but not pack them up for fear of creating noise. The procedure is called 'Stand To'. This transformation of individuals from night routine to day routine is done in absolute silence.

It is the coolest time of day and the jungle is very, very quiet. The men sit or lie on the ground depending on their field of view into their allocated arcs of responsibility and watch their fronts as night slowly ebbs into soft daylight. It is still quite dim under the jungle canopy.

About half an hour later when the light has improved, a couple of men from each section move quietly to the designated gun position to move out and sweep the position. The direction of the sweep is varied every day to avoid setting a pattern and to keep everyone on their toes. The clearing patrol, after sweeping the area, return to their positions to give the all clear and the platoon commander orders 'stand down'.

This is the signal for the platoon to do one of two things. If the platoon is in the habit of moving straight after first light to another position to conduct their morning routine they will quietly pack up their equipment and move off in single file to another harbour. If the threat is determined to be virtually zero, the platoon may opt for conducting their morning routine *in situ*. The danger in this is that thirty dirty grunts can create a fair amount of odour in one position from their cooking and toilet, and the odour is not dissipated in the still air of the early morning.

Many platoons opted to move straight after first light and an hour later would again harbour and conduct their morning routine. This entails the platoon going to about 30 per cent alert with sentries posted on likely tracks or approach routes or just in front of the machine guns as was normally the case in thick bush. Each man would usually buddy up with another and they would take turns cleaning their weapons so that not all weapons were being stripped and cleaned at once. The machine guns would be cleaned one at a time. Weapon cleaning took precedence over any other activity.

While weapon maintenance is being done, water is heated for tea or coffee, always called a 'brew', and meals are cooked out of the selection of cans in the ration packs. The section

2ICs circulate and issue malarial suppressives. Up at platoon headquarters the platoon or patrol commander will be finalising his orders for the day's patrol and once he sees that his section commanders are able to accept orders he calls them in and gives navigation data for the next half day of patrolling to take the patrol until lunch time.

Some company commanders believed that daily shaving was important for morale; others, like Major Jerry Taylor, took an oppostive view:

> There were some very sound practical reasons for not shaving—it saved time; it saved water; and I really could see no point in shaving off perfectly good home-grown camouflage and then replacing it with greasepaint. In my view there's a lot of nonsense talked about what the indicators of 'good' discipline are. I've always considered that the place to worry about individual and collective turnout is in barracks and on the parade ground—and then the standard should be immaculate. But shaving and polishing one's boots on operations is completely irrelevant to discipline.[37]

The company medic, Corporal Mick O'Sullivan, insisted that soldiers shave a strip down their throats in case he had to conduct a tracheotomy to create an airway if a soldier was seriously wounded. Most of the Diggers complied with this request, knowing it would make Mick's job easier if they were ever going to be in that predicament. Another good reason for not shaving was the smell of soap applied as lather which is quite strong. Deodorants and the like were banned from being taken to the field because of their strong odours which were a give away in the jungle. Body odour was something that took about three or four days to get used to but once everyone smelt bad it didn't matter any more and people just got on with the job. Washing was a luxury and confined to crotches and arm pits if done at all. The emphasis was placed on other more important issues as Jerry Taylor explains:

> We in Delta Company didn't shave, we didn't clean our boots, we didn't wear badges of rank, and after Day Three of any

operation we all stank like polecats. But I venture to suggest that you could have stripped down any weapon in the company at any time of day and found it immaculate. And I recall, shortly after returning from Vietnam, a very senior and well respected Australian Army officer telling me that in his opinion Delta Company 4 RAR was one of the best rifle companies to come out of Vietnam. So I rest my case.[38]

Once the morning routine is completed the platoon rubbish is deposited in the central latrine called naturally 'the shit pit' and then covered over. 11 Platoon liked to have its soldiers empty their bowels onto the rubbish before patrolling for two reasons. One, it helped reduce gut problems if a man took a stomach wound, and two—and probably the reason most Diggers participated in the ritual—was that the enemy were known to dig up rubbish pits and the Diggers wanted to ensure that the scavengers received a nasty surprise. Soldiers were forbidden to 'cat crap' or defecate wherever they liked and never outside the platoon perimeter. One of the first smells usually detected from enemy camps by Diggers was human excrement. The Viet Cong were notoriously ill-disciplined in the manner in which they fouled the jungle. But the smell was often not just from excrement; the fact that 'we are what we eat' is fairly true and for the enemy who had a diet of mainly dried fish and rice often spiced with chilli, there was an unmistakable odour that came with them. Sometimes its olfactory effects had a startling result as Rifleman Wally Burford recalls:

> I went to sleep and I remember waking up, just wide awake, every nerve just seemed to be pulsing, and I couldn't work out why—and then it hit me—I could smell the nogs. I thought, Holy shit, I was laying in this bloody little hootchie, in a hammock, and had a mosquito net around me. So, the smell was that strong I knew they had to be very, very close.[39]

After the morning routine is completed, the platoon is off and moving. The radio operator sends a short code word for 'moving now'. Movement was usually in single file unless in cultivated areas, such as rubber and coffee plantations. The lead section commander has his bearings and distances written on his shirt sleeve or in chinagraph pencil on his piece of laminated map strapped to his weapon stock or in his pocket. The emphasis is on searching—quietly. Every soldier has his sleeves rolled down and any exposed skin is covered with camouflage cream.

The scouts tentatively push their way through the jungle as silently as possible, kept on course by occasionally looking around at their section commander who silently indicates whether to veer left or right to maintain their heading. Each soldier searches his arc, treading softly where possible and looking through the bush for any movement. The scouts also concentrate on the ground to pick any sign of foot movement. Tracking in Vietnam was an art form and those who were good at it would always be consulted to determine how old the track was and in what direction the enemy were last moving.

As the men continue their patrol, they randomly halt, kneel on one knee and listen. These listening halts were good for two reasons. One, it allows everyone to listen to the bush and second, it allows one to shift the weight of the back pack and relieve the aches. Even in the slightly cooler months and under the jungle canopy out of direct sunlight, the heat is still oppressive and the humidity enervating. After an hour's patrolling the jungle green shirts and trouser waistband start to look black from sweat. Listening halts can be ordered by anyone at any time, not just by the scouts or commanders. A snap of the fingers and the signal of a cupped hand to the ear brought the patrol to a sudden halt and the Diggers move off the line of march to the nearest cover and drop onto one knee. This listening halt technique paid off handsomely one day for 11 Platoon, when a Digger in the lead section called a listening halt. An enemy squad was scrub-bashing noisily on a compass heading and walked straight into the waiting platoon with dreadful results for them.

After an hour or so of patrolling, the men halt and send a radio message called a Locstat or location state, in code, detailing their location and what they are doing. Codes were used because it was known that the Viet Cong actually monitored very high frequency radio traffic in an endeavour to locate and attack the Allies. The Australians deployed counter measures against these listening posts and on several occasions destroyed and captured enemy intercept stations.

Paces and bearings are what navigation in the jungle is all about. The task of the sections, back from the front of the platoon, was to allot check pacers who would count their paces so that the platoon commander could calculate the distance travelled. It was important that the platoons knew exactly where they were so they could call in indirect fire support in time of contact or to summon a helicopter for resupply or casualty evacuation (casevac). The mortar fire controllers (MFCs) from the battalion mortar platoon and Forward Observer party bombardier assistants, colloquially called 'FO Acks', were very good at calculating where they were because their lives and, some thought more importantly, their reputations depended on it. As the platoons progressed through the bush the FO Acks and MFCs would adjust their 'On Call' targets which were silently registered to give them a list of targets that could be called down within a minute of contact breaking out.

Contact, wait out

These words were often heard on radio nets. It is usually screamed by some radio operator undergoing a huge adrenalin rush as he passed back to his next higher headquarters that they were in contact with the enemy and shots are being fired. The message is then passed quickly over the radio net, so that several agencies can prepare for action. At the company headquarters, the Forward Observer records the last known position of the platoon and is waiting for the next radio message which usually contains a very brief situation report along the lines of: 'Callsign 42 in contact, grid reference 123456, ten armed enemy, black dress, moving east. 42 initiated contact and following up, two enemy KIA (killed in action), no casualties, wait out'. The call sign sending the contact report at this stage does not even wait for acknowledgment that its message has been received. All other stations on the net minimise their traffic and keep the air waves clear until the situation is resolved. This allows for a fast reaction to requests for support. If the contact results in a casualty, the radio operator includes the words, 'Stand by Dustoff'. Back at Battalion Headquarters when this message is received, the helicopters designated to evacuate casualties from the field are told where the likely contact is taking place and what the general situation is. If the enemy is heading east, the chopper pilot's approach will be from the west to avoid taking ground fire from a withdrawing enemy or over flying a possible enemy camp.

Back on the ground, every man is now fully aware that his patrol is in contact and drills are being put in motion to gain the initiative over the enemy. This is sometimes difficult to do because of the terrain or vegetation or if the enemy is dug-in to some form of protection, such as a bunker system. Battle drills now take over and the built-in mental and then physical mechanisms induced by the repetitive nature of drills drives the soldiers into action. This is a strange situation, because the normal reaction is to take flight from danger but instead the Diggers are now plunging headlong toward it. Corporal Warren Dowell vividly remembers his first contact, 22 years after the event:

> The initial part wasn't too bad. I found that training took over and we just went into our drills and did everything we were supposed to. I wasn't scared at that stage—the adrenalin was pumping—but it was only after things had stopped that I started to get the shakes and the adrenalin started to really make me tired and it hit me that way. It is unbelievable how tired you get. I don't know what is in the drug adrenalin but it certainly knocks you around. It keeps you going while it has got to, but it takes its toll after it wears off, and because of this we tend to let our guard down and we become vulnerable.[40]

The adrenalin 'rush' that Dowell speaks of is a surge of blood sugar and insulin which subsequently overshoots and causes a rebound hypoglycaemia. This can manifest itself as lethargy and fatigue, and in some cases can last for several days depending upon the fitness level of the individual and the amount of stress to which they have been exposed.[41]

I remember my own first contact. Everything went just like we had practised so many times at Canungra and on exercises. I was very impressed and excited that the whole thing was coming together so very well, with machine gun teams deploying, Diggers putting down covering fire as their mates raced forward into fire positions. I could hear information being passed back on where the enemy were, how many and what they were doing. It was all going like clockwork. Then suddenly the contact drills stopped and nothing was happening, until I realised that everybody was looking at me as the platoon commander and waiting for me to give the next order to do something about the enemy that we had pinned down.

One of the principal reasons that drills are put in place is that it is a starting point for what will always be a confusing situation. No two contacts are ever the same and the enemy will always do his best to ensure that the fire fight takes place either over, above or around an obstacle of some kind. The contact will never be exactly head on but at an oblique angle. Guns will have stoppages, Diggers will fracture ankles, grenades won't detonate, the enemy will have a captured machine gun that sounds just like yours. There will be a dozen different things that make every contact unique.

The difficulties in contact vary from job to job for the infantrymen on the ground. For everybody, the biggest problem is noise. In Vietnam, the Belgian Fabrique Nationale (FN) 7.62 mm SLR was the standard issue personal weapon and carried the nickname 'elephant gun' for good reason. It went off like one. It was extremely loud and had great penetration and hitting power which was quite reassuring if you were firing at an enemy taking cover behind a small tree. Noise has a very unsettling effect in battle and makes communication difficult and is something that you cannot fight. One has to work around the noise. There are always grenades exploding or RPG missiles slamming into trees and detonating every time you want to yell an order or pass information to your mates.

Patience—which will sound somewhat strange given the desire to close with and kill the enemy as quickly as possible before he slips away into the security of the jungle—is required to make sure the right message is passed and people are not committed into battle ill-prepared. Section commander Warren Dowell felt this communication link was important to the riflemen because

> . . . you have got to keep the Digger informed all the time. With section commanders, platoon commanders, the company medic, the radio operators, they had things to do which kept them busy. Where the soldier had to not only do his own battle craft, he had to wait for the other people to direct him to do things. That must have been hard for them; waiting if they were in support to move forward or whatever. We commanders had things to occupy our minds. That is where if you keep your soldier informed of what is going on they understand *why* they have to move forward and do different things.[42]

Dowell makes the very good point that Diggers should know why they are being asked to do something. It doesn't have to be a drawn out lesson in minor tactics but a short burst on what you are trying to do goes a long way in motivating men in battle. Major Jerry Taylor agreed, but added that sometimes it was hard because of the noise:

> For the rifleman, it's noise—not being able to hear what his section commander is telling him, and the difficulty of passing information against the noise of close-quarter battle in a confined space; and also keeping contact with his neighbours.[43]

Pitting a rifle section or a platoon against an armed enemy is no mean task owing to the co-ordination required. All the training in the world can prepare you for battle but until you actually get into a fire fight and experience the noise, the smells, the adrenalin and the ordered chaos, it is difficult to convey the reality. The greatest fear I always had was that we would accidentally shoot our own men as we tried to pin the enemy to inflict a fatal blow by sweeping or rushing them on an angle. For the commander of the rifle section, which is considered for counter guerilla warfare to be the basic manoeuvre unit, Taylor added:

> For the section commander, it's also noise and also one of perception—trying to pass and receive accurate information; pin exactly where the enemy is, his size, what he's doing and what he will do; and then manoeuvring his section to keep it cohesive as a fire unit, but at the same time responsive to the platoon commander; and finally controlling movement.[44]

Contacts could range from seconds of brief shots and flight by the enemy to fire fights lasting for over half an hour or more. Anything over 30 minutes I consider to be more than a contact—it is an engagement, otherwise the enemy would have fled or countered with another form of manoeuvre. Every time the Viet Cong or North Vietnamese fought for longer than 30 minutes meant that we were facing a dug-in position and they needed to buy time to extract themselves or prepare another position to fight from. The fact that the enemy would often dig in called for caution when rushing headlong into contact situations. It was always a judgment call on how vigorously one launched into a contact. Good, hard information was required from the scouts to avoid having men caught inside a bunker system or where it would be very hard to extract them back to relative safety. This was where the platoon commander had to earn his pay and as Jerry Taylor says:

> For the platoon commander—it's as for the section commander, plus the difficulty of gaining sufficient, accurate information to make the decision to either press the attack home on his own, or to wait for the rest of the company.[45]

Another platoon commander, Second Lieutenant Kevin Byrne from 10 Platoon, summarised his thoughts with these well chosen words:

> I think the thing that shook me in the first encounter was it was mayhem. For those people that had never been in a fire fight it was just, 'Christ, what is happening here?' And it takes you several seconds and I guess as a platoon commander, the interesting thing was you shook your head after a while and thought, 'What the fuck is going on?' And then you realised well why am I saying that because I'm in charge of this show and you try and steel yourself and steady it and that was the biggest shock to me. It is like you're entombed in this bloody monster noise machine. It's terrible.[46]

Captain Peter Schuman believes that success in contacts comes down to the passage of information:

> He who has the information usually wins the day. And the information source, of course, comes from your intelligence assessment of the area and what you find. And from that you should be able to work out what's likely to happen. When it does happen, it is the forward scout, it is the training of the forward scouts and the corporals, the section commanders, to get that rapid information back, so that you can do something that is all important.[47]

For most of the Delta Four contacts, emphasis was really on instinctive reaction and speed. Later in another chapter we will look at sustained battle where the emphasis changes dramatically and becomes one of something more akin to conventional infantry fighting.

In the meantime, the fleeting contact is over. There is a strong smell of cordite hanging in the thick, tepid air of the jungle accompanied by grey blue smoke from grenades or rockets. The jungle is now deathly quiet and the commanders have to switch their men from yelling and shouting in the maelstrom of contact back to stage whispers to get the reorganisation drill under way. Men quickly check their ammo states and pass to their section 2IC how much ammunition they have left, so that a redistribution can be effected. People check to see if anyone has been hit or is missing; they check their kit is secure and has not come loose while crawling around on the jungle floor during the fighting.

I have deliberately used the words 'crawling around on the jungle floor' because unlike combat scenes in movies, men who want to stay alive do not run around upright exposing themselves. Occasionally, the various commanders, especially at platoon and section level, have to stick their heads up to see just what the hell is going on. I found that the only way I could see was to kneel and try to get as close as possible to the action without becoming too embroiled and caught up in the section's fire fight. The platoon commander has also got to learn to shut up at times and trust his subordinates to do the job. It's not easy, but gives great confidence to the section and their commander.

Reorganisation includes sending formal radio messages, detailing what has happened to whom and where and what results have occurred. If there are any friendly soldiers killed or wounded, they are evacuated by the fastest possible means along with enemy wounded who will be treated and then interrogated for intelligence purposes. The enemy dead in Vietnam were buried *in situ* and their graves marked with a marker made from local materials. The identification of the dead was recorded; sometimes the dead would be photographed for the Battalion Intelligence Section to keep their records intact. The grave site would be recorded in the platoon log held by the radio operator. The enemy were not buried if the situation called for a hasty withdrawal.

The first contact can be a turning point in a soldier's attitude and future behaviour in battle. Lance Corporal 'Jethro' Hannah recalls what happened after the first contact his platoon experienced:

> After we had done the initial search and all that, the platoon commander brought the bodies in and they were searched for all documents and stripped. Because this was our first contact in country, the area was secured, the platoon

commander then brought the whole platoon through, a section at a time so everybody could have a look at the dead enemy. These enemy had varied wounds. One looked like he had a mask that the bullet had gone through the skull and took off half of his face. It looked as though he had been hit by a machete straight in the middle and one half of his face was there and the other half was missing. I thought that was very valuable for everybody in the platoon. I remember later that evening in the harbour that the platoon were very appreciative of what and how he did that, because otherwise the blokes at the rear wouldn't have seen anything.

I don't think there was any fear whilst the contact was going on, but afterwards when you see the three enemy laying there dead, it starts to sink in. You think, well shit it could have happened to me. I think after that for the next three days the patrolling became very, very aware; the pace was slowed down; the movement was excellent. For the next three days everyone was so aware—'shit, we are not firing blank rounds any more'.[48]

Once the reorganisation has been concluded the platoon moves off and continues on its mission. If the patrol doesn't move off straight away it must watch its security very carefully because Diggers start chattering through the excitement of it all and, as described earlier, some men will suffer from their adrenalin surge and become careless and lethargic.

Patrol duration

For Delta Four the average time spent on operations, outside the wire and scrub bashing, was around six weeks. I asked every person interviewed for this book how long they thought patrols should be and the consensus was no more than a month. Soldiers need to have their batteries recharged and 42 days on patrol can be very demanding both physically and even more so mentally.

I remember vividly one particular patrol. We did not have a contact in the entire six weeks, yet we saw the enemy on several occasions but were unable to engage them owing to our own vulnerability (recce party) and distance. The stress that the strain of constant alertness imposes is quite considerable and unless soldiers can get relief from that intense pressure, then fatigue and mental tiredness can creep in. Rifleman Wally Burford got down to tin tacks about six-week long patrols:

> You can't stay switched on for that period of time. If you're not having contact, you're not finding regular sign of the enemy and everyone starts getting blasé. You start getting a bit too casual. You start making a little bit more noise at night. When you're patrolling you're not as alert. A patrol of three weeks means you can keep your mind on the job the whole time. Six weeks—with the exhaustion, when you're patrolling in jungle all day, it's very debilitating. You're sweating, it's a lot of physical work; you're not having your sleep. You're not having what you would call a first-class menu with green vegetables and all the stuff you need for stamina. During nights, you're laying awake a lot. Operating in the rain—the rain keeps you awake and you're out on sentry and you have got to come back and try to get sleep. You're operating on exhaustion a fair bit and trying to go that long on six weeks, means that you do start to lose your sharp edge. And when you start to lose your sharp edge, then you can start losing blokes.[49]

Several platoons had a system of establishing a firm base and sending out a strong half-platoon patrol, usually with a radio and two M60 machine guns. They would search using a 'fan' patrol to clear a sector of a platoon AO. This had the advantage of letting tired and wet feet dry out and recover, enabling everyone to recuperate within the space of two or three days. Knee and ankle sprains can be a problem, especially in the wet. Often a day's rest can be enough to allow a recovery for a slight sprain.

Diet is another concern. Many infantrymen who served in Vietnam suffer today from gut-related problems stemming from a lack of fibre and fresh food in his diet whilst on operations. The constant and often unchanging diet of canned, concentrated rations is monotonous. Many a time I have seen a Digger open a can of food without bothering to see what it was because 'it all tasted like shit anyway'. One platoon in

Delta Four suffered four weeks of canned turkey as the main supplement to their diet because of some administrative oversight. It was not unusual for men to carry chilli and other condiments to give their tins of meat some spark to relieve the boredom of their diet.

Every 10 days a resupply chopper would come into the platoons. The choppers would bring in rations, replacement equipment and clean greens to replace the filthy clothing the Diggers had been wearing for the last 10 days. Mail would also accompany the 'big resup' as it was known. Most platoons would spend the rest of the day allowing the Diggers to catch up on news and to write letters, which would be taken back with the dirty greens.

It was not uncommon on these resupply days to find that one of the Diggers was having a birthday during the next 10 days or so, and for Sergeant Joe Ryan, the Delta Four cook, to bake a cake in a tray and send it out on the resupply chopper. The celebrant would then be paraded within the platoon, which would form a tight circle around the birthday boy—with sentries posted of course—and the Digger would be made to kneel on the ground in an upright fashion. A thick application of shaving cream would be applied to his head to form the 'icing' to support a paper wick to substitute for a candle.which would then be lit. In a stage whisper, the rest of the platoon would then sing 'Happy Birthday' to the Digger and then help him demolish his cake. This was important for the men, many of whom were celebrating their 21st birthday a long way from home and without the traditional fanfare and family that accompanies this event.

Night movement

In the next chapter, when discussing the battle at Nui Le, it will become evident how difficult it is to move and fight in the dark. Of course, technology today has turned that problem around and indeed when 1 RAR deployed to Somalia in 1992, the bulk of their contacts were at night but they were equipped with night vision goggles which meant they could operate quite effectively 24 hours a day. Under the jungle canopy with very little ambient light it would still be very difficult, unless operating with infra-red equipment which is still heavy and expensive for a personal issue item. But in 1971, night movement was rarely done unless for a reason of operational necessity. On one occasion, 11 Platoon had to move at night because of a US Air Force B-52 bombing mission, known as an 'Arc Light', was to take place in Long Khanh Province and the platoon had to move some 1500 metres to place itself outside the danger zone of the 500 and 1000 lb bombs that would descend close to where they were then situated. The greater problem was that movement itself was fraught with danger. Even with a good moon, night vision in the jungle is difficult and soldiers can easily poke their eyes out on branches and more likely spend most of their time on their backsides from tripping over vines, logs and deadfall.

Consequently, platoons would prepare for their night routine well before last light. If circumstances allowed, most platoons would stop for their evening meal about an hour and a half before last light and allow the soldiers to cook a hot meal and have a brew. Once that had been completed, they would then patrol for about half an hour or longer and then go through a series of drills that would get them on the ground in a quick, silent and well co-ordinated fashion. This was called harbouring and became known as the platoon NILOC or night location. It also meant implicitly that you did not intend to move again until the next morning. The area was swept by clearing patrols and all that was done in the night harbour was to prepare shelters for the night, without erecting them, and wait until dark. Communications cord would be placed along the ground to guide people from their sleeping site to the gun where the picket would be run during the evening but not raised to waist height until after Stand Down. This meant that a track plan was laid out and meant that the noise of people moving at night when visibility would be very low would be minimised. The track plan is an essential part of noise discipline again and aids security. Important also was the need to ensure that the track was cleared quietly of any material likely to cause noise or be an obstacle to foot movement. As last light approached, the order for Stand To would be given and every man would sit and watch his arc of the perimeter in absolute silence. Kevin O'Halloran remembers Stand To as an enjoyable part of his daily routine and when he felt 'good' out on operations:

. . . strangely enough it was out in the scrub. It only happened a couple of times, it was either early morning or on sunset when things were quiet. Being up in the Nui Dinhs, right up, we were well and truly up one morning and I woke up and it was cool. It wasn't bloody hot and it hadn't rained, so it was nice, that was dandy, and everything was quiet and I looked across and I could see the whole of the countryside. And you say, 'Jesus, is there are a war going on here?' You just really didn't realise it. And you would say, 'Yeah, this could be a nice country if it wasn't for the war.[50]

While the sections were preparing their night routine—laying out their comms cord, setting up their Claymore mines in front of the machine guns and clearing track plans—the platoon headquarters signallers would be busy encoding messages by the light of red torches to minimise the glow and sending situation reports or encoding Locstats for the night position. The platoon sergeant could possibly be sending off requests for equipment needed on the next resupply or sending strength statements on how many people were actually on the ground and who needed to be sent back on the next resupply chopper for a rest or some other reason, such as dental or medical treatment. The platoon commander would be going over his plans for the next day's activities or preparing orders for a special activity such as a likely ambush target. He would inform his OC and the other platoons what he had done and planned for the next couple of days.

The MFC or FO Ack would encode the artillery targets for night defensive fire tasks (called for some reason, 'Tin Trunks') and they were all radioed in before last night and plotted on large maps at the fire support co-ordination centres at the battalion and Task Force command posts. Anyone moving at night would place these targets in jeopardy by moving near or through silently registered target locations. Consequently, night movement was actively dissuaded and it was taken as a given that anyone moving at night was therefore usually the enemy. It was less confusing, safer and more predictable that night movement by the Australians was not undertaken.

Once darkness had settled in and one could no longer sight through the iron sights of the rifle, the platoons would Stand Down and adopt their night routine. The percentage of alertness would be told to all the Diggers. If the platoon had had a contact during the day or seen, smelled or heard enemy in their area they would often stay on 60 per cent Stand To until an hour after dark, to see if the enemy were aware of their presence.

Sometimes when situations were desperate for manning, platoons would adopt a very low profile and seek very thick scrub or thorny bamboo to back up against and man a half-moon perimeter with only two guns manned to allow the soldiers to get some rest. There is not much advantage in stopping for the night and only having three hours sleep after a hard day's patrol. Tired Diggers will be the end result and ones that are not alert usually are the first to become casualties—or their immediate neighbours. About a half an hour before first light, the morning routine starts all over again and another day of patrolling commences.

Ambushing

Sometimes during a patrol, information would be received by the battalion or company Intelligence cell that allowed platoons to target a track or some other site for ambushing. For Delta Four, who did a lot of scrub bashing during their tour, this was a rare occasion and the reader who is keen to learn more of the experiences should read the Eighth Battalion (RAR) History, *The Grey Eight in Vietnam*[51] where some very good examples of ambushing are recorded, especially one involving Sergeant Chad Sherrin who conducted a very successful ambush which involved relocating his ambush patrol to a better site during the night with all of the dangers that incurred.[52]

Ambushing is a very difficult tactic to employ because it will usually involve night fighting, when the enemy were more likely to move to avoid the Australian patrols and artillery and air strikes. It requires troops who are highly trained and have a high degree of noise discipline and battle-craft. They have to have the discipline to stay in the one place for considerable lengths of time and to be able to act on their own initiative. The orders for ambushes must be very detailed but paradoxically the ambush *must* have a simple plan.

The execution must be simple, violent and complete. The aim is to kill everything and anything that walks into that ambush site. I was once taken to task by a journalist who thought that my platoon's practice of clearing the ambushed track was not in accordance with Geneva Conventions. When ambushing, 11 Platoon's SOP was to spring the ambush and when clearing the ambush site, the search parties would be covered by the machine guns who would deploy onto the side of the track and cover each flank—looking out to where more enemy may appear. The killing group would usually comprise the search party and they would quickly advance onto the track, placing their rifle barrel against the head of any enemy laying on the track and despatching the enemy with a head shot. Naturally if there was an enemy sitting or laying on the track and attempting to surrender he would be captured and treated as a POW. But for those enemy laying motionless, they were despatched and the search party would sweep past, searching off the track about 15 metres in case enemy had been blown off the foot pad by the blast of 18 Claymore mines or crawled away wounded. The search group would then sweep back and drag the bodies back into the ambush site where they would be stripped and searched for papers and any identification. If time permitted they would be then buried as described earlier in this chapter. The despatching of the enemy as I have described meant that any enemy feigning death could not 'rise from the dead' and inflict casualties upon your own troops, as was reported to have happened in previous encounters in ambushes with Australian troops.

One memorable ambush involved a 10-day stint with 11 Platoon, which was ambushing a known resupply rendezvous point at the intersection of two tracks in a rubber plantation. Cover was afforded by one quarter of the intersection being over-grown coffee. The platoon had set up a Claymore ambush and set up a rest area some 50 metres back from the ambush site in a depression in the ground. In that rest area, the soldiers could sleep and eat. No cooking was allowed and the Diggers had to eat cold rations for the duration of the ambush. One afternoon about five days into the ambush, a group of civilians collecting firewood, who probably came from a village about a kilometre and a half away, wandered into the ambush rear protection group without seeing any of the Diggers but saw a few Claymore mines sited to protect the rear of the ambush. That night the rear protection group heard movement to their front and flank and a small group of five to six enemy attempted to penetrate the ambush position. The Claymores were fired and the enemy fled onto one of the tracks leading back toward the village. The artillery fired in an attempt to cut off the enemy but more probably just to give them a bit of a hurry up as they withdrew, but when illumination was fired to see if any enemy were on the track, the carrier shells for the flares crashed down onto the Diggers in the ambush positions. No casualties were reported by either side and blood trails the next morning petered out after about 100 metres, so the likelihood of serious injury was probably minimal. The ambush had to be abandoned, but that village was always marked for a random sweep whenever Australians were in the area.

Return to Nui Dat—Exercise Lifesaver

When the platoons from Delta Four came back from their patrols, they went through a process of shedding their old and dirty equipment and cleaning and re-issuing new equipment. Every time Delta Four came in off an operation they would, while back in Nui Dat, be put through a bull-ring exercise known as 'Exercise Lifesaver'.

Sergeant Daryl Jenkin
hones his shooting skills
between patrols on the
improvised 'range' of
Nui Dat.

Each and every man of the company would be tested on
his basic TsOET on all weapons in the platoon, including
mines and grenades; basic radio procedure for encoding and
decoding messages; first aid for shock, heat treatment and gun
shot wound bandaging; posting and briefing sentries, marrying
procedure which laid down the exact procedure for platoons
and units to marry up in the field and not accidentally clash
with each other. It also covered the siting and aiming of
Claymore mines, and the Rules of Engagement had to be
recited and understood by everyone. A good knowledge of
the various types of weird and wonderful camouflage uniforms
worn by the many and varied military and para-military groups
operating in the 1 ATF area was important. The sections
would then be put through various drills such as 'Mine Freeze',
which laid down the procedure in the event of someone
triggering an anti-personnel mine and the method for clearing
and evacuating a safe path for the platoon to extricate itself.

The platoons would then go down to the 'range' and fire
off the old ammunition and Claymore mines not used on the
patrol. This allowed everyone to become familiar with the
various weapons that the platoons carried, and it meant that
ammunition was constantly turned over and not affected by
too much exposure to moisture and damage whilst being
carried on patrol. I found that a 9-volt battery placed inside

a water bottle split to accept the large power pack and then resealed with soldered alligator clips and waterproof tape made an excellent, silent firing device. On one memorable occasion over two dozen mines were set off in this fashion on the range, but unfortunately the Task Force Headquarters were not warned of the impending mini-Hiroshima and thought the base was being rocketed.

Full medical checks were undertaken by the platoon commanders with assistance from the platoon stretcher bearer and company medic. Men were treated for varieties of ailments from sprains to other exotic tropical diseases mainly centred around skin and heat problems. It was important that no-one escaped this medical dragnet and pass on infections in the close environment of communal living and showering.

Soldiers then attended to a range of administrative detail, including receiving and sending mail, getting paid, attending to a plethora of admin detail, such as pay allotments, sending parcels home and tidying up their tents which became dirty and dishevelled during their absence.

After the administration had been attended to, it was time for rest and convalescence (R & C), which was taken in the seaside resort town of Vung Tau to the south of the Task Force Base. Once R & C had been taken, the soldiers returned to be briefed on their next operation and the cycle would start all over again.

This chapter has endeavoured to show the basic life of infantrymen on operations. It was a far from glamorous life. It was instead hard work, demanding both physically and mentally and often frustrating. Survival and success rested above all else on being professional:

> I couldn't believe the actual professionalism and that's some-thing that I have really been proud of, the fact that I have been a part of a team that was really professional in their bush work. It didn't have to be forced on them, it didn't have to be pushed on them. We are no more 'kiddies', we are at war, so we need to be pretty schmicked up, we need to be clued up and know what's going on, switched on. I was really proud to be part of the company—I really was. The professionalism was great.[53]

4

'IT HITS THE FAN'

Battle . . . is essentially a moral conflict. It requires, if it is to take place, a mutual and sustained act of will by two contending parties, and if it is to result in a decision, the moral collapse of one of them.

JOHN KEEGAN
THE FACE OF BATTLE

CONTACTS IN THE AUSTRALIAN EXPERIENCE in Phuoc Tuy and surrounding provinces were, for the most part, short, sharp and often fleeting affairs. Rarely did a contact last for more than 15 to 30 minutes. Once the enemy knew he was outnumbered or out-gunned he would do what any self respecting guerilla would do—withdraw and wait for when he would have the upper hand. He did this because he knew that the Australian forces hardly ever operated outside of artillery or mortar range and usually had air support on call if they really got into trouble. For Delta Four there were two occasions when the Australians were outnumbered by the enemy and when they decided that for better or for worse and for tactical reasons they would stay and fight.

THE BATTLE OF THE SUOI CA

The first was in late July 1971, elements of 4 RAR were searching for enemy believed to be from 274 Viet Cong (Dong Nai) Main Force Regiment in Phuoc Tuy Province. Delta Four was conducting a mounted operation code named IRON FOX with a troop (1 Troop) of APCs from A Squadron, 3 Cavalry Regiment and a troop of Centurion tanks from C Squadron, 1st Armoured Regiment.

Charlie Company 4 RAR located an aggressively defended Viet Cong bunker system on the afternoon of 29 July. Seven Platoon was following a track when they made contact with a considerable number of the enemy. Several Viet Cong were shot. The Viet Cong fired rocket propelled grenades, machine guns and crude, home-made Claymore mines which were located in the trees. Contact was maintained for over an hour before the platoon could be extracted.

The bunker system was along the line of the Suoi Ca river, also called the Song Ca, close to the Long Khanh Province border in the north of Phuoc Tuy Province. The bunkers were hit with considerable artillery and aerial bombardment as Charlie Company manoeuvred to attack. Night fell and thwarted their attempts. When Charlie Company moved against the position at first light the next morning, the Viet Cong had withdrawn.

On the morning of 30 July, Delta Company had just dismounted from the APCs of A Squadron and was about to continue its search and destroy operation when news of the Charlie Company action came over the battalion command net. The men of Delta Company hastily regrouped with the tanks and then moved from its area of operations to assist Charlie Company. The men of Delta Company really busted a gut to reach them, despite the incredibly thick jungle and broken terrain. Delta Four spent that morning searching the abandoned bunker system, and then destroyed it. Afterwards, the commanding officer, Lieutenant Colonel Jim Hughes, decided to clear down the line of the Suoi Ca river, in a south-westerly direction, with Charlie Company on the southern bank and Delta Company on the northern bank.

Around two o'clock in the afternoon, Delta Four started to move out along the line of the river. The armoured personnel carriers and tanks were sent off to refuel as the company made their way along the side of the river through very thick jungle with huge trees and interminable vines hanging everywhere. Visibility was down to about 15 to 20 metres and the light was subdued under the jungle canopy. Because of the numbers of enemy the company expected to encounter, they were moving as a whole company and it was a slow process indeed. The thick vegetation had forced them to move in single file and whilst it was easy to control, it was pretty boring for those stuck at the tail end of the column.

It didn't stay boring for very long. Eleven Platoon, which was at the tail, had not moved from their company harbour position when all hell broke loose at the point. Delta Four had hit another bunker system even though they had not even travelled 200 metres out of the one they had just destroyed! The enemy turned out to be 1 Battalion and the headquarters of 274 Viet Cong (Dong Nai) Main Force Regiment. The 'Dong Nai' is the VC name allotted to the regiment and which the province of Phuoc Tuy and Long Khanh is named today.

Ten and 12 Platoon were both shaken out into a two-up formation where they could ascertain how big the system was. From the amount of small arms fire that could be heard from the rear, there was no shortage of enemy or ammunition up ahead. Major Jerry Taylor decided to push forward as a company to see what Delta Four were up against. The tanks were given a call on the radio and told to get back from their refuelling to join the company as quickly as they could. This would be no mean feat as scrub bashing in this type of thick jungle in a Centurion was near to impossible. Quick reconnaissance by the forward platoon commanders, Kevin Byrne and Graham Spinkston, showed that Delta Company were up against a reasonably sized system and that the enemy were not about to withdraw.

Charlie Company were tasked to cover Delta Company's southern flank and as soon as the tanks joined Delta Four, they were going to assault the bunkers. Even though Delta

Four had been working with the Centurion tanks on the previous phase of the operation, they had never rehearsed a full blown company attack with tanks in direct support, but this is exactly what was about to happen. It speaks highly for the flexibility and adaptability of the troops when one considers they were not able to rehearse or discuss in detail the manoeuvre before they launched into the attack. It was going to be tricky and it was going to be a case of 'suck it and see'.

The initial reactions of soldiers in contact, especially when it is their first contact, is always remembered vividly. In this battle Private Bob Meehan of Nine Section, 12 Platoon, was in contact for the very first time and he recalls what happened when rounds started coming his way:

We were heading towards a bunker system, we all knew there was a bunker system there and we were heading towards it and we had seen the enemy first and they were pissing off. I had a forward scout, [Private A. C.] Alan Ottway, and he turned around and gave me the enemy sign and pointed which way they were going. By the time I was just about to yell out, 'Gun's going right' to let Spingo [Second Lieutenant Graham Spinkston] know exactly where I was going, all hell broke loose off to our left. Ten platoon had hit the enemy. I took off anyway and when I hit the ground there was a bunker in front of me and thank Christ no one was home. The next thing I know, I'm copping rounds across the top of my head and I could hear an M60 going. So, I thought, 'Shit, I have walked into our own people', and I held my fire as did the other machine gunner in the platoon, because initially for the first couple, seemed like hours, but for the first couple of seconds we thought we had walked into each other. We then found out the enemy had an M60 and so I went forward again. I found another bunker which was occupied, so I put as much firepower through as I could and I was told that I was copping rounds, but really I never heard them. So, I was just doing my job and trying to get the enemy but I was also trying to put down so much fire so that none of our blokes got hit—but we got word that one of our other blokes, [Private C. D.] Sedgwick, who was a couple of hundred yards back, copped a round through the calf muscle and here I am up the front, I'm not getting hit, but the blokes down the back are getting hit. So, bullets don't stop they just keep going until they find something to hit.[1]

The company would be assaulting with two platoons forward, each with two sections in assault formation, with a tank central with each platoon. Company Headquarters would be travelling in the centre just behind the assault sections and my platoon would be centre-rear. Artillery from the Battalion Direct Support (DS) Battery was being called in from Fire Support Base 'Cherie' which was to the west and behind the assaulting troops some five or six kilometres away. The Forward Observer, Lieutenant Greg Gilbert, had a difficult time dropping the rounds onto the enemy as the shells were coming from the rear and catching the very tall trees and spraying live shrapnel amongst all and sundry, and we took a few minor casualties from our own artillery fire. The wounds were not too bad—mainly shrapnel wounds to the backs of the legs. The plan was that he would keep the artillery falling just in front of the assault, so as to keep any enemy from interfering with the attack.

The attack started in earnest and before long the battle was in full cry. The rifle sections were crawling forward and clearing about five or ten metres in front of the tanks, which would then drive slowly forward and come just past the men lying on the jungle floor. The Centurions would then engage any bunkers they could see and hit them with high explosive shell and machine gun fire. The golden rule was not to get forward of the second road wheel when the tanks fired as the 84 mm main armament blast would severely injure the infantrymen hugging the ground. If the tanks couldn't see anything to their front, they let rip with a canister round to clear the vegetation. The tank troop commander, Lieutenant Bruce Cameron, had done this sort of thing before on Operation OVERLORD with 3 RAR, so he was a source of inspiration to the infantrymen embarking on their first full blown company attack. Major Jerry Taylor was co-ordinating the assault and trying to keep the assault platoons level so they didn't expose a flank to the enemy in the fire fight.

It was extremely slow going. Fire and movement had to be done on stomachs all the way, for to stand up in the assault line was asking for trouble and a quick death. The enemy were raking the assault area with long bursts of automatic fire—most of which was just above the men's heads as they crawled forward. Ten Platoon had their first casualty when one of their riflemen, Private Bernie Pengilly, stood up to get out of the way of a tank. He was hit in the chest by a large calibre machine gun bullet which knocked him backwards about a metre.

I was forward, carrying an ammunition resupply from the APCs to the forward platoons, who by now had been fighting through the bunkers for over 30 minutes. I grabbed my medic Private Frank Wessing and got him to go forward to where Pengilly had been hit to see what he could do. Frank crawled forward and reached Pengilly, who was mortally wounded. While Frank was treating the wounded Pengilly, he put his rifle down on a foot track. A Centurion passed and then another, and ran straight over his rifle. It was a mess. The woodwork was completely shattered and the barrel was bent almost at right angles.

Pengilly was now dead. The stretcher bearer, Frank Wessing, was preparing to put him in a collapsible stretcher to move him out of the battle area. After he had evacuated Bernie Pengilly to the APCs to our rear, he came back to where I was watching the fire fight. He was shaken by Pengilly's death and was concerned at what had happened to his rifle. He told me he was shit scared and feared retribution from the Company Quarter Master Sergeant, on his return to Nui Dat. I told him to take Pengilly's rifle, stick his own smashed SLR in with Bernie's body and forget about it and that he should be more scared of the enemy than Bob Hann, our CQMS.

By now the company was right inside the bunker system and the fighting was pretty fierce. The thing that one noticed almost immediately was the incredible noise of the battle. Training at Canungra and on exercises in Australia had not prepared me for the unbelievable din of battle. Weapons like the SLR, AR 15 or M16 and the AK-47 are noisy, but when the tanks let loose with their 20 pounders only feet from

where we were taking cover, the blast and noise was staggering. Many soldiers couldn't hear what their commander was
saying as they attempted to pass messages, and they had to
either crawl over to their men to make themselves heard or
send a runner. Corporal Warren Dowell remembers:

> You had to rely on people passing the word on and in the
> 'J' with six man sections, even then you're not that spread
> out. I found that if I started to give orders a lot I would
> draw enemy fire. The enemy will tend to zero in on people
> talking, if the section can't hear you, you had to stand up
> and run—certainly bend over, scurry over, and get across
> to whoever you wanted to talk to or they would have to
> pass the word on for you.[2]

The tanks were the key to Delta Company going forward.
The Viet Cong were fighting from behind the lids of their
bunkers and occasionally from inside the stepped entrance.
Most of the bunkers were about six foot square and had a
raised roof which was very well camouflaged and which was
only a foot or so above the level of the ground. They were
not the classic Second World War bunker everyone imagines,
with a slit firing port and made out of concrete. In fact the
roof was constructed of three or more layers of logs with hard
packed clay between each layer of timber. They were primarily
designed as protection against US B-52 air strikes and artillery
fire. The camouflage on the bunkers was so good soldiers
found themselves literally sitting on top of one before they
knew it.

Fighting through the bunker system was hard, because
fire-lanes had been prepared between each bunker in order to
give mutual support to one another. The fire-lanes were used
by the enemy to allow them to sight their weapons through
the undergrowth and aid detection of human movement. They
were about a foot wide and cut from ground level to knee
height and you could not see them until you were literally
looking down it. That was then a pretty bloody awful feeling.
Knowing where all the bunkers were was vital before we

could push forward; otherwise men would be cut down in the fire-lanes.

Ten and 12 Platoon were finding the going very tough and progress was naturally slow. After an hour or so we had probably advanced no more than 100 metres into the system, yet the firing from the enemy was still intense. The Army Aide Memoir suggests an advance rate faster that that, however, I suspect that the author of that document had not taken into account the problem of fighting through smashed vegetation and fallen trees and a very determined enemy who didn't want to leave home.

I asked Warren Dowell if there was ever a problem of getting men to go forward, and he replied:

> I never had any trouble in getting them to go forward but having said that, I had never seen any of them get up and run forward like they do in the movies. Going forward is either a leopard-crawling sort of affair, or on your stomach going forward. I didn't see any long rushes or 'Banzai' sort of stuff. It was all moving forward slowly, but still moving forward.[3]

It must be remembered that this is close contact stuff in bunker fighting. The enemy are often only 10 to 15 metres away and it becomes a case of being pretty careful lest you lose your life for not looking before you leap.

But now it was 11 Platoon's turn to launch into the attack. Major Jerry Taylor decided to push 11 Platoon through 10 Platoon to maintain momentum. I will now recall my memories of that eventful afternoon when I was committed to the attack:

> With my heart pounding, I dashed back to where my platoon was lined out, gave quick confirmatory orders to my section commanders who were waiting at platoon headquarters with my sergeant, Daryl Jenkin, and we moved forward in extended line to start our assault. By now radio voice procedure had been drastically abbreviated; in fact Major Taylor was calling the platoons by the platoon commander's first name. It saved time and saved confusion

between the radio call signs 41, 42 and 43 and company headquarters being 40. (These are pronounced 'four one, four two' and so on.) Besides, the noise from the small arms, the screaming motors on the Centurions and firing of the 20-pounder main gun on the tank, meant that it was bloody difficult to hear what was being said over the radio. I linked up with the tank which would be pushing forward with our platoon and we started assaulting. I have to admit I still had no idea how many enemy we were up against but from the amount of firing it sounded like a 'one on one' battle to me. I guess the fact that we had the firepower was the reason we were determined to push home our attack.

The soldiers were told to watch their ammunition usage, as the company had run out of ammo several times already and the armoured personnel carriers only had so much left on board. Keeping my men moving forward in a straight line was a difficult task. Every time I tried to yell a command, someone would either fire a rifle or a tank would let go with a canister round or enemy fire would force our heads down. The only way I could get my message across was to move across to the section commander I wanted to speak to and talk into his ear at close range. I was now beginning to comprehend the lesson at Officer Training Unit, Scheyville on the 'Position of the Platoon Commander in Battle'.

We made reasonable progress and 'caterpillared' forward with the tank. When the tank fired its canister round, it was a stunning sensation and had the effect of drowning out all other noise for some time after. But the tank was keeping us going forward: it was devastating bunkers with high explosive shells or running over the roof of the bunker and then doing a track turn and collapsing the lid. At the same time we were providing flank protection for the vehicle and crew, and spotting enemy who were firing at the tank or at our own men. While all this was being done we were also desperately looking over our shoulders for trees and branches being knocked down by the tanks as they crashed forward.

As we fought our way through we came under fire from an M60 machine gun. Instead of the high pitched 'chat chat chat' of the AK-47 assault rifles we were now hearing a slower 'Dug, dug, dug'. It was firing at the tank and ricochets were going everywhere. The tank wasn't being damaged by this enemy gun but it was stopping my men from going forward as it ripped through the trees and logs we were using for cover.

Finally we were able to get a reasonable fix on where this machine gun was firing from. I was unable to communicate with the crew commander of the tank on the tank telephone at the rear of the tank. The phone must have been designed by someone who had never been shot at, as I had to stand up to talk because the cable was too short to allow me to take cover. I jumped up onto the back of the tank and gave the crew commander a target indication. The tank then raked the area with its machine gun and before long a Viet Cong gun crew broke from cover and withdrew along a footpad between the bunkers. I heard the tank crew commander on his radio yell, 'Traverse left, canister load, fire!' and the enemy gun crew were hit at a range of about 20 metres at most and that was the end of them. The canister round literally blew the scampering gun crew to smithereens.

This was the first time my platoon had been under heavy enemy fire. The sensation was incredible. Most of the enemy rounds were passing above our heads and the noise of the bullets going overhead was eerie. There was a high pitched cracking noise like a thin bull-whip as the round went overhead. After the 'crack!' came a 'thump' which was the sound of the weapon firing the bullet. As their rounds were going overhead pieces of tree and foliage would spit down on us. Every now and then there would be a big bang as the enemy fired their rocket propelled grenades. This was primarily an anti-tank weapon but was useful if fired into the trees above and rained shrapnel down upon us. Most of the rocket propelled grenade rounds were detonating behind us and luckily no-one was hit by these rockets.

It was now around 4.30 pm and as a company, we had been fighting our way through the bunkers for two hours. The enemy's resistance to our assault now seemed to be weakening. We were able to keep crawling forward now with less fire being directed at us. To see what was going on in my forward sections I had to position myself almost level with the assault line and right in the middle between the two sections. It was difficult to get a picture of the enemy and where he was fighting from. It wasn't until we had been fighting for another 30 minuters that I saw that the enemy was in fact firing from behind the bunkers and not from inside the stairwell. It was almost impossible to get an aimed shot away at the enemy as the vegetation kept obscuring the view. If you moved to a better fire position the target area looked completely different and one had to start searching the area all over again.

The platoon was slowly moving forward, a routine had been established with our tank and we started to capture a few bunkers. I had not had to tell the Diggers to keep moving forward at all. They knew what was required and got stuck into their job. It took quite some time to ensure that men weren't going to get caught in a fire-lane as we advanced. The section teams were working well, but it was something that just couldn't be rushed. I noticed that we were all covered in sweat and our shirts were so wet we looked like we had been caught in a tropical downpour.

What made our forward movement harder were the trees in our path which had been hit by the artillery or blasted by the tanks. We had to somehow get through the tangled debris of branches, without getting our arses shot off. The enemy was conserving his ammo and now was firing only when we moved. We didn't have any M26 grenades to throw into the bunkers to clear them as they had all been withdrawn from issue, because a batch of grenades with instantaneous fuses had been mixed up with the normal seven-second delay fuses.

Fortunately we hadn't been issued any of the wrong grenades, but now we needed grenades badly. It was asking for trouble to stick your head into a bunker even if it looked empty as the enemy could quite easily be in a corner and kill you as you entered from above. The noise of the fire fight was starting to decrease as we neared what appeared to be the end of the bunker system.[4]

By now all the firing had ceased right across the company front. Major Taylor gave the command to secure the position and to very carefully clear all the bunkers. Reorganising had started. Delta Four had to move quickly as it was almost five o'clock; night would soon be upon them. Eleven Platoon swept forward to where they were pretty sure the bunker system ended and searched for enemy signs. It appeared that those enemy who hadn't been caught in the bunker system had withdrawn west, back along the creek line. After positioning sentries on the footpads that led out of the system, the company started a systematic search of the bunkers. Company headquarters was still central and the Centurions were now grouped together and allocated a part of the company perimeter to defend.

Suddenly firing broke out up front: one of the sections was letting all hell loose at a bunker. Riflemen in 11 Platoon yelled back that they could see the enemy. They pointed out where they had seen him and men started to search for the bunker. No firing had been directed back at the company, so I told the section commander to push forward and clear the area but to be bloody careful.

Corporal Ken Moore moved his men forward toward their objective. After about 10 minutes of careful movement, they halted and I was called forward and shown what all the action had been about. In the steps of the stairwell was a Viet Cong soldier who had been shot. But the riflemen hadn't killed him. Sometime earlier in the fighting he must have stuck his head up out of the bunker—at about the same time that one of the tanks had fired a canister round into the jungle. For there, right between this unfortunate soldier's eyes, was a piece of the steel out of the canister round. This soldier had been dead for over half an hour, judging by the dried blood on his forehead and mouth. He had dropped where he had been hit. Eleven Platoon had carried out a contact drill on a dead man.

There were no more bunkers containing surprises. As it was almost dark, we settled into our night routine. It was far from a routine night as the wind came up during the evening and trees and branches which had been shattered by artillery and tank fire started to fall. There was so much deadfall coming down that many Diggers were seriously considering sleeping in an enemy bunker. One particular tree, over 20 metres tall, came down with a tremendous crash. Many remember spending a long time staring at the roof of their hootchies and listening to creaking timber before falling asleep. I later wrote in an article for a magazine:

> It had been an incredible day. I hadn't been scared as I thought I might have been even when we actually led the assault. I think I was too busy driving the platoon and telling my MFC where I wanted the artillery fire to be worrying about my feelings at that time. I knew I was exhausted both physically and mentally by the time we finished the attack. As a platoon commander I seemed to have spent most of my time keeping my sections pointed in the right direction. I hadn't fired directly at an enemy soldier, as they had been too hard to identify and get a clear shot at. When all the fighting had stopped and the noise from the artillery and tanks had finished, I sat down on my pack sketching the layout of the bunkers we had cleared; my hand started to shake so badly I couldn't draw a straight line. Once all the danger was over my system must have finally let go and took the time out to remind me just how dangerous battle can be.[5]

The company had lost one man killed and four wounded. Those wounded were primarily from our own artillery that had been firing from their rear—raining shrapnel back on top of them as the impacting rounds hit the tall trees. They had been pretty fortunate considering the experience most people had when they attacked bunker systems. There was no doubt that the Centurion tanks had made all the difference.

Trying to count the enemy dead was not easy. Searching some of the bunkers was impossible because the Centurions had crushed the lids in, no doubt with the occupants inside. The total body count of enemy was placed at 12. It was a little useless digging up bunkers to find another handful of enemy bodies. The haul of weapons was five AK-47 assault rifles, the American GPMG M60 which had caused us so much trouble and confusion when initially we thought it was being fired by one of our platoons, and a couple of B40 (RPG-2] rocket propelled grenade launchers. In addition there were hundreds of rounds of machine gun ammunition, AK-47

Captain Peter Schuman makes his way through a clearing made by the Centurion tanks after the company attack against 274 Viet Cong Main Force regiment on the Suoi Ca in July 1971. (*Photograph courtesy of 4 RAR Museum*)

magazines, folding shovels, 18 back packs, and about 100 kilograms of rice.

The bunker system was laid out in a pattern which resembled a large letter X on the ground. The cross point of the 'X' was a command bunker to others which were sighted along the arms of the cross. Light blue signal wire was found connecting the bunkers, and small torch globes conveyed the signals to the bunker occupants. Some of the bunkers were situated a little further out; these were sentry bunkers. Once the Australians were able to lay down behind the bunkers they could see the fire-lanes which they had just assaulted through. If they had been standing, the enemy would have seen them between their ankles and their knees. This impressed upon them the enemy's intense preparation of his defences and their need to be on their stomachs when fighting through bunkers.

After the re-organising, the company began clearing up the battlefield which looked like an atom bomb had hit the place. Bunkers had to be cleared and the enemy dead located, stripped and searched. Enemy weapons had to be gathered and made safe and any hiding places for 'stay behind' parties or snipers eliminated by the use of CS gas or explosive devices.

In one bunker the section commander told me that they had heard voices and believed the enemy were still trapped inside and there was obviously no escape tunnel. I yelled out to the enemy in Vietnamese to surrender and received no response. My 'splinter team' sappers from 1 Field Squadron, RAE, had come forward and one of them by the name of Smith decided that he would have a look with the aid of his torch. He had hardly stuck his foot down onto the first step when a burst of AK-47 fire ripped up out of the bunker. Sapper Smith leapt about a metre in the air in his hasty and somewhat inelegant retreat from the stairwell.

The enemy refused to surrender and after several attempts to get them to surrender they were despatched with the aid of grenades and an M18A1 mine thrown into the bunker. Later it was learnt that the men in the bunker were officers and one was the battalion intelligence officer. One of the 11 Platoon Diggers remarked that for an intelligence officer he hadn't shown much of it by not surrendering—but in the same breath he acknowledged his bravery and determination to fight to the end.

Reorganising is also a time for reflection when men look back on what has just happened and think how lucky they were or unlucky others might have been. Wally Burford reflected on his first contact and the crucible of battle:

> The first one, you know the rush of adrenalin. You just about become an adrenalin junky after that first one. The sense of adventure, here it all is, this is what we have been training for, you know it was absolutely awesome. But of course in the first one we had [Private B.M.] Bernie Pengilly killed and when you get the word after a few hours that someone is dead you think, 'Oh Christ, who was it?' Early in the piece you knew every bloke in the company well. It makes you think a bit more about it. When I knew it was Bernie, a bloke that I knew and liked very much, it hit home very, very hard. I think from there on, from the first contact—which was huge—I think the subsequent contacts we had, a person was a little bit more introspect and most certainly not as gung ho.[6]

Me (*left*) and my radio operator, Paul Howkins, grab a quick bite amidst the devastation of the enemy position on the Suoi Ca.

Without doubt, the trump card on 30 July was 1 Troop, C Squadron, 1st Armoured Regiment commanded by Lieutenant Bruce Cameron. The tanks created havoc for the defenders of the bunker system and either blew them out of their cover or crushed them by track-turning on the lid of the bunkers. War is about the total use of force and this was absolutely uncompromising. But using tanks in close quarter battle can be difficult and, for the Digger clad only in his green shirt and carrying a rifle, he can feel somewhat vulnerable. Lance Corporal 'Jethro' Hannah recalls:

> Probably the most scariest part for myself, and I remember talking to 'Beetle' [Private D. G. Bayliss], my offsider, was hoping that one of these tanks didn't run over us. However, with the noise of the battle plus the noise of the commanders trying to control our movement and the revving of all these tanks that were going in to support us, it made it quite scary

"Strange—it wasn't extraordinarily difficult to get us here . . ."

A cartoon from the *Daily News*, ironically, six days after Delta Four faced off against 3/33 North Vietnamese Regiment and were fortunate to escape a mauling at the hands of the well trained enemy. (Daily News, *27 September 1971*)

because you could hear the noise of the tank but you actually couldn't see it. At stages I remember 'Beetle' turning around and saying 'watch out' and probably a silly thing to do, but we both looked around to our rear together and really all it was was a tank moving across our rear around to a flank. At the same time I remember getting a boot in the arse by the Platoon Commander to concentrate on what we were doing and not worry about what was behind us. To me that was quite scary. Not so much as to what was happening up the front but what was happening at the rear because of the tanks, and afterwards seeing what a tank can do, it was quite scary at the time.[7]

The oft heard expression 'the fog of battle' well and truly descends when 120 riflemen, with a troop of tanks in direct support and a battery of artillery are all firing and smashing the jungle to pieces. One man who was able to observe all of this mayhem from the epicentre was the Forward Observer, Lieutenant Greg Gilbert:

There were so many things going on at the same time and so many conflicting things coming in. Trying to get information and then you can't get information. It is very difficult to know exactly what is going on and where. Especially so for the Company Commander who is trying to get a clear idea of just what the dispositions of his platoons are. Certainly in those situations, from what I saw, it was usually too confusing for the Company Commander to be able to direct much himself and he just had to try and keep an overall picture of it.[8]

In summary, the attack was highly successful. The attack took about three hours and covered a distance of assault of about 150 metres total. The next day, the battalion Assault Pioneers, supported by more sappers from 1 Field Squadron, RAE came in to blow up any remaining bunkers. 274 VC Main Force Regiment had been dealt a blow in that one of their strongholds had been destroyed, they lost several officers from their headquarters and were forced to re-deploy back outside the province.

By the next day, the dead were now fairly putrid as the heat and humidity had taken its toll. Private Phil Asprey from Five Section was one who volunteered to go down into the stench of the bunker to clear the bodies, on the understanding that he was given a fair share of any decent souvenirs. He tied a handkerchief around his nose and down he went. The bodies were a real mess, and Phil certainly earned his booty.

ONCE MORE UNTO THE BREACH: NUI LE AND THE NVA

By August 1971, 4 RAR was the only Australian battalion left in Phuoc Tuy Province as the withdrawal from the Vietnam War started to take effect. The tanks from 1st Armoured Regiment had been withdrawn by some clever staff officer who figured they wouldn't need armour as they were winding down and withdrawing south from Nui Dat into the 1st Australian Logistic Support Group Base at Vung Tau.

The North Vietnamese Army were keen to inflict a bloody nose on the Australians before they withdrew from the province. They set up an elaborate ambush involving an attack on a Vietnamese Regional Forces (RF) post at Cam My some 10 kilometres north of Nui Dat, an anti-armour or motor transport ambush on the main north-south road called Route Two, and a regimental ambush in the jungle just south of the Courtenay rubber plantation which was about seven kilometres from the battalion's forward Tactical HQ on Courtenay Hill. A Bravo Company platoon, commanded by Second Lieutenant Dan McDaniel, discovered the NVA laying out the forming up place and assault line markers in the bush to the east of Cam My. They subsequently had a running battle which resulted in the platoon being mortared and taking heavy, if not serious, casualties.

In the meantime, 11 Platoon had been having heavy contacts for several days with NVA squads and platoons moving further to the east of Bravo Company. On 20 September 1971, 11 Platoon had a contact with an enemy NVA platoon strength group on a track they intersected over which at least 200 enemy were estimated to have moved. No casualties were taken by 11 Platoon but they despatched four NVA soldiers who were dressed in greens, with chest webbing and small back packs. They carried no personal or unit identification and their battle drills—including the use of a bugle—indicated that they were well trained. The platoon harboured for the night some 400 metres from their contact position and 50 per cent Stand To was maintained all night as everyone in 11 Platoon could sense they were deep in the 'Bad Lands'. The next morning, 21 September, 11 Platoon moved out to find a place to conduct a resupply as they had no rations and very little water left among the platoon. They had not gone more than 500 metres when they intersected another track which had all the signs of at least 200 enemy moving over it. This made a total of 400 enemy in the local area unless they were walking around in circles. This disquieting information was passed to Major Jerry Taylor at CHQ of Delta Four, who gave orders to 10 and 12 Platoons to move smartly toward and to close with 11 Platoon before they were over run by a numerically superior force. As the company was concentrating, the enemy clashed with the now static 11 Platoon and the Australians were assaulted twice by very large numbers of enemy who appeared intent on simply over running 11 Platoon with a mass attack—almost Korean war style. Over 60 enemy clashed with 11 Platoon as they desperately held their ground and waited for reinforcements.

To the west about two kilometres away, just before 0900 hours, 12 Platoon found one of the tracks that 11 Platoon had recorded in a contact report and they started to close with the now fully alerted NVA who were well dug in a bunker system. The forward scout of 12 Platoon was killed in an opening burst of fire and several men fell wounded in the lead section. The platoon commander Graham Spinkston recalls the events that followed:

> We found the track that 11 Platoon had seen the day before and had started to follow it. We had probably only followed it about 100 metres and we noticed another little track running off to the left. So I stopped the platoon and they were deployed and I took [Corporal C.R.] Charlie McKenzie who was a section commander of 7 Section, [Private] Jimmy Duff, or James Duff as he was called, and my sig [Private T.B.] Trevor Gorringe and myself on a recce and hadn't gone 20 metres and all of a sudden there were people shooting at us. At that stage we hadn't seen anybody but they had obviously seen us and started firing. We pulled back to about the vicinity of the track and went to ground and at that stage it became obvious the enemy were using fire-lanes and started firing RPGs [rocket propelled grenades] into us. An RPG hit Jimmy Duff, or it went off in a tree right next to him, and killed him instantly. The platoon at that stage was basically deployed facing the enemy, two sections up. The third section was to the rear. Once the firing started, the last section pulled around to the left and that was [Corporal D.W.] Dave Carlyon's section— he was a new section commander that we had picked up about three weeks before and he put in a lot of fire from the flank because he in fact could see them better than we could.
>
> By then we had had about seven or eight casualties including one killed and about six shrapnel wounds. No bullet wounds to my recollection. All shrapnel from RPGs. At that stage it was obvious that we were in a big contact.

There was a huge amount of fire from both directions. I was concerned that we were using a lot of ammunition, even at that early time, particularly [Corporal D.W.] Dave Carlyon because he kept firing and I suspected that at the rate he was using it, we would have run out very quickly, and I had to tell him that if he didn't have a target not to fire. So, we pulled the whole platoon back about 20 metres, back across the other side of the track, and called in artillery initially onto the position.

I didn't know at the time how many casualties there were, and I didn't even know I had been wounded myself. I was aware of someone hitting me with a big flat board. That is what it felt like, like the flat blade of a cricket bat. It was only when I got back that I realised I had got some shrapnel, and my platoon sig, [Private T.B.] Trevor Gorringe, had a shrapnel cut across the back of his neck. I knew about that, but it was only as we pulled back and [Private C.J.] Kempy started talking about the casualties that I realised what had happened and how many we had. We were just getting back far enough so that we could call in some artillery. Kempy had, to his credit, gone straight to [Private] Jimmy Duff, because it was close to Platoon Headquarters, and he determined that he was dead and there was nothing we could do for him.[9]

So, with two platoons already in heavy contact and still an hour from morning tea, Major Jerry Taylor looked like he had his hands full. The battalion commander now had three platoons in contact and two companies reporting large numbers of enemy—and this was supposed to be the withdrawal from Vietnam!

By late morning, Delta Four had concentrated and it was decided to soften the enemy up with air power and indirect fire from artillery. No tanks could help Delta Four on this one.

After hammering the enemy position for several hours the airborne forward air controller reported that he could see the enemy departing in a northerly direction (Delta Four was south of the position) and heading toward the feature called Nui Le. If what he was saying was true, then the bunker system must have contained hundreds of enemy. The fighter ground attack (FGA) aircraft and gunships began pursuing the fleeing enemy and it seemed as if it was all over bar the shouting.

Not so. A decision was made to advance into the bunker system and clear it of any enemy before nightfall. It was now about three o'clock in the afternoon. The company would attack with two platoons up and one back. Twelve Platoon on the left, 11 Platoon on the right and 10 Platoon in depth. Company Headquarters (CHQ) and Support Section would travel central to the whole affair. The attack would be supported by artillery which would be silent until contact, if any, broke out. This was one of those times when I, as a platoon commander, was very uneasy about what was about to happen. I wasn't sure we had pegged the enemy down completely, I was also unsure of exactly how wide the enemy position was and given the way the enemy had assaulted 11 Platoon earlier in the day I knew that this was going to be a tough assignment. With legs feeling like jelly, I returned from the Orders Group to make out a very quick set of orders. We had barely enough time for the word to get around the platoon when we started to shake out into our assault formation. The attack was set on a compass bearing as there were no large features to align the assault onto and Delta Four cautiously started their assault.

The men were advancing in extended line (line abreast) in a crouching sort of walk and we were still wearing our packs, probably in the hope that we would not have to drop them as the enemy had 'bugged out'. There was no sound from the enemy position as the Diggers worked their way through shattered undergrowth, smoky, cordite-filled air and shrapnel scarred trees. After 10 minutes of gingerly stepping our way into the enemy bunker system, all hell broke loose. The din was electrifying and deafening. It was as if every nasty in South Vietnam was shooting at Delta Four.

The riflemen instinctively hit the deck and attempted to pass information on what they could see and hear. Diggers started crawling forward and looking for cover from fire. Sporadic return fire began as men found their bearings and started to get a feel for where the enemy were located. The thick undergrowth made this task even more difficult. The shock of the initial burst of enemy fire had a big impact on many of the Diggers. Private Kevin Benson from 11 Platoon recalls:

> I think every bristle of hair that I had just stood straight on end. You know you never, ever forget it. I was up the back again. Didn't have a bloody clue what was going on, what was actually happening. That is my most vivid memory of Vietnam.[10]

Private 'Jethro' Hannah said, 'I don't think anyone in 11 Platoon that survived and lived through that day would ever forget it'. Company Sergeant Major Noel Huish remembers vividly the ferocity of the attack and mentioned the surprise that he felt when the enemy were found to be still in the system—and in large numbers—when they usually withdrew after an artillery barrage and FGA attack. Private Garry Sloane recalls his impressions:

> I am sure we were going up the side of a hill and then there was this one, almighty horrific bang and it just sounded like a hundred machine guns going off, and everyone just went everywhere. We were all over the place; running forward, I tripped over a bloody log and nearly knocked myself out. It was just mass confusion once we got into it. Nobody, from where I was at the time, could see anybody or any enemy. There were bullets snapping twigs off round your head, and you were just trying to get yourself into a position where you could try and establish where the Viet Cong were. I got in behind a log and I could see them firing out of a trench or it was coming out from underneath a log. I was just plunking away into that. Every time I would shoot into it, they would just pull their rifle barrels back in, and then you would move position to try and get into another place to have another go at them and they would move and had gone down a bit further. It was incredible. [Lance Corporal J.A.] Johnny Bergmans and myself were together and three or four of them ran over the back, and they were that bloody close you could almost

reach out and grab hold of the mongrels. I didn't think any of us were going to get out of it. The firepower that was coming in was that intense. I remember there were jets going everywhere and I thought that this was it. We've had it today. There was fear in the mind that this could be the last day of your life, but it wasn't a fear that was going to stop you from going on. Everyone was just prepared to just let fly with everything. The firepower was phenomenal.[11]

Even in the midst of this maelstrom the Digger humour surfaced. Private Garry Sloane continues on the mood of his platoon:

I wouldn't say it was jovial, but people were still able to laugh about things that had actually happened in the morning when the battle was going on. It was all whisper, whisper, you know. I remember when the count came around on who had been knocked over the guys went quiet for a while. There was still a bit of the Aussie humour there. I remember [Private] Geoff Maple saying, 'I'm a fucking Nasho and I shouldn't be doing this.'[12]

Despite the ugliness and the tragedy that accompanies armed conflict, the protagonists can often find relief from this unreal situation and bloody carnage through the medium of black humour. It is a relief valve that allows men to express themselves and escape from the grim reality of their murderous task.

Once the battle had been joined in the bunker system, Delta Four discovered to its surprise and its chagrin that the 33rd Regiment had left behind a substantial number of their soldiers who were very well sited and prepared to fight to the end. After the initial withering burst of fire which caught most of 11 Platoon in several fire-lanes, there was a lack of co-ordinated response as the two leading machine gun teams of that platoon had been destroyed. Contact distances with the enemy were now down to no more than 15 metres. Both the number one and number two on the machine guns in 11 Platoon had been killed and the lack of automatic fire in return gave the enemy, who were firing from behind their bunkers, some cause for optimism. They began to advance on the Diggers using their bunkers and trees for cover, and throwing wooden grenades and firing RPG into the trees above the Diggers' heads.

Most of the action in this company attack was now centred on 11 Platoon, who were trying to establish what was going on. Sergeant Daryl Jenkin had been shot through the right upper arm and was bleeding badly, however, he had not suffered any broken bones from his wounding. Two things stick out from this event. The trees in the contact area were not substantial but numerous. They did not afford really good cover as they were only about one foot wide at their base. The men had dropped their packs and were using them for cover from fire. Private Hannah recalls the wounding of his sergeant:

We advanced and then all hell broke loose. I was on the far left-hand flank with Daryl Jenkin as the platoon sergeant at that time, carrying an extra radio we had got in to the platoon. Right beside us was 6 Section and the gunner was [Private K. M.] Kingston-Powles. I remember as soon as the fighting started, him hitting the ground and getting about 50 rounds away. Then Daryl got hit. He was approximately 10 feet in front of me. I looked across again at Kingston-Powles and there was no movement from him whatsoever. He was just slumped with his head on the butt of the gun. And then Daryl asking me to get him back because he had been hit.

At that stage I turned and said to Daryl, 'What?' And he said to me, 'I've been hit'. I can remember saying, 'What do you want me to fucking do about it?' And he saying, 'Mate, you've got to get me back'. I then crawled forward, got him back to where my pack and the radio was and he said, 'Mate I need to be bandaged up'. So, I took up my knife and cut his sleeve off and started to put a field dressing around it. I remember him saying to me, 'Watch over there'. I watched, and there was movement to our left front. It was was the enemy coming out of a bunker and using two big trees with buttress roots as a route from that bunker to wherever they were going. Once Daryl's arm was bandaged, he laid there and I saw him personally kill, well hit

four, I don't know whether he killed them, but they didn't
move anyway. As they got out of the hole and ran for this
buttress tree he just knocked them off.[13]

This was the biggest contact that Australians had been
involved in since the Battle of Coral and Balmoral with 1
RAR in 1969. And the battalion and Australia Forces were
supposed to be withdrawing from this tragic war. The interesting thing is that in all of the large battles, armour in some
form or another played a significant part. The infantry very
rarely can fight it out alone when they are outnumbered and
especially when they are fighting someone who is fighting on
his own ground as it was on this fateful day in September
1971.

Meanwhile, Delta Company was ordered to withdraw.
The Company Commander, Major Jerry Taylor, was faced
with the awful dilemma of pushing on as light was fading or
of withdrawing in the face of an obviously larger group, with
the resultant chaos that normally ensues when soldiers have
to withdraw under fire. The astute reader will have noticed
that I did not mention the word 'retreat', as it is strictly a
'no-no' in infantry culture to talk of any rearward movement
in terms other than 'withdrawal'. This has a psychological
purpose as the word 'retreat' carries implications of defeat,
whereas 'withdrawal' implies a movement or manoeuvre
designed to resite or reposition the force to continue operations.

So, Delta Four withdraws and evacuates what casualties it
can. Three members of 11 Platoon who were killed were left
on the battlefield because their extraction under fire would
certainly have resulted in more casualties. Soldiers rarely train
for withdrawal, as it is not an aggressive or offensive action.
Rather it is one of fire and movement to the rear. It has to
be controlled very strongly by the commanders at all levels,
so that the movement does not turn into a race for the rear.
Once the company had pulled back into a reasonably tight
defensive posture it was decided that further air and artillery
strike would be required to suppress the large numbers of
enemy who were pressing onto the company. The order was

given that the company would move approximately 500 metres in a southerly direction and then harbour for the night in a defensive posture.

Light was failing rapidly as the company stepped off in single file. It was becoming increasingly obvious that the enemy were not going to relinquish their advantage and they pressed harder to close with the withdrawing Australians and attempted on several occasions to inflict casualties by trying to outflank the company as it withdrew. No friendly casualties were taken, but some members from Support Section commanded by Warren Dowell shot and killed some NVA.

The company executed a hasty harbour drill and automatically went into a very tight circular formation in the deep gloom of the dusk under the jungle canopy. Ten Platoon had led the way and as they started to settle onto the ground, they passed back a message that they thought they had heard voices to their left flank as they moved in to the harbour. As 11 Platoon started to move into its position in the harbour, Private Bob Simms, who was now carrying a machine gun, looked up and saw a group of four or more enemy sitting on what appeared to be a bunker and eating a meal from bowls. He involuntarily let out a loud, 'Oh no!' and let loose with about 50–60 rounds of sustained machine gun fire which dispatched most of them.

Once this shooting started, all hell broke loose again and it was painfully obvious that Delta Four had withdrawn up against another bunker system. As they say in the classics, 'shits were trumps' and Delta Four now moved rapidly to consolidate as best they could in the maelstrom erupting around them. The pursuing NVA now closed around the Australians in the dark of early evening as the platoons struggled to find out who was where and what gaps, if any, they had in their defences. From the top, where Major Jerry Taylor was trying to co-ordinate his company, the action unfolded like this:

> I think probably the worst thing that can happen to any commander is to experience the feeling that there is no longer very much he can do to influence events during a battle, and that things will just have to take their course. I

experienced this towards the end of the battle at Nui Le, and I think it provided one of the bleakest moments of my life. The Nui Le battle started for Delta Company at 0851 hours on the 21st September, 1971, and 14 hours later we were still at it, having advanced, attacked, and withdrawn. Now, in the dark, with unworkable direct communications to Battalion Tac, no other company closer than five clicks [kilometres], with five dead and several wounded, and the guns almost at maximum range, we had forced up against yet another bunker system, and were encircled by elements of Regimental Headquarters and the 3rd Battalion, 33rd NVA Regiment.

There had been no time to properly co-ordinate the defence, and certainly no time to dig even a shell scrape. In fact our perimeter now measured about 35 metres across, and any attempt by commanders to move about, give orders, or return fire, provoked a hail of small arms. I was able to communicate with [Lieutenant] Greg Gilbert, my FO, who was about 20 metres from me, only by an ad hoc airborne relay manned by Captain Greg Shannon, the Battalion's ingenious signals officer.

I'd passed the word that everyone should stay still and be quiet; not shoot unless directly threatened; and that the guns would begin firing Danger Close to dislodge the enemy—who we could see and hear moving about round us. I had arranged with Greg that the guns would fire on the four cardinal points of our perimeter, and that we would 'walk' the fire in until we started to pick up live shrapnel. We'd used this technique against 274 Regiment on the Song Ca, and although it got fairly exciting, it worked well and caused no own casualties.

Obviously we needed this defensive fire as quickly as possible. We had already skittled with small arms fire an enemy squad that had come charging into the north side of the perimeter. Grenades were also landing among us, but most of them failed to detonate. I had the distinct impression that the movement and talking around the perimeter indicated that the enemy were preparing a concentrated attack. However, there were difficulties in getting clearances from Arty Tac at Nui Dat, so the guns were unable to shoot. And now, on the south-east side of the perimeter, the small arms fire redoubled in intensity, and it was suddenly obvious that, after everything else that had happened this day, our perimeter had forced up against yet another bunker complex. In the gloom I realised that everybody close by was looking straight at me. Nobody said anything, but the message was obvious—'For Christ's sake, do something'. At that moment I realised that apart from bringing the fall of shot from the guns steadily closer to the perimeter, and giving the best possible account of ourselves when the enemy finally launched their attack, there was nothing else that could be done except hang on.[14]

Down at the soldier level, the position was very confusing as sections from various platoons had become misplaced in the dark and the organisation as a whole was under extreme stress. This was made worse by the evacuation during the day of one of the platoon commanders, Graham Spinkston, who had been wounded in the leg and could no longer remain on duty. He was evacuated with Sergeant Daryl Jenkin and so one third of the company's command and control was missing before this untimely contact in the dark. The company was in bad shape. As we have heard the distance across the perimeter was very small and in danger of being over run. The survival of Delta Four came down to several things. It was essential that the men didn't panic and indiscriminately shoot off their remaining ammunition as resupply now would be virtually impossible until first light. They had to make sure that there was no penetration of their position and they had to maintain an intact perimeter in the dark for the next 12 hours until the sun came up. Once that happened the Australians could once again rely on close air support and be able to adjust their gun fire and make better use of their small arms capability.

As the company struggled to organise its perimeter, the enemy continually sniped at those trying to co-ordinate the defences. During this phase of the fighting, at around 6 pm, I was severely wounded and 11 Platoon was left with no command structure. This was the platoon's darkest hour, as Lance Corporal 'Jethro' Hannah recalls:

A bit of confusion went through the platoon because the platoon commander, who was organising it, was down now. The platoon sergeant had already been choppered out. For a little bit of time until one of the other section commanders took command, there was a little bit of, how could you say, I suppose panic set amongst us because there was no more information once the platoon commander went down. How he was getting the information, we still don't know, but he was getting information to us. Once he went down it stopped, and we were all no more than I suppose four foot apart, that is from man to man to man, all facing the one direction.

Someone asked, 'The boss is down and what the fuck is going on?', and no one could tell us for a good half an hour before the word got to us what we were to do. But at that stage, we just wanted someone to keep telling us that we were going to be all right and just keep doing the job. I suppose for 20 odd minutes we just laid there, but we never got any further instructions until later on that evening, when a runner did come around and tell us that we were to remain at 50 per cent Stand To until the next morning. I don't think it ever struck the other section commanders that, 'Hey, I've got to be in charge.'[15]

Fighting in the dark is never easy and when the leaders are gone and there is total confusion, it can be a disorienting and terrifying experience for anyone, especially so for the Digger who is at the very end of the information chain. Hannah continues:

My personal feeling was absolute fear. I can remember the three blokes closest to me, all of us and I don't believe I ever went to a church parade unless I was ordered to go, however, all of us were saying some type of prayer. We had heard about the Battle of Long Tan and things like that, and now we felt that we were close to being in one. One minute we were going forward, and even when we withdrew we ran into some more enemy, and then they seemed to be surrounding us. There was terror there—there are no two ways about that.

But actually when the fighting was happening, there was no panic. But after that when you had time and your adrenalin was stopping and you were starting to think, you were starting to think about the dead, your own blokes that had been hit. Yes, fear was there.[16]

The Forward Observer, Lieutenant Greg Gilbert, now held the key to Delta Four making it through the night. The enemy were prevented from assaulting Delta Company because of the judicious use of artillery which was being called in at very close range known as Fire Mission—Danger Close. Greg Gilbert recounts his time when he found himself in the spotlight and every infantryman around him praying for accuracy by the gunners:

I had just got my map out to start to work out where we were and all hell broke loose with rifle fire. So, I can remember lying there and seeing the green tracers going over my head about 18 inches away. I couldn't put a light on and it was too dark to see my map and I couldn't talk to the company commander because he was maybe 20 feet away and as soon as he and I tried to talk to each other we drew aimed fire, so we couldn't talk. I then had to get the artillery in, so I had to try and remember what the grid reference was where I was during the day, and try and remember how far I had walked, what direction I had walked and I was lying there with all this rifle fire going on trying to do a trigonometrical equation in my head—I was doing a right-angled triangle saying, 'If I had walked this far, this would be the hypotenuse, so it would be this far down and this far across' and working out this is where I think I am. We were out of range of most artillery, except for three guns from [Lieutenant] Brian Stevens's section of the artillery, which were just within range. We were at the extreme end of the zone of the gun, which means there was quite a large error [factor].

I then called the artillery, put it out a little from where we were and then was absolutely terrified when the rounds were on their way as to where they were going to land. But they landed out and then I bought them in until we started copping the shrapnel on ourselves and I reckoned it was close enough. Then I just tried to move them around the perimeter a bit to cover it as best I could.[17]

Many of the soldiers, and in particular the officers and those in positions of leadership or command, recognised that they were frightened at some stage. However, their training drives them to automatically overcome that fear and get on with their job. Gilbert illustrates this point, when he says:

> While the battle was going on I don't think I was scared. In fact, I remember being quite calm throughout the whole procedure. I spoke to Brian Stevens and he said the gunners were getting tired. I had slowed it down and said not only was it the enemy at this end, but the psychological comfort of hearing our own artillery landing and I said it provides a bit of comfort, but we agreed that I would stop about midnight. It was all calm then. I do remember being convinced that we would be attacked at dawn, but I was quite calm. I think I had made my peace.[18]

For the next five hours or so, from the time that Private Bob Simms initiated the last contact during the battle at Nui Le, the Forward Observer party called for and adjusted the artillery which began slamming down as close as 50 metres on occasion from the Delta Four perimeter. This forced the enemy away from the company and made 'hugging' the Australians a dangerous tactic for them. Around nine or ten o'clock that evening the sporadic incoming rifle and automatic weapon fire from the enemy had ceased. There was no reorganisation of the company in the normal tactical sense that usually occurs after contact. One of the Diggers, Private Garry Sloane, still shudders when he recalls the latter stages of this momentous day in his life:

> I don't know what time it was, but it went quiet and then you would just get sporadic shots coming out of the trees and the word came down not to shoot back, because as soon as you shot back they will pinpoint you and you are into it. But you could see them walking around and they

were kicking over the bloody foliage with the phosphorescence coming up. They were everywhere.[19]

Major Jerry Taylor continues his recollection of the late hours and aftermath of the battle on 21 September:

In fact the final attack never came. Three weeks later, a badly wounded sergeant from the 3/33rd surrendered, and during questioning, said that RHQ and the Third Battalion thought they were being attacked by an Australian battalion. Consequently those who had surrounded us in the dark had been sent to pin us, while the rest withdrew. Then they, too, melted away.[20]

The next day about late morning, the New Zealand Company attached to 4 RAR as part of its ANZAC contingent, Victor Company, arrived in the battle area and assisted Delta Four in the battlefield clearance. The three dead from 11 Platoon were recovered intact, as was equipment dropped and misplaced in the dark during the fighting. I was evacuated by winch onto a 9 Squadron RAAF helicopter around 0900 hours and flew via 6 Platoon, Bravo Company, who had taken 19 casualties in an exciting afternoon with another group from 33rd NVA Regiment.[21] One of the platoon commanders, Second Lieutenant Dan McDaniel, later to be a Sabre Squadron Commander in the elite Special Air Service Regiment, was winched up onto the same chopper as me and together we were evacuated to the 1st Australian Field Hospital at Vung Tau.

Delta Four came second in this battle. Despite the fact that they forced the enemy to evacuate his bunker system because of the incredibly heavy use of close air support—which included cannon, rockets, mini-guns and napalm strikes—and medium and field artillery, they lost five killed and about 10 wounded. Tanks sure would have been handy on that day.

The jungle was not easy for the tanks—but neither was it impossible. The men from C Squadron, 1st Armoured Regiment earned our admiration at the battle on the Suoi Ca when they fought with us against a determined and resolute foe. Most of the time they operated with their heads sticking out of their turrets, as they were unable to see and the Viet Cong were throwing heaps of fire their way. The impact of the armour on the enemy—with its protection, mobility and advantage in firepower—must have been devastating. Those machines were awesome, terrifying, and thank God, they were on *OUR* side!

In battle a soldier can expend his ammo in pretty short order if he is ill-disciplined. The trick is to ensure that soldiers only fire at seen targets and not fire 'on spec'. Ammunition for each company was stored in the company Q stores back at Nui Dat and was ready to be flown straight into the battle sites when required. It was the job of those back in Nui Dat to get it sorted and packed for distribution. Jerry Taylor remembers what happened when Delta Four was calling for more ammo:

> An incident which illustrates the very strong sense of family and team which existed in 4 RAR in 1971, and of the commitment throughout the Task Force generally, took place at Nui Dat on the 21st September during the D and B Company battles against 33 NVA Regiment. D Company around Nui Le, and B Company about four kilometres to the south, had suffered five killed and more than 25 wounded throughout the day. Ammunition usage, especially of small arms ammunition, was very high. In fact, D Company used three first lines, and ammunition resupply was difficult to achieve because of the close proximity of the enemy. Towards the end of the day, ammunition, in pre-filled magazines and packed in sandbags, had to be thrown out of hovering helicopters to the troops in contact.
>
> As day turned to night and the battles continued, members of 1st Field Squadron, Royal Australian Engineers, set up lights at Eagle Farm so that ammunition preparation and forward loading could continue unhampered. They, and members of other units from throughout the Task Force, then continued to help 4 RAR personnel charge magazines, pack them into sandbags, and load them into the helicopters as they came in. As the night wore on, Left Out of Battle

personnel from 4 RAR particularly, but also from other Task Force units, gathered unasked at Eagle Farm with their weapons and equipment in case they might be needed as reinforcements. I was much moved when I discovered later that the majority of those who stayed throughout the night were from my old admin company.[22]

These two battles have, hopefully, highlighted the fact that soldiers must always be prepared for the worst and that their training must reflect what might happen. If it was not for the fact that Delta Four had been honed to such a fine point by their hard, tough training, they may not have seen it through to dawn on 22 September 1971.

5

RELATIONSHIPS, COMMAND AND LEADERSHIP

Discipline is then not the end, but a means to an end—the end that each man shall be imbued with a spirit of loyalty to leader and to organisation, which will result in unity and promptness of action in instant response to the will of the leader.

CAPTAIN L.C. ANDREWS
UNITED STATES ARMY

APART FROM TRAINING, WHICH IS A CATALYST that drives men together, there is another set of intangibles which transform men from being merely soldiers into becoming comrades. Their organisation becomes a confraternity in the truest sense, where they are united in the same purpose in the profession of arms. There is no denying that the experience of war brings this union to a very high state, but how is it formed? What brings the riflemen and their leaders together, so that they are a tight unit and able to withstand the pressures that force other human groups to disintegrate?

This chapter attempts to explore and discuss those actions, feelings and emotive issues which are very difficult to describe and analyse but which at the same time are so critical for success when men go into battle. I also delve into the area of relationships between these men and attempt to dissect what are the essentials for leadership amongst men in battle. I will look at those aspects of command which Australian soldiers consider important when they are facing an armed enemy and those aspects which give them the drive and motivation to continue when they really want to stop.

THE EMOTIONS

Men have been notorious in the past for hiding their emotions because it has, and in some countries still is, seen as a man's badge of honour that he not display or show his emotions, or express his fears in public. Some countries insist that a 'macho' image be maintained at all times, however it is not the Australian way despite the image portrayed in movies or in novels or even in advertising. The Australian Digger is a fairly honest sort of character and will tell you what he feels up front and to your face—most of the time.

Fear

The primal emotion that affects any sane man in battle is fear. George Patton is reputed to have said that no sane man is unafraid in battle. All of the respondents for this book stated in one way or another that at some time during their tour of duty they were scared or frightened. It was not something they saw as being ashamed of, rather it was the fact that they were being honest with themselves.

The natural reaction to combat is to be afraid. It makes sense. Someone on the other side of that bush or mound of dirt is trying his hardest to end your life. He is shooting at you, firing rockets, mortar rounds or even shells and throwing grenades. He may even be enticing you into a booby trap or a mine so he can blow you to smithereens. So, why shouldn't you have the shits up? One of the platoon commanders, Kevin Byrne, has this to say about fear:

Oh, the thing that scared you the most was the fact that you might get killed, I think that's a natural fear. But fear, if you train properly, has a positive result and that is that it *drives* you. The fear of death provides in you a driving force to make you stay alive, and that, if you train properly, is a positive thing. Now, we were trained to react instinctively in a contact and in a fire fight. The initial response was an instinctive one, then you thought about it. You did your appreciation of where the enemy was and what he was firing at and how best to silence him. Battle was part and parcel of our life and our training and the reason we were there, and it was frightening. If anybody suggests that going into battle is all fun, well that's bullshit, it's a terrifying experience. And so there is a natural fear when you're on operations about death.[1]

One of the men from Delta Four who had a reputation as a pretty hard sort of bloke and was always willing to mix it either on or off the footy field was 'Jethro' Hannah. He said that he had been scared and went on to say:

I think it would be a lie, and I think most people would lie if they said they weren't scared. Probably the thing that scared me more than anything was after the initial first rounds were fired. If you didn't actually see or know what was going on, I think that was the more scary part of it. If you were up the front and you knew what was going on at that stage of the initial few minutes of the action, you had the advantage of being able to see or knew exactly what was occurring. Once you were in action and your adrenalin really does hype up, I believe you were more afraid of offending or letting your mate down who was beside you. But, after the action was finished and you had time to sit and think of maybe a stupid move you had done or whatever, then fear came into play.[2]

Fear is a very raw emotion and it has the unsettling effect of 'unmasking' individuals. The look of fear on someone's face or in their body language is extremely difficult to hide. The adage that you can run from tigers but not from your fear is very true. Fear or a real terrifying situation brings everyone down to the same level. All men are stripped of the cloak of privacy brought about by position, rank or privilege. However, the act of facing fear together creates a very strong bond. Among soldiers it creates the 'family' and it creates the respect for each other that everyone sooner or later has to earn in battle.

There are many things that can trigger fear in a person and it will depend upon their level of training and confidence and the trust and confidence they have in each other. Every man interviewed said the thing that scared him most or made him frightened was the thought of letting himself or his mates down. Major Jerry Taylor echoed these sentiments when I asked him what he thought drove men to overcome fear when in battle:

> I think there are two principal motivators for overcoming fear in battle. The first is that no man wants to let *himself* down. In my view, the conquest of mortal fear is the greatest test that a man can face, and when he has done that, and won through, he knows that he never again has to justify himself to anyone, and that he has got the right to stand in front of the world and say, 'I can hack it'.
>
> The second motivator is that no-one wants to let the *group* down. In my opinion, men in battle fight for their primary group—the section, the platoon, the company, or the battalion. I don't believe that men fight for 'Queen and Country'—and I don't believe that when the chips are down they ever really have done so. It's loyalty to the group. comradeship, what we in Australia call 'mateship', that really causes men to overcome fear. So the stronger that loyalty is, in my view, the better men fight. In the end, it's mainly a function of morale.[3]

Not being in control of the situation can be a cause for fear. Some of the improvised mines laid to ambush the armoured vehicles were often devices containing up to 100 kilograms of explosive. Crude as they might have been, the anti-tank mines laid by the enemy were devastatingly effective and some apprehension and frustration on the part of those whose job it was to carry the infantry was normal, as Lieutenant Chris Stephens, an armoured personnel carrier (APC) troop commander, explains:

In the end for me it was mines. Constantly. They were the most frustrating thing that I came across. They would do a lot of damage and you could do nothing back, you could not find anybody nor do anything to anybody to deal with it.[4]

Apart from anti-tank mines, the enemy would seed anti-personnel mines which were either lifted Allied mines from poorly protected minefields or improvised devices which were still shatteringly effective against the foot soldier. Some Australian battalions suffered badly at the hands of these vicious weapons, but thankfully Delta Four escaped fairly lightly. However, the threat was always there and when Delta Four first arrived they were very conscious of the mine threat in Phuoc Tuy Province.

The Forward Observer who was attached to Delta Four, Lieutenant Greg Gilbert, RAA, was apprehensive when he was first deployed on operations during his familiarisation operation:

One of the FOs ahead of me in the class at Duntroon had been killed by a jumping jack mine and that heightened my awareness of them, so the first time I went out, I was extremely apprehensive about treading on a mine. I remember being absolutely terrified walking along and every spare bit of ground that didn't have leaves on it, I was looking to see if there were three prongs sticking out of the dirt—terrified of these jumping jack mines. If we crossed a track I would be terrified that there would be mines on the track. Then I soon got to realise that not every spare bit of ground was laced with mines in Vietnam.[5]

Other men like Corporal Warren Dowell had a fear of being captured. Even though the Australian forces had never had anyone captured during their entire time in Vietnam (six men are posted as Missing In Action), he still had this phobia about being dragged off by the Viet Cong in the middle of the night:

I didn't want to get captured. The most scared I was was at night time when I was moving around the perimeter seeing how things were on the perimeter or going to a gun position. I don't think I could have handled being captured. That was the only thing I was scared of.[6]

National Serviceman Wally Burford also hated the nights when men spent their evenings on gun picket duty guarding their mates who were sleeping:

Nights to me were the worst part of Vietnam. Nothing much happened at night in the scrub whilst I was in Vietnam, but that was the part where my nerves started to pack up, it was just the thought of what can happen. It is what goes through your head when you're stuck out in the bush, sitting behind a gun. It was that black. You could wave your hand in front of your face and not see anything—it would be pissing pick handles—just laying there just thinking the worst for the whole time.[7]

It probably comes down to not being able to control your environment, much the same as being carried in the back of an APC where you cannot hear or see where you are moving. Fear of the unknown is as potent as that of the known and when a man cannot see or hear, the two most important elements for an infantryman, then he feels very vulnerable.

The role of the leaders—cool, calm and collected

What is important in a combat environment—where probably everyone is scared—is the manner in which people control their fear. Fear is a contagious emotional disease and can spread rapidly. For the man saddled with the responsibility of being the leader, he has a very important part to play in battle apart from making the correct tactical decisions—he must *appear* to be unafraid. Major Jerry Taylor's reaction to the dilemma was very cool, as described in the previous chapter. Nobody panicked when they were withdrawn to a safer position—they just did it calmly and without fuss because the leader was displaying absolute calm. Inside he wasn't—as he admitted later—but it was important at that very moment that outwardly he be cool, calm and collected. Jerry Taylor did that again in the Battle at Nui Le on 21 September, when Delta

Major Jerry Taylor, officer commanding Delta Four, taken after the announcement of his award of the Military Cross in early 1972. (*Photograph courtesy of Jerry Taylor*)

Four was obviously surrounded and, to a man, everyone looked for leadership from the man in charge. I had been severely wounded at this time and had been dragged back into the centre of the very tight company defensive position. I overheard Jerry Taylor telling battalion headquarters of his dilemma. It went something like this, however, I cannot swear to the exact words:

> Zero Alpha this is Four Niner, brief Sitrep. I have nasties to my north, east and west. All of my call signs are in contact with large numbers of enemy and more enemy movement has been detected to our south. It would appear that the nasties are all around us, over.[8]

I must add that this brief Sitrep was given in a calm and re-assuring manner despite the extreme danger that the company was facing. Delta Four could have easily been over run and wiped out. The perimeter was tight and relatively unco-ordinated. Ammunition holdings were low and artillery defensive fire tasks had not been registered. Yet, every man in the company stuck to his guns and nobody panicked because the leader apparently had everything under control. It was a very close run thing and Delta Four survived because the leader appeared in control.

Another example I often cite in leadership lectures is when I had to give my attack orders to 11 Platoon before the assault into the enemy bunker position on 21 September. My platoon had been attacked twice before on that day and we knew that this attack had a good chance of being a real ding dong fight. When I came back from the company orders group, my stomach was churning, my legs felt like jelly and I was quite concerned about the forthcoming battle. But I had to be positive, assured and aggressively convincing when I gave my orders to the section. The *delivery* of those orders was probably more important than the content. I had to appear cool, calm and collected—but in reality I was as scared as anyone else there that day. As it turned out, we were forced into a withdrawal, but everyone did their job because they were looking at their leaders at all levels who did not panic or start to show fear.

It is a fine line that the leader has to walk between exposing himself unnecessarily to enemy fire and getting around the battlefield and setting the example and encouraging the troops. Obvious 'give-aways' that someone is 'losing it' are rash decisions; an inability to make a simple decision; screaming and expressing defeat; or perhaps taking a pessimistic view of the situation. The leader stating in the heat of battle that, 'This is starting to get untidy' will always be received better by the men than, 'We'll all be killed!' Major Jerry Taylor should have the last word on this topic of combating fear because I think he sums up most of what has been said:

Obviously everyone must be well trained; must be physically and emotionally tough; and morale must be very high. Those are the basic ingredients, because confidence in yourself, your mates, and in the people who lead you will help to offset fear. I also believe that officers should talk to their men about fear, so that everyone realises that it's a normal concomitant of battle, and nothing to be ashamed of. The next step is to undertake some form of training that will challenge individual determination and courage.

I don't think that we in the Australian Army understand, nor have exploited sufficiently, the training value—for war—of adventure training. Getting people 'close to the edge' allows them to experience fear, to understand it, and then bring it under control. I believe this to be a vital piece of self-knowledge that no soldier should be deprived of. It was Clausewitz who said, 'It is of first importance that the soldier high or low should not have to encounter in war things which seen for the first time set him in terror or perplexity.'[9]

Overcoming fear

One aspect of soldiering that is seldom explored is the method of training so that men can overcome fear in battle. Captain Peter Schuman, MC, who himself was taken to the edge many times on 'Claret' operations in Borneo as a trooper with the SAS, believes that it depends on training and the skills of the trade:

> Training and knowledge. When you're good, when your training is right, when you are all focused to what you're doing, you get this state of mind. You get this, and its individually I think, you get this feeling of confidence that 'tomorrow I am going out onto the battlefield and I am going to do all my drills well and if something happens, I am going to kill someone'. Instead of, 'Jeez, I've got to go out today and I might get killed'. It's really just that turn of mind where you feel so good in yourself and the team around you.[10]

Handling or managing one's own fear is always going to be a very personal, a very individual thing. Each man must find his own way. Schuman found the approach that worked best for him was again:

> Training. I had always classed myself as a hard trainer, and I learnt this from the Brits that trained us [SAS] at a place called See Kong, near Seria in Borneo. This was the first

campaign that I was in. They taught us the battle drills of
the 'shoot and scoot'. We always knew that when we got
up against the Indonesian Army there were going to be
more of them than us. There was just no doubt at all. We
had either three or four man patrols and they were in at
least platoon strength—at least. The whole thing was
worked out on a drill of shoot and scoot, that is blinding
the forward scouts, killing the forward section commander
of the enemy and getting out. And we used to practise that
for eight hours a day, five days a week, until you could ask
the forward scouts on the fifth day, 'What do you see?' and
he would say, 'Grass, I just see bloody grass'. And they were
exhausted. That is the way we used to work our scouts.
And we could guarantee that these guys could pick up a
bird flying. A strange bird flying in an area would indicate
something moving, either a man or an animal, and that
would put us on the alert straight away. We could tell by
flies leaving an enemy shit pit coming towards us. We
worked out that flies could fly 50 metres in the jungle when
they saw or smelt us. Now it would either be a dead animal,
a shit pit or another human being. So that alerted us. We
were 50 metres better off than anybody else in the jungle.
It was just knowledge. That was the training system I
suppose we went through and that just carried for all my
time after that. It's really just practice, practice, practice.
And if it works—don't change it until you have to.[11]

There are a few twists that can be placed on all of this
and it has to do with the immortality of young warriors. The
old belief that 'it won't happen to me'. Lieutenant Chris
Stephens was an Armoured Corps troop commander and
carried Delta Four to many places on many occasions during
his tour of Vietnam. He saw the experience of battle and the
collective effect in this way:

There is amongst most of the men a desire to give it a go
I believe. For a lot of them, they were there; they had the
equipment; they had the vehicles; they had the guns; they
had the chance; they were young! There's a certain 'testing'
of self which people want to do and I found that I was as
much of that I think as anybody else. How would it be?

What is it like and how will I go? And perhaps you worry a bit about that at times. First up, it's a bit like a game, let's get out there and give it our best. The overcoming of the fear first of all is quite clearly knowing the situation as best you can; knowing your enemy; knowing what you're probably getting into. It is a question of drills immediately. To overcome that initial fear, it's a question of being confident in those that are leading you, so that the boss is going to—as best he can—put you in a pretty reasonable situation so you can get out of this mess. And then there's a certain amount of 'well, he's going so I'll go too'. A certain amount of 'crew commander's up there, he's telling me to go, I'll take him, he's coming with me, so, I can't not go and he's got to get there so we'll go on'. So, there's a certain amount of not follow the leader, but because your mate's going in there, then you go too.[12]

There is no doubt that having an automatic mechanism that will get men moving and acting in a way that protects them and their team will help to defeat the inertia or panic that can come from the shock of a contact, the blast or detonation of a mine or impact of an incoming mortar or artillery round.

Several men from the Delta Four group expressed the opinion that because they were in a leadership position or position of responsibility, they didn't seem to be scared until after the event, and that they had more important things to do first before being scared or fearful. When Delta Four was surrounded on the night of 21 September, artillery was the only thing apart from hand-to-hand bayonet or machete fighting that was going to save it.

Fear of failure, or a fear of letting the team down is a great driver in ensuring that men do the job expected of them. Kevin Byrne, a platoon leader, says that his position of responsibility was the most important thing and:

. . . the biggest thing, from my point of view, was the fact that I've got this platoon out here and if I don't do my job we might all get bloody well killed.[13]

For the men of Delta Four, who were raised in the machismo climate of men being tough, resolute, emotionless and 'stiff upper lip' in the chauvinistic and homophobic fifties and sixties, it was a shock to their system when confronted by the stark and uncompromising reality of fear on the battlefield. What became very important to the men, especially the leaders, was how they controlled their fear. It is generally accepted that it is a common reaction to be afraid in combat, but to lose one's control or to succumb to fear is not accepted. One of the Diggers who completed his tour as a junior leader, National Serviceman Wally Burford, thought what he learnt most from his exposure to combat was:

> I think how to control your fear. Fear is a bloody invidious thing, it's a bit like a toothache. When you're frightened you know all about it, but five minutes afterwards, it's pretty hard to remember what being frightened is like. But when you have been frightened and had the fear creep through your body and know that you have still done what was required of you—that's the sort of thing that you learn about yourself that you could not learn in very many other environments—ever.[14]

The control of fear is easier said than done and it would be presumptuous to list a set of guidelines on 'How to Control Fear'. That is not saying that it could not be done, but because the psychological make-up of each and every one of us is so different and so affected by a variety of conditioning and programming factors.

Courage

The control of one's fear will depend a lot on one's personal courage. I will not try to re-invent the wheel on this much writ subject, but will instead give examples of what the Australian soldier looks for in himself and his leaders. When I first broached this subject with my ex-company commander, Jerry Taylor, and asked what he thought courage was he replied:

A day or two before I left to join the Regiment in Singapore, my father and I were discussing soldiers and soldiering. I asked him what he thought courage was, and he said that in his opinion it was the determination to hang on five minutes longer than the enemy. I've never to this day found a better definition.[15]

Like fear, courage has a contagious property. The act of one brave man can have an enormous impact out of all proportion to the event or action at the time. During 11 Platoon's major battle in late September 1971, one of the Diggers from 11 Platoon was Private K.G. Casson, known affectionately as 'Fred', for reasons I have never been able to determine. He was not found wanting when the machine gun team in his section had been killed and his section was in danger of being over run, or at the very least picked off one by one. Without being told or ordered by anyone, Fred went forward into a fire-lane where two men had just been shot to death and he recovered the M60 machine gun and the ammunition from the dead gun crew. He did that under intense enemy fire and where he knew that it was a deadly place to be. I asked him later why he had done that and he said that he: '. . . thought "Kiwi" [Private Kingston-Powles] was in strife and needed a hand'.[16] I cannot overstate enough the enormous effect that Casson's actions had on the rest of his section, which was about to go under. They remained *in situ* and fought resolutely until the situation swung back in their favour and the North Vietnamese found themselves once again facing an operational machine gun and their plans for a quick rush on the section position were thwarted well and truly.

Physical courage is listed in many leadership manuals around the globe as being a prerequisite for successful leadership and I would not dispute that fact. It is essential, therefore, that courage is evident in those who we anticipate will lead soldiers into battle. There are many devices one can use to test the presence of this required quality in people, ranging from abseiling, parachute jumping and other hazardous pursuits, to simply playing a contact sport. The use of contact sports has long been employed in the Armies of the British Commonwealth to bond their soldiers together and so that they can enjoy themselves at the same time. Some regiments, like the Duke of Wellington Regiment, have in the past taken rugby to the extreme and used it as a recruiting medium and as a means for promoting their unit's physical prowess and, probably subliminally, their ability as warriors.

There is no doubt that a man will face some physical danger on the sporting field. So, apart from the obvious team building and bonding that results from a team contact sport, there is something to be said for exposing men to danger and preparing them in some way for what may lay ahead on the battlefield. Many officer training institutions have used (and some still use) boxing as a means of testing whether officer aspirants had the desired mettle to get into the square ring and slug it out with another person.

Courage can also be bred and fostered from within the group. Much as mass hysteria affects a group, so can courage. The team that is tightly bonded will find the path to courageous and brave action easier to follow than one which is fractured with disunity, low morale or poor teamwork. Strong inter-personal relationships are essential for this climate to evolve and it is assisted by good teamwork and the spirit— even *esprit de corps*. Corporal Warren Dowell saw courage coming from the teamwork that 11 Platoon had established:

> The greatest strength of the platoon and the section was that we knew each other, that in the main we could depend on each other and we were pretty honest all the way along with each other. When you have got that sort of thing going for you and everyone can depend on each other you have a pretty good putsch.[17]

The strong personal relationships which create the teamwork and spirit do not come easily, nor overnight, and it has to be remembered that courage does not exist in inexhaustible supplies within us. I have heard it expressed that every man has a store of courage much like a bank account. Every time we face danger we use up a bit of courage and unless the store is replenished by giving the individual a chance to regroup and rebuild his confidence, then his supply or 'account' of courage will be exhausted and becomes bankrupt. When a man reaches that stage, he faces the problem of battle fatigue which could result in panic, sheer terror or shock.

Can men run out of courage? I certainly think so and so did many of the men from Delta Four. Captain Peter Schuman, MC, whose bravery need not be questioned, gave a graphic example of running out of courage:

> Yes. I've been there. It happened to me while working in small groups in Borneo. The training with these drills was so good and so fast that we could escape. But you knew at some stage, you had to run out of luck. When you ran, you were running blind. And you had to run into the canyon, and the old Indians would get you one day. You just knew it would happen, it was just luck. You would either ran into a river you couldn't cross, or you ran onto the edge of a clearing and you were surrounded. It just had to happen. But it didn't, we were always just that lucky, but it was always that. The first phase always went well, it was that second phase when you were trying to break the contact, that used to wear you down. And sometimes it used to last for five minutes with no follow up and other times it would go for a day where you were just hounded and hounded and hounded, and you would be fighting and knocking off the next scout, or trying to knock off the next section commander to blind them. Getting lower and lower on ammunition and you could feel yourself, you really get to the stage where you say, 'Bugger it, let's just fix bayonets and just sort it out.'[18]

To have your men run out of courage would be tantamount to a racing car pit crew letting their driver run out petrol when leading the race with the finish line in sight. In combat it could lead to disaster and it becomes the responsibility of all the leaders to ensure that their men have the intestinal fortitude to carry on through the uncertainty and stress of battle and emerge as victors on the other side. The

The strain of operations shows on the faces of company 2IC, Captain Peter Schuman (*left*) and platoon commander Second Lieutenant Graham Spinkston, as they listen to patrol orders after the company's first contact in May 1971. (*Photograph courtesy of Peter Schuman*)

company commander of Delta Four, Major Jerry Taylor, thought that men could run out of courage and added:

> Yes, most definitely. And it's yet another task of the leader at every level to know when his men have had enough. There are numerous ways of doing that. If you know your men really well, you'll find that they undergo subtle changes in personality. The normally cheerful man will start to become quiet or withdrawn—or be uncharacteristically aggressive, or perhaps he'll start drinking too much. There are a thousand signs. But the surest way is to look into a man's eyes. If he's had enough, you'll see it there. It can never be hidden.[19]

The type of courage men expect from their leaders will depend very much on where they are situated and the prevailing circumstance. The courage required may be moral courage, when a leader will be expected to admit he was wrong or made an error of judgment, or stand up when he knows damn well he's going to get knocked down, for something he believes in. Failure to act with moral courage may be as damning and crucial to the morale and *esprit de corps* of the group as cowardice. An example, cited by Private Greg Stuchberry, was when an officer from another unit failed to discipline a soldier. A Digger was misbehaving and the officer said he would charge the man if he didn't behave. The reply from the malcontent Digger was an indirect threat using the words, 'A fucking bullet will travel quicker than an A4.'[20] The officer turned and walked away, and by so doing walked away from his command responsibility and at that moment, at that very instant, he lost the respect of his platoon for failing to take a stand. In Stuchberry's words, 'he lacked leadership'.

RELATIONSHIPS

For leaders to be effective and for teams to work together there is a web of relationships that need to be formed. The number of sub-groups that can exist in just one rifle platoon is almost endless, so I will keep this discussion strictly to the hierarchical structure that exists between the officers, the non-commissioned officers and the other ranks. The responsibility for establishing a good working relationship in a military environment rests principally with the senior person involved. This is because it is easier within a rank-oriented culture for the senior person to initiate the discussions which will hopefully blossom into a good working relationship.

The commanders

Most things that work well do so because the people at the top of the hierarchal tree have got 'their act together', to use the vernacular. In Delta Four, the command changed once during the tour and for most, it was a welcome change because of the unpopularity of the first company commander. Without labouring the point, his command and leadership style was seen by almost all of the company as being inflexible and dogmatic, with a dictatorial, untrusting and unapproachable personal style. When the replacement commander, Jerry Taylor, arrived in the company, it was seen as a God send because of the manner and style of the man and the relationship that quickly developed between the commander and the company. The artillery officer attached permanently to Delta Four observed the effect it had on the whole command chain:

> I think my position as the neutral observer in Delta Company, in terms of looking at the way the Company operated and the way the platoons operated, it was mostly to do with the style of the commander, be it platoon commander or the company commander, and the next one down. More so in the platoons. I think it is a sort of three-way thing between the platoon sergeant, the platoon commander and the platoon, and to a lesser extent the company commander and the CSM and the company. I think if the platoon commander and the platoon sergeant were a good team together I think they influence the way the platoon operated. With the company, I guess it was less the CSM and more the way the platoon commanders interacted with the company commander which made a lot of difference.[21]

The role of the company second-in-command (2IC) is important because he has a two-way role both as understudy for the commander and as a sounding board for the subalterns who seek advice and guidance without bothering the very busy company commander. Captain Peter Schuman saw the role of understudy as being feasible but also observed:

> The words have been written about understudying but you can't understudy a man's style. All you can have is your own style and if, as happens, the leader falls over, the first thing you have to do is paint your own style on the troops. You can't be somebody else's man. You can understudy the battle procedures and the drills, but not the style.[22]

What Schuman says is very true. Copying someone else's style will do nothing but produce a facsimile of someone else, which the soldiers will see through very quickly.

The platoon commander and the sergeant

It is vital in a rifle company that people can talk honestly to each other without getting their noses out of joint. This is particularly so of the platoon commander and his sergeant. Some see the job of the sergeant as an understudy to the platoon commander, which can be something of an anachronism because the sergeant often has more combat experience, or at least line experience, than his younger platoon commander. The sergeant of 11 Platoon, Daryl Jenkin, expressed his relationship in this way:

> I certainly think you should understudy the platoon commander and know what's happening in the platoon in case the platoon commander suddenly isn't there. As far as 'understudy' a platoon commander is in a learning-type role, that is probably six of one and half a dozen of the other. I think that they both learn off each other. That must be done freely. I did see in different places where there was something, not quite jealousy, but something between platoon commanders and platoon sergeants—they weren't even close. They completely went down their own tracks, and the result of it was that the platoons were generally a shambles. Not that we have to mix socially, you can. It certainly doesn't hurt. But you don't have to. But something must be there between the platoon commander and the platoon sergeant; and if it is not there, then that platoon can't possibly succeed. It must fail.[23]

That 'something' that Jenkin refers to is the honest, frank and open relationship which allows the two men to work together to get the best out of their men. They have to project an aura of confidence, commitment and harmony, which will then filter down to the soldiers and make for a close and happy team.

The platoon commander and the Diggers

The view from the 'bottom up' is often a more accurate perspective of the relationship between the platoon commander and the Diggers. One Digger from 11 Platoon saw the relationship from this perspective:

> You look up to them through their leadership. I think the platoon commander or platoon sergeant were more or less part of the team. That is the way I felt. I think that is what is has got to be. I think that works with anything, any employee/employer. He has got to be approachable and if you have a problem he will listen. I don't like anybody who thinks they are any better than anybody else. I don't care who they are or what sort of social standing they have or whatever job they have, I don't think anybody is any better than anyone else.[24]

This openness and everyone being able to contribute regardless of who they are, will give everyone in the team 'ownership' of the decisions and thus commitment to the team's direction. Military leadership is not about industrial democracy, but it is about teamwork, and Captain Peter Schuman also saw great benefit in this approach. He thought it helped to make a sub-unit 'click':

> This might sound funny, but discussion periods with your subalterns and senior NCOs all as one group. Even down to the rank of corporal, getting them all into a discussion period on problems, on procedures and drills. Now there are certain things that have got to happen within a thing like a battalion with the SOPs that everyone has got to go along with, and you have just got to teach those things. But within your own sub-unit there are things that you can implement that are pretty slick and new and innovative that everyone can contribute to. Like the method of rapid redeployment; the method of Stand To in crisis; things that are not the norm. You can discuss these and come up with pretty good operational drills.[25]

That 'involvement' that Schuman talks about is what provides the cement that helps bring the various elements of the company together. Leaders, especially the younger ones, must overcome any fear of losing control of their men because they provide input. In fact it can create a very strong union between the leader and his men, when they feel they have contributed in some fashion to the tactical design of the operation.

The sergeant and the corporals

One of the more difficult relationships, not so much to establish but to maintain, is that of the senior non-commissioned officer and the men directly beneath him whose ranks he will have left not so long before. Daryl Jenkin saw this as one of the hardest things in being a sergeant:

> Something that is more difficult than anything else, is the fact that the longer you are on active service, remembering the corporals are all friends of yours and you've knocked around with them for many years, is just being able to remain the sergeant. There is no doubt that you are the platoon sergeant. There is never any time, or you do not allow a time or situation, where they are going to question what you say. And that is not because you are the platoon sergeant. It is because they have faith in what you say is the right thing.[26]

This is something that Jenkin had to work on continually as a sergeant and, in my opinion, did so successfully because he was able to 'leave the door open' and he was approachable.

Sergeant and the Diggers

The link between the Diggers and the platoon commander is normally the platoon sergeant. Even though the young officer is the commander and leader, he would always be wise to take heed of the advice of his usually more experienced sergeant who will have a good feel for how the platoon is reacting to the young officer's leadership style. Consequently, the sergeant has a role to play in maintaining a good relationship with the men and not be just an administrator or disciplinarian within the platoon. He must be a conduit to the men and vice versa. Sergeant Jenkin continues:

> The thing I think that is very important is that even though you are set aside a little as a platoon sergeant, you should never be that way. It is all right in peacetime because you knock off at four o'clock and go to the Mess and you get away from your platoon and it is very easy to grow away from them. But on active service when you are with that platoon all the time, you really must be one of them. However, whatever you say, they must do it out of respect. Not because you are the platoon sergeant. They do it because they know what you are talking about. They believe that whatever you say is the right way to do it and that takes experience. It is not something you can just read in a book and learn about.[27]

The 'respect' that is so often talked about only comes through because of the competence displayed by the leader. If the leader lacks confidence then it will become very hard to convince the men he is leading that they should follow.

> The relationship was . . . you would say casual, I suppose, but it was pretty good. I used to like [Sergeant D.K.] Daryl Jenkin, I had great confidence in him as a platoon sergeant because he had been there before, done that. I looked up to him for that reason and looked up to him for that leadership, and I think he gave us that leadership as a platoon sergeant. I always see the platoon sergeant as the guy like the mother and the father in a sense. I remember at times, he used to come around when we were on operations, and have a yarn and sit down and talk to us, just explain things to you and I appreciated that. I thought it was good. It showed that he was interested in us.[28]

Corporals to Diggers

The men that are closest to the Diggers are the section commanders—the corporals. They have an enormous responsibility as young men because they are the ones who physically command the Diggers. They are the ones who tell them what to do, when and sometimes how. They usually do not have that much more experience than some of the soldiers and in Delta Four's case, many of the section leaders had been conscripted and were only six to nine months senior to the men they commanded. Consequently they had to earn the respect of their men if their command was to work. A National Serviceman who reflected on this aspect of relationships thought:

> Warren [Dowell] was younger—that didn't worry me—he knew what he was doing. The corporals that I was directly associated with knew what they were doing, gave the orders, you had to obey them, but they would also listen to you and they would have a beer with you at the end of the day. I think communication is a lot to do with it. If they wanted to be isolated—away from you—that's OK. I suppose it's a fine line of being one of the boys and then when it needs be, to have enough command and respect for the other people. For them to have that respect for you too.[29]

Respect is a two-way street and the leaders must have respect for their men and not just as pawns for the battlefield. Australian soldiers are generally a fairly egalitarian lot and often all they want is to be treated with some respect and given a fair hearing. Lieutenant Chris Stephens, RAAC, considered the input from all ranks in his troop to be an important facet of leadership and teamwork, and he also saw the input of advice as a two-way street, with the art of listening just as important as talking:

> Rank has its place and it's a very important thing in the way that we have the hierarchy, but it must be thrown asunder when it comes in terms of fighting the battle; in terms of giving the advice; in terms of taking advice; and in terms of learning and so forth. You have got to respect the individual for the individual. Same as a trooper—he is well worth listening to at times, when he is talking about what he knows. He has advice to pass on and you're silly

if you don't take it on board. You may reject it in the
end.[30]

LEADERSHIP

Let's not beat around the bush. There is no such thing as man
management in battle—there is only 'command'. Man management is a part of leadership and not the other way around.
Men in battle do not want to be managed—they want to be
led, and not up a garden path.

There are scores of books on leadership and the approaches
to leadership are just as many. But what is important to know
is what the led look for from their leaders at various levels of
command, and give the bottom up perspective, which is
usually more frank than a top down view. One Digger saw
the requirements of leadership as:

> I suppose the quality of a good leader is to get the best out
> of his men with the least amount of effort, but in turn, to
> get that, there is a certain amount of respect that you have
> got to earn—between men. We can look upon officers; we
> can look upon any leader and if he has got a wimpy little
> voice and can't exude that little bit of authority, you would
> say well, this bastard is a pushover, we will fix him. So, I
> think it's just men amongst men. You have got to be able
> to do your job. Do your job competently and have the
> welfare of your men in your heart—first and foremost.[31]

Jerry Taylor was more philosophical when it came to
discussing what leadership is and what it required of him as
a leader:

> As a company commander, the most important thing to me
> was being able to trust my subordinates. I needed to know
> that they would follow through any task they were given
> to the best of their ability and resources. Or, if they were
> not able to complete the task, that they would come and
> tell me that it was incomplete. Reliability is in my view
> one of the most important characteristics of the infantryman,

138

whatever his rank. The first question I always ask myself about a subordinate, a peer, or a superior is, 'Can I trust this person?'[32]

In fact, trust reared its head time and again during the research for this book. Like loyalty, trust must go several ways. Leaders have got to trust their subordinates and let them learn by their mistakes. To not trust a trained soldier or young officer is tantamount to saying he cannot do his job and that will stymie development in teamwork.

Leadership is both an art and a science, and is definitely not an easy one at that. It requires many personal qualities which at times will run against the natural behavioural patterns of the individual, such as the normal psychological want of being liked. As humans, we like to be wanted, it is part of group psychology. We want to be part of the group or team and thus be popular so that we are accepted. However, in war there is no place for popularity for its own sake. Corporal Warren Dowell found this to be one of the hardest parts of his job as a junior leader, when he was a section commander and just 19 years of age:

The hardest part was finding a happy medium between being a popular person and getting the job done. When I was just starting out, I thought the best way to do things was to be popular and not necessarily get the job done 100 per cent. But that is not the way to do it—you have got to balance both those things out, and the hardest part was constantly reminding blokes that they were doing something wrong. They used to get pissed off with that too, but they had to be told if they were doing things wrong. That was hard. I didn't find ordering them to do anything overly hard; if they had to go forward under fire or anything like that, they did that because of their training, so I didn't find that hard. It was the being on their back all the time, and not only that, it fell back on me too, because if I was on their back all the time I had to be better than them to set the standard. So it got tiring in that way.[33]

Dowell was 'on their back all the time' because he was after a standard of excellence which would keep his men and himself alive when they got into combat. There is no pardon for letting standards slip, because when the judgment day comes, it will be easier to look in the mirror afterwards and say to one's self, 'I did all that I could to be good at my job'.

People are very rarely born with that innate quality of natural leadership and there are those to whom the art comes easier than others because of their personality and psychological make up. The recognition of who has 'got it' and who has not, can sometimes be seen in other arenas (no pun intended). Captain Peter Schuman explains:

I really believe that the senior and junior leaders of the military are born on the sports fields. And it doesn't matter whether you play volley ball or rugby or Aussie rules, as long as you get out there, take a bit of bark off, get smacked around the ears a few times by your soldiers and smack them around the ears a few times. That's the essence of it.[34]

Almost all of the men from the lower ranks mentioned that they expected their leaders to set the standards and lead by example. One of the riflemen gave this example of how leaders can earn respect and gain confidence from their men:

The platoon commander never asked us to do anything that he wouldn't do himself, and on many occasions he did that. I can remember an obstacle crossing we came to which was a pretty deep creek and there was a log across it, and to bypass it would have meant delay and we had a job to do at that time. He had made his decision that we were going to cross and he set up a machine gun on the bank we were on to cover. The river was flowing pretty heavily. The platoon commander would cross first because if he fell, he was a reasonable swimmer and he didn't want anyone else in the platoon to take the risk of doing it. So leadership wise, there it is in the middle of the 'J' [jungle] and he led the river crossing. All because if he fell he believed that he could swim to safety and he wanted to see if the log would hold. That is the type of leadership that people look for.[35]

The platoon commander's perspective

The men who led the platoons were usually in their very early twenties and had been serving for at least 12 to 18 months. Their own selection and training process was specifically aimed at identifying and nurturing good leadership behaviour. All of their own instructors were role models from which they could emulate and form their own style. Second Lieutenant Kevin Byrne saw the role of the leader as being one of extracting the best performance from those under one's command:

> People always ask the question, 'What is leadership?' Difficult thing. I think you have to be determined; you have to have confidence in your own ability; and you have to have ability. You can't lead in battle unless you have the rudiments of tactics; and how to get on with people and how to extract the best out of them. It was one of the most pleasant things I've experienced, when I was instructing at Portsea and Duntroon later on—passing this experience on, and I remember years later seeing the film called *Dead Poets' Society*. Robin Williams had a quality of leadership in that environment which was very similar to the military. You are extracting the best out of young people and I equated that situation to the military. I loved that movie because I could see he was eccentric, but that he had an ability to get the best out of people.[36]

Several themes have emerged during the examples cited from the men of Delta Four when discussing leadership. The Diggers want their leaders to have a go, not necessarily be the star player, but have a go and give it their best shot. They want to be heard and given a fair hearing if they have an idea. They also want another thing from their leaders—honesty. Frank and open relationships have been mentioned as prerequisites for successful working relationships and the personal quality of honesty is seen as being a basic ingredient which will endear a commander to his men. Corporal Dowell explains that it encompasses several areas:

Honesty is the big one, or one of the big ones. When I say honesty, it is honesty to yourself, honesty to your platoon commander and honesty to your soldiers. If you are honest with those three groups everything else falls into place. You have got to be honest enough with yourself to say, 'I am not as good as I should be and I should be able to do better', or 'I don't know what is going on and need to find out more'. Be honest with your soldiers, if you don't know, you tell them you don't know and don't try to bluff it out. Be honest with your platoon commander because he has to have respect for you too, and if he finds that you lied to him, then he is going to have second thoughts about either getting you and your section to do a job or relying on your judgment.[37]

Being 'tough' was not mentioned once. It seems 'toughness' is more aligned to physical and moral courage as opposed to being a Neanderthal wearing infantry clothing.

Approachability

What has been mentioned in almost every interview is the requirement for approachability. Yet, this quality does not seem to be spelt out in any current training pamphlet that is on issue in the Australian Army. Hopefully it will be listed as a desirable quality in any new publication on leadership. It does not matter at what level in the military hierarchy, the more successful leaders are those with whom people feel comfortable and can approach and discuss freely their thoughts and ideas. When a leader has an approachable style or manner, it has many benefits beyond allowing the soldiers to express their opinions and share their ideas. Platoon commander Kevin Byrne found that in his relationship with his company commander it became a case of requiring an open relationship regardless of rank and approachability should be a two-way affair so that dialogue is capable at every level. Quite simply, if your men cannot come and talk to you freely, you are starting behind the eight ball and will have to work very hard to open up the communication lines.

Discipline

The leader of any group of infantrymen knows that he commands a group of highly trained, fit, lean and mean warriors. They are not 'panty-waists' as the Americans love to say, but are men who are prepared to close with and kill the enemy. They get dirt under their finger nails and go for weeks on end without a bath. So, how does one maintain discipline in this group? How did the leaders of Delta Four keep these infantrymen in line? In fact it was not that difficult a task and while the men were on fulltime patrolling operations or in Nui Dat, there was very little trouble. It appears from the consensus of the respondents that discipline in a well formed and motivated team comes from within. The discipline is self-imposed and individually it is self-discipline. Very few men from Delta Four were charged with a military offence during their time in Vietnam, which is an indication of the morale within the organisation.

A few of the soldiers who were formally disciplined in Delta Four suffered at the hands of Company Sergeant Major (CSM) Noel Huish. The reason for getting into trouble was explained by the CSM in this plain but honest fashion:

> The two 'Ds' get the Australian soldier into more trouble than you can poke a stick at. And the two 'Ds' are drink and dick. But, that's the Australian soldier. There's no problem with that, it's just, hell, the Australian soldier hasn't liked discipline since he galloped off into the sand in World War One. We never had a fulltime reprobate in Delta Company. Beyond the AWOLs [soldiers absent without leave] and the drunk and disorderlies, there was no real problem.[38]

Discipline is therefore probably a reflection of how the people in the group see themselves and regard each other. It becomes a matter of respect for their mates, the team and their company. If the men have pride in their unit, their company or their platoon, they will be less likely to damage the reputation or smear the name of that organisation. Second

Lieutenant Graham Spinkston believes that discipline evolves through the men forming strong teams, and

> . . . from teamwork. If you are in a good team you do things because you don't want to let your mates down. There is no doubt about that. I am not saying they were perfect. There were little things that they did, but there were never any serious breaches of discipline where people would let their mates down. When the crunch came to it being done, they would do it without question.[39]

When I questioned Spinkston further on whether the discipline in 12 Platoon was imposed by him or his sergeant, or was it a case of self-discipline, he replied:

> I think self-discipline. I am certainly not into the forced discipline business. It is not my nature and I don't think many successful platoons had to force discipline. They did what had to be done because they were part of the platoon and wouldn't let anyone down.[40]

Another soldier saw it as being a combination of imposed discipline and self-discipline:

> I think a lot of it was self-discipline, but obviously it comes from the top. The standard came down from our platoon commander, that was passed down to the sergeant. Daryl [Sergeant D.K. Jenkin] used to mete out the discipline at times, when you needed a kick up the backside, bang, he would do that. I think the guys used to accept that and I remember Dowelly, [Corporal W.W.] Warren Dowell, was a section commander, he used to keep us in gear a bit at times. As for the self-discipline, I think a lot of that was there. I think we realised that we were going to war and we weren't playing kiddies games—we weren't just in there for a couple of years and getting out, so I think there was that professional attitude that we had to get some sort of standard here, got to pull our socks up a bit.[41]

There were, however, some breaches of discipline, as when Private Garry Sloane succumbed to demon drink and a small bladder. The incident and subsequent punishment occurred when Delta Four was occupying quarters at the Peter Badcoe Club at Vung Tau near the end of their tour of duty:

> I just got a bit too much grog into me one night down in town and came home, went to bed, the room started to spin and I wanted to go to the toilet. I couldn't be bothered walking downstairs and pissed over the balcony and our CSM, [Warrant Officer Class Two] Noel Huish, was walking past and I got him. In fact, he never said a thing that night, but the next day I saw him with his uniform on a coat hanger and he asked me if I made it a habit of pissing on the Duty Officer, and then proceeded to front me up to Captain Schuman to get charged.
>
> I think 'Shoos' [Captain Peter Schuman] could see the funny side of it, but the old military discipline in war zone—28 days field punishment and away I went. It started at 6 o'clock in the morning, full battle order, full front line ammunition and a flak jacket, and tin helmet. And one of the biggest bloody bladed shovels I've ever seen in my life, and a small red fire bucket. I had to tactically patrol down past the swimming pool, through the barbed wire, down on to the beach, fill it full of sand and tactically patrol back. This is about 100 metres either way. Then [I would] dump the sand into a blast wall and I did that up until breakfast in the morning, then it was normal day duties from then on. As soon as I had finished work in the afternoon, it was don the gear again and go down and fill the bucket up. Plus a bit of rifle drill in between. I didn't piss on the CSM again, I can assure you.[42]

A sense of humour

With all the stressors that men face in a war zone, plus the separation from loved ones at home, the strain of operational service can be quite palpable. The infantrymen are often living on the edge, and continuous stress such as six-week fighting patrols can be fairly tough. One of the release mechanisms for this stress was the Diggers' macabre sense of humour. Soldiers in a combat zone exist in a most unreal environment, where the protagonists are doing their damnedest to kill or maim each other. Consequently, the sense of humour is reasonably macabre. The style of humour could probably never be described as side splitting or uproariously hilarious because often the situation would not allow much more than a snigger or a quiet chuckle. The incident was usually highly situational and one had to be there to fully appreciate and understand the ambience of the moment. To illustrate that point this anecdote from Private Kevin O'Halloran shows how something so simple was considered at the time to be just bloody funny:

> We were out going along the paddy bunds. Walking out, we had full packs on, bloody heavy as anything. One of the guys slipped, it was Ian Boulton actually, in front of me. He slipped and he went backwards into the paddy field—it was full of water. Here's this guy laying on his back, hands up holding the M60, legs up in the air kicking and he couldn't get up because his bloody pack had been pulling him down into the water.[43]

This seemingly innocuous incident does not seem that humorous to those of us sitting back in a chair and reading, yet it acted like the pressure release valve on a pressure cooker and anything like this helped ease the tension that built up on long patrols where men lived off their nerves.

Other incidents at the time were quite unfunny, as Bob Meehan recalls:

> Now, as I look back at an incident that happened, at the time it wasn't considered humorous, but I can now see the funny side. We had harboured the afternoon before in thick scrub: closed canopy, poor visibility. At first light we were put on 50 per cent Stand Down. To [Private R.B.] Ray Davis was brewing up when all of a sudden in the distance we heard noise to our front. Nothing was said to the rest of the platoon as they had also heard the noise and were already dousing hexy [hexamine] stoves and getting down behind their weapons.
> The noise increased and we could hear screaming. I turned to Ray and said, 'It sounds like half the fucking

North Vietnamese Army's coming!' I had already linked up 200 rounds to the gun and Ray had positioned his rifle onto a forked stick. The noise just kept getting louder and louder. Next thing I felt something pulling on the back of my legs. It was [Lance Corporal J.A.] Johnny Bergmans, he had decided to inform me that he thought this was the big one—which was the last thing I wanted to hear at this time. Then, all of a sudden at the top of the trees a mob of the biggest fucking apes I had ever seen in my life appeared. They had spotted us below and proceeded to break off branches and pelt us. They started pissing on us and I heard that one had shit in his hand and singled [Private J.A.H.] Jeff Croymans out as his target for this messy missile. For about four to five minutes they let us have it, but as quick as it started—it stopped. For that short length of time the noise made by the apes was deafening. I can still vividly remember the gigantic teeth on the animals. [Corporal A.C.F.] 'Tassie' Wilkinson told us later that they moved at that time of the morning in search of food and water before it gets too hot.[44]

Being pelted by excreta by angry apes could hardly be considered amusing but it is typical of the black humour that soldiers appreciated, and evidenced by the fact that it is recalled as something funny.

It was often a sign of good leadership that men could use their sense of humour to stop an incident from being taken too seriously or when some kind of relief was called for. One good example was when Delta Four was in deep trouble on 21 September 1971 and a last ditch stand was being taken as darkness started to envelope the company. Cover was hard to come by and the order to dig shell scrapes was passed around and one Digger made a comment, as recalled by Garry Sloane:

Somebody yelled out to try and dig in if you can and someone yelled out 'Yeah, you're digging your fucking grave here.'[45]

For the National Servicemen, whose lives were totally uprooted for two years as they fought in an unpopular war, humour was probably needed even more. The following example told by Wally Burford illustrates this:

> We had this bloke [Private W.T.] 'Dirty Douglass' in 10 Platoon and he was due to get out. He was in the National Service intake one or two ahead of myself. Anyway, it was his last day in the bush effectively, and I can still bloody remember, we were laying up where we were, everyone was shooting and shouting, you could hear 'Dirty' screaming out from the 10 Platoon lines, 'The cunts have got me, one day left in the fucking bush and the bastards have got me!' and that broke everyone up. The seriousness at that stage, and here is 'Dirty' screaming out through the bush, 'They've got me again the bastards! Bloody one day, one day in the bush!' And you could hear it, he would have carried on for about five minutes before someone put a gag on him. In a very serious situation here was everyone stopping to have a bloody giggle, that's a pretty rare thing you know, everyone being shot at and shooting back. For everyone virtually looked at each other and start smiling and kind of giggling.[46]

Another way of letting pressure off was to indulge in practical jokes. The toilet system in the Task Force Base at Nui Dat was reasonably crude but relatively hygienic. The urinals were simply 44 gallon drums with the ends cut out and sunk into the ground save for a foot or so of clearance and covered with fly wire. These devices were placed strategically next to boozers and mess buildings and in each section tent lines. They were not screened from public view as no women were on the base—unlike American bases—in the war zone. The latrines were a little more sophisticated and were usually screened with hessian or corrugated iron walls. Such was the scene for this practical joke recalled by Grahame Tooth:

> We used to have those toilets that were just a screen sort of thing around you, and half a dozen seats to sit on. Anyhow, [Private] Corey Van Amstel, he was a Dutch bloke, belonged to 10 Platoon, funny as bloody buggery he was. And [Private C.A.] Col Fisher was in the dunny one

day, sitting on the seat, and Van Amstel walks in, swings the door open, pulls the pin out of a hand grenade, lifts the seat up next to Col Fisher, drops it down and walks out! Of course Col comes bolting out the door with his strides down around his knees. But Van Amstel has put a rubber band or a bit of tape around the lever so the hand grenade wouldn't go off. And here is poor old Col Fisher running out of the shit house with his bloody strides down around his ankles, and of course nothing goes off, and we are all sitting back outside the door watching him and laughing at him.[47]

It was rare to see practical jokes that were ever malicious or designed to humiliate a man, they were more for the simple fun of seeing someone else in bother or embarrassed. Greg Gilbert thought that having a sense of humour was essential and placed it high on his list of priorities for leaders to have:

I think it is important. War is a serious business but you can't take it too seriously all the time. When there is a job to be done, you get in and do the job but there has to be room for a sense of humour—a sense of light heartedness, when the pressure is not fully on and not fully off.[48]

Mateship

The camaraderie, or in Australian terms, the mateship, is a large factor in team cohesion. It is the strength, the cement or glue of the small teams and the underlying base of the friendships. Mateship evolves from the bonding through the hard training, the shared experiences in combat and simply living in each others' pockets day in and day out for months on end. The common purpose the men share and the inability for individuals to escape from the situation forces them together. They either swim with the tide or have a very lonely existence.

One of the Diggers had a nice analogy on what he thought mateship was in his group:

I think it's because you rely on each other. I'm one of these people who believe in machines and if you have got one part of the machine breaking down, the machine won't work. So, you all work to the best of your ability. There's a good thing in the *Fighting Fourth* (4 RAR Battalion book on Vietnam second tour) about Delta Company; that you're only as strong as your weakest member and we didn't have too many weak members. And that's one thing good about the Services, that they combined you, they bring you together to such an extent that you rely on each other and everybody knows everybody else's weaknesses and their strengths and you can either draw on it or you can support that other weak member and it works out great. So, that's where the mateship is, and then over a period of time you can 'read' a person—he's like a book. You know everything about that person: you sleep, eat, bloody do everything else with them and you become like a football team. It's like a good little team where everybody works together.[49]

Mates were there to look after you, back you up regardless of whether you were in the right or not. Mates are supposed to be there to support each other. For Garry Sloane breaching that reliance was the ultimate sin. So for him, a man he couldn't stand or tolerate would be

. . . the bloke that wouldn't back his mate up, irrespective of whether he was right or wrong. You always had this thing of camaraderie pushed into you—look after your mate and all that sort of thing. If you knew your mate did something wrong and he was to get in the shit for it if you backed him up he would probably get out of it. The guy that wouldn't back you up used to piss me off.[50]

Esprit de corps

Many believe that *esprit de corps* is a fancy word for mateship, but in fact they have two totally different meanings. The *esprit de corps* tends to be an emotive element that exists at the group level and not at individual level. At the same time, both coexist and to an extent feed off each other. If the morale is good in a unit, company or platoon, it is usually because there is a strong team spirit. That spirit is born out of good, hard and relevant training and good leadership. The training is usually

Private Bob Meehan (*left*) enjoying time in the boozer and 'telling lies' with Corporal 'Dogs' Foley. This photo was taken in the high humidity of the wet season as evidenced by Foley's damp shirt. (*Photograph courtesy of Bob Meehan*)

the catalyst that bonds the Diggers together and the mateship, that reliance on one another, is fostered from that teamwork. Platoon commander Kevin Byrne thought that the rivalry between the platoons was a good tool for building up the *esprit de corps*, as he explains:

> I'm a great believer in competitiveness. I temper that statement by saying that it has to be healthy competition and not competitive because it's a 'one-up-manship' thing. When we played inter-platoon sport, I remember saying to my boys, 'We've got to beat Gary McKay's platoon, we've got to beat 11 Platoon'. It's not because we didn't like you guys, it's just that we wanted to be a bit better than you and have you people shout the first drink. I think it's tremendously important. I used to always say that Delta Company was the best company, and Four Battalion was the best battalion. Because I worked bloody hard to make sure that my platoon was the best, the company was the best, the battalion was the best. And I think throughout the battalion, if everybody had that sort of philosophy, then it would only be to the benefit of everybody.[51]

The Fourth Battalion was a healthy, competitive battalion that engaged in inter- and intra-company competitions from shooting to swimming, rugby to cricket and all manner of military events. Those competitions developed a spirit and pride in one's own small team and organisation, and for men going off to the field of battle, pride and belief in each other is very important.

The final word on this chapter should probably go to someone who has explored and researched the nature of battle in enormous depth. He writes:

> The study of battle is therefore always a study of fear and usually of courage; always of leadership, usually of obedience; always of compulsion, sometimes of insubordination; always of anxiety, sometimes of elation or catharsis; always of uncertainty and doubt, misinformation and misapprehension, usually also of faith and sometimes of vision; always of violence, sometimes also of cruelty, self-sacrifice, compassion and above all, it is always a study of solidarity and usually also of disintegration—for it is towards the disintegration of human groups that battle is directed.[52]

6

DUSTOFF

The common soldier's blood makes the generals great.

ITALIAN PROVERB

ONE OF THE ENDURING IMAGES OF THE VIETNAM WAR is of the Iroquois utility helicopter clattering above the jungle canopy and swooping into clearings to unload or load its cargo of green clad soldiers. These helicopters carried soldiers right onto the battlefield, sometimes with tragic results, and it was used as an airborne weapons platform to support Allied soldiers on the ground with close air support. More importantly, for many soldiers it was a quick evacuation from the battlefield. The relationship between morbidity rates and survival is related directly to the length of time before a wounded soldier receives proper medical treatment. The longer he spends on the battlefield after wounding, the greater his infections; the greater the chance of shock claiming him and consequently the greater his chance of dying on the battlefield.

Another image of the Vietnam battlefield is a direct result of American television news footage. Mention soldiers being wounded and the general populace conjure up visions of an American GI screaming 'Medic!' at the top of his lungs and a very frightened, dirty, sweat stained face imploring God not to take his comrade. Often those images were captured after a mine incident or during a rocket or mortar attack where civilian camera crews had relatively easy access to the turmoil happening around them. In reality—at least for the Australians locked in mortal combat deep in the jungles of South Vietnam—those images were the antithesis of what combat and the associated wounding and dying were *really* like.

The best film footage to illustrate the brutality and truth of battle was captured by an Australian, the late Neil Davis. His outstanding work features in a David Bradbury documentary film entitled *Frontline* and to my mind it is essential viewing for anyone contemplating a career in the services.[1] The stark truth is that when men are wounded there will often be only a grunt or low moan; perhaps an apt expletive, such as 'Fuck it!', or sometimes nothing at all. When there is massive trauma, such as occurs in a landmine or artillery shell blast, where men have their limbs literally ripped from their bodies, there can be screaming as they attempt to cope with the horrendous pain racking their torn and mutilated bodies. The author saw enemy soldiers struck down and their reaction was not unlike that of the Australians. Hollywood movies have done very little to realistically portray the felling of humans by shot and shell and the celluloid version of being hit is a long way from what actually happens. One medic who saw several soldiers wounded, and subsequently treated them, recalls:

> The portrayal on TV and the screaming and carrying on is not the way I saw it in Vietnam. Some of the guys were very strong-willed and I think it refers back to their pain threshold and that they were able to handle it better than others. In fact on some I could have very easily—owing to the traumatic aspects of their wound—administered morphine or pethidine to accommodate their pain, but those individuals were able to suffer through that pain threshold and in fact I didn't have to administer it when I very well could have.[2]

The best way to imagine a man being shot is to see him as a puppet. When he is shot, it is as if the strings supporting him to the puppeteer are cut and so he collapses much like a rag doll to the jungle floor, often being sat literally on his backside. There is no dramatic staggering and reeling; no clutching at trees or branches. It is just 'bang' and down he goes.

I was struck twice by a burst of AK–47 7.62mm 'short' bullets, one of which shattered the head of the humerus and dislocated my shoulder joint. The feeling was similar to being kicked with a steel-capped boot and even though I was lying on the ground, the impact still moved me a good six to seven inches (150mm—175mm) along the ground. I heard what I thought was a large explosion and assumed that an RPG round had detonated against the small tree I was using for a fire position. The 'noise' was in fact the shock wave of the two bullets hitting me in a burst. There was no immediate pain that I recall, just a numbing effect. I was to endure the real pain later, when I reached hospital and surgeons started pulling rounds and broken bone out of my shoulder. My Diggers told me later that they only heard me grunt when I was hit and then say 'Shit' or words to that effect under my breath.

AFTER THE HIT

When a Digger was wounded in Vietnam a series of actions were set in motion beginning with a radio operator calling 'Contact, Wait Out'. Once he issued the next cue, 'Stand-by Dustoff', a well-drilled standard operating procedure commenced and dozens of people in many places swung into action. Before the soldier left the site where he was wounded, he was treated first by those immediately around him. In Delta Four every platoon had several men who were trained specifically in first aid and the treatment of gun shot and shell wounds. They had been trained by the Regimental Medical Officer (RMO) Captain Paul Trevillian and his senior personnel from the Medical Platoon. Those 'first aiders', as they were colloquially known, would render treatment if they were able and assist the platoon stretcher bearers to dress wounds and help in the evacuation of the wounded man. They would only do this once the contact or fighting was over and the platoon sergeant called for assistance. This concept of winning the battle then looking after the wounded is drilled into every Digger from the time he starts his infantry training. Captain Peter Schuman offered these comments on battle casualties and the priority one should place on casualty evacuation:

> There is comfort that if someone does get wounded, and the first time that you have a casualty in your particular unit, don't stop the battle and look after the casualty—never get fooled into that, but get the casualties into a safe area and win the battle first—then look after your casualties. You might lose guys, but as long as you have got that drill and everybody knows about it within the company it is a great comforter with guys. Otherwise if someone gets hit they will start thrashing around the place, screaming and yelling, 'Everyone look at me, look at me, help me, help me,' and people will—because it's a natural instinct. So, no that's not the way we are going to go fellas. What we are going to do is put you into a hole for a while, put your tin hat on your balls so they don't get shot off, you hold that and we'll win the battle and come and get you later on.[3]

This 'buddy system' meant that there was a pool of people who could assist and help reduce the onset of shock and stem blood flow. The important thing was knowing that sooner or later you would be collected. The next step in the evacuation chain was to get the wounded soldier out of the line of fire and the stretcher bearers would get the casualty back to a chopper pad or winch point.

THE STRETCHER BEARERS

These men were permanently detached to the rifle platoons from the Medical Platoon in Administration Company and they were quite proficient in first aid. These private soldiers were infantrymen but were under the 'technical control' of the Company Medic who was usually located at Company Headquarters. The stretcher bearers would render first aid and were usually the first men that treated the wounded soldier. His prime task was to stop bleeding, treat the patient for shock and move him to a safer place than where he was hit and finally, prepare him for evacuation from the battlefield. Being a stretcher bearer was risky business because these men were often required to go directly into the area where the casualty occurred.

Stretcher bearers in the Australian Army are armed, but their principal role is to render first aid and evacuate casualties. In addition they assisted the platoon commander and sergeant by treating the men in the rifle platoons for minor ailments, scratches, sprains and other injuries. After six weeks slogging through tropical jungle there are plenty of medical problems which arise ranging from sprained ankles, knees and wrists when men take a tumble over logs, hidden stumps, vines and unseen holes in the ground. In the wet season there will always be skin and other fungal problems associated with being unable to bathe or carry out normal hygiene.

THE COMPANY MEDIC

Each rifle company in the battalion had a medic permanently attached from Administration Company. The soldier was a corporal in rank and highly trained in first aid. He was a member of the Royal Australian Army Medical Corps (RAAMC) and on the posted strength of the battalion. He too was armed, however, this was purely for self-defence and he was never looked upon as an infantryman despite the fact that he had done all the training to allow him to participate in infantry action. The Delta Four medic was Corporal Mick O'Sullivan. He saw his role as

> . . . a member of a large team, I was primarily a rifleman within that team with a secondary role of having a very good expertise in the medical field. I saw my primary role to operate in whatever area that the rifle company superior wanted me to

Corporal Mick O'Sullivan, Medic, wearing his recently awarded ribbon for the Military Medal he was awarded for his actions under fire in September 1971.

operate in, and in the time of a battle situation—then come to the forefront, and with my experience and knowledge, help save the lives of my mates around me. That knowledge of having more expertise than most was probably comforting I guess.[4]

Mick O'Sullivan went by the nickname of 'Doc', as did probably almost every rifle company medic who was ever deployed to South Vietnam with Australian platoons. He was also an adviser to the rifle company commander on medical matters. The company medic had another role which is not in the medic's manual and it is about relationships. O'Sullivan continues:

In personal relationship with the guys in my company, I like to think that I had become very close to the majority, and maintained that close link with them which I felt would be important later on in the time of trauma or injuries.[5]

The relationship the medic establishes must be close so that the Digger can trust the medic and not get too excited or apprehensive about his treatment. This reassuring presence of the medic may help calm the Digger and help offset shock

caused by trauma and fright. O'Sullivan became very important to the men in Delta Four. The company had several
incidents where they operated as a complete sub-unit and had
two major actions which saw O'Sullivan at the forefront of
action and later decorated with a Military Medal for his
bravery.

The company medic needs to be far enough forward to
assist the wounded yet not get killed or wounded himself. So,
how far forward should the medic go? I asked O'Sullivan that
very question:

> Well, the policy is that he goes no farther forward than the
> Company Headquarter group. That is where he is to be and
> then your platoon stretcher bearers/first-aiders, their role is to
> bring the casualties back in to the Company Headquarter group
> where you then complete the stabilisation and prepare the
> casualty for evacuation.[6]

On several occasions O'Sullivan had to drag wounded
soldiers out of the line of fire after they had been hit. He did
his job with coolness and purposeful intent. And that's all that
Mick O'Sullivan saw it as. He says he was 'just doing his job',
but any rifleman who has been in a serious fire fight knows
that it takes courage to move exposed over ground where
others have already been hit.

DUSTOFF

Dustoff is supposedly an acronym for the American term
'Dedicated and Untiring Service To Our Fighting Forces',
which was used by the chopper crews who flew the missions
to evacuate wounded from the battlefield. The Australians who
were wounded were often collected by American helicopters
who then flew the men to either 8 Field Ambulance at Nui
Dat or, if the wound was serious, to the 1st Australian Field
Hospital at Vung Tau. If the American crew were advised
that they had a head wound victim, they would take the
casualty directly to the hospital at Long Binh which had

neurosurgeons on call. The golden rule in medical evacuation is to go to the most appropriate facility as quickly as possible without endangering the life of the patient.

The helicopters that the Americans used for casualty evacuation or casevac[7] were especially equipped for that task, unlike Australia's own 9 Squadron RAAF helicopters. Evacuation was often dangerous. If the contact was still in progress, then it was often recommended to the chopper crews that they not come in. The aircraft crews would monitor the VHF radio nets and if they heard that someone was in a bad way they would take a chance and come in and get the wounded man out. If the aircraft landed behind the action it was relatively easy to get the patient on board. If the helicopter couldn't land close by, then the patient would be winched up into the helicopter. This made the evacuation pretty tricky, especially if the fire fight was still in progress or if the exact withdrawal direction or movement of the enemy was unknown. The chopper would hover over a spot and let down the winch cable and a wire framed Stokes litter. The patient would be strapped in, hoisted up and hauled into the chopper. If the jungle was too thick for a litter, then a 'jungle penetrator' would be lowered which resembled a heavy, steel, upside-down umbrella frame. When this lump of metal crashed through the canopy to the jungle floor, it would then be folded out to reveal a platform seat and the patient would be strapped onto the penetrator and hauled back up through the trees. I experienced this unusual extraction method—being smashed into tree trunks and branches, and holding on for dear life with my one good arm.

Guiding a chopper to the area for evacuation was never easy. Throwing coloured smoke always drew a sharp response from the enemy and some enemy units even went to the trouble of throwing similar coloured smoke to draw the helicopter into their small arms fire range. Marker panels were always carried but not always easily seen. Delta Four tried using marker balloons which were an American device consisting of a bulky tin of chemical powder which when activated with water produced a gas capable of lifting a large bright orange balloon tethered to 100 feet of nylon cord up into the air. The disadvantages were the weight of the tin of powder and balloon and the fact that it needed about five litres of water to create the gas to lift the 1.5 metre diameter balloon. Second Lieutenant Graham Spinkston recalled his own platoon sergeant, Kevin Philp, having to urinate in their tin because the platoon was almost out of water. Another disadvantage was trying to get the balloon through the canopy so that the aircrew could see it. It also did not aid one's camouflage.

WOUNDED

Seeing one's own mates get wounded is a traumatic experience. Section Commander Warren Dowell reflected on the aftermath of battle:

> When I saw my own people get shot it bought it back to you how vulnerable you were too. But having said that, we had been trained enough to know that you had to leave the casualties where they were at that time because there were people like Support Section and the medics that would help out. It was afterwards when things had quietened that it would really come to you that your own blokes had been hit. It was then that it knocks you around again. It does take a little while for you to bounce back. But the job of the platoon commander, section commander, platoon sergeant, is to say 'Hey, let's get on with it.'[8]

What should not be underestimated is the impact of seeing your mate ripped and torn by bullets and his pain and bleeding. The tearing and sometimes shredding of flesh and bone by high velocity bullets or fragmentation is quite shocking and very ugly. It can affect the Digger who is having second thoughts about going forward or continuing to fight. I asked one Digger, Wally Burford, what was the hardest thing or the toughest time he experienced during the fighting on 21 September. He replied:

I think when I saw [Private R.J.] Ralph Niblett. Ralph was being brought back—he was one of the gunners with 11 Platoon. Once again a bloody good friend and one of the nicest blokes. He came past and he was being carried on a stretcher. He had a hole in his chest, bloody insignificant looking bastard of a thing with just a little bit of blood dripping out of it. He said, 'Oh shit this hurts, Wal, shit it hurts'. Anyway he went past and I thought well it didn't look too bad, but then we heard pretty well straight away he died. But that to me was the hardest part of it. That really brought it [home], I thought we could be in a fair bit of bother here. We already had [Private J.] Jimmy Duff down; we tried to sweep forward—we couldn't; and just the thought of what the outcome could be was the hardest part in that.[9]

Exposure to this side of battle as soon as possible after commencing operations is very important. Even visiting the local casualty ward of a hospital before going to a war zone can help prepare men for the carnage of the battlefield.

Some reactions to wounding and death are difficult to come to terms with, especially if the perpetrators are not present so as to allow some reaction such as returning fire. If the loss of a comrade is caused by a mine, then frustration becomes the principal emotion. Sergeant Daryl Jenkin explains:

The worst thing about any mine incident is that most times it doesn't involve a contact and you just feel so useless. All of a sudden you have had people killed and wounded and there is absolutely no retaliation. In a contact I think you can let off steam. But when it is just a mine incident it sorts of sticks in your mind longer because it is all bad news.[10]

Several of the men interviewed for this book were wounded themselves. Private Garry Sloane was hit by what is often termed 'live shrapnel' when the gunners were required to bring the artillery into danger close limits to stop the NVA

from swamping the Diggers and wiping them out. Sloane
explains:

> I got a bit of shrapnel in the head that day from our own
> artillery. I felt like I was out cold for a while. You seem
> to have a blackening effect but I don't think I was knocked
> out. I remember this big hunk of steel, burning steel,
> hanging out of the top of my head and trying to flick it
> out with my bloody fingers, and it wasn't working. That is
> our artillery for us I suppose, isn't it? Actually, they were
> good on the day and they came right in on top of us.[11]

However, he was somewhat more pragmatic when asked
what he felt when he saw others around him being killed and
wounded. In a forthright manner he states that he was:

> Thankful that it wasn't me. But I had a sick feeling in my
> stomach for anyone. You know it is going to happen in
> battle but you don't want it to happen, and when you do
> see the guys that copped it, it is a funny feeling. Even if
> you hated the guy, you still wouldn't want to see him cop
> it.[12]

Wally Burford, also wounded, highlights the extremes of
emotion that one can face on the battlefield:

> It was after our first battle, the whole place had been shot
> to the shit house by the tanks the day before plus the artillery
> of course. Anyway the very next morning, where we had
> slept, we had slept right on a bunker, so everyone was pretty
> jumpy but we weren't too sure of the extent of the bunker
> system at that stage. So, Spingo [Second Lieutenant G.D.
> Spinkston] asked me to take out a small clearing patrol about
> 20 metres around the front of our area. Anyway as we
> started moving out, choppers started coming in to drop out
> ammo and resupply. Anyway, because everything had been
> shot to pieces, bloody branches started falling, I just turned
> around to the blokes behind me and I said 'Look, jump
> down beside a big tree', and as I said that the big branch
> from the big tree I was under came straight through and
> hit me straight across the scone. I knew what had happened,

I knew I had been pole-axed but I couldn't speak and with the noise of the choppers, everyone just saw me go down and they thought I had been nailed. So the bloody gun opened up. (laughs) [Corporal M.J.] Mick O'Sullivan [medic] comes down in his normal dash and there is a person you know should have had more than one bloody Military Medal—Mick. But out he came and that's reassuring when you see him coming through the bush, but he came out and he wasn't too sure if I had been shot or not, you know he is asking me, 'Have you been shot?' You know all I could do was gargle and point. I must have been pretty heavily concussed at the time I think. So, anyhow it took a while to realise it had only been the bloody tree that had got me and not the nasties. Anyhow, Mick [O'Sullivan] took me back into the area and he's trying to stitch up my head. And he is saying, 'Gawd, fuck Wal this cotton is rotten'. And I could feel him pulling on the scalp as he is trying to stitch up my head and 'plonk' you could hear the cotton go and I suppose he had tried about ten or twelve stitches before he said, 'Oh, look, no, it's no good I'll just have to stick a bandage across it and get you back on the chopper'. And I am pretty sure it was the same chopper that caused me the smack on the scone that eventually took me out. So back to camp I went and I had the head stitched up at the hospital back at Nui Dat. Well it was a bit of a hollow feeling but at that stage it was after our first big battle and I think I really wanted to be back out there with them. I kind of felt cut adrift because they kicked me out of the hospital in the afternoon which was crazy I think in retrospect now, I really haven't got much recollection of the next couple of days. In the end I was looking forward to getting back in the bush.[13]

So, here we have a soldier who wants to leave the safety and cleanliness of a hospital ward and get out into the bush with his mates and risk getting shot at again. But reflect for one moment on a man more seriously wounded, and owing to his wounds taking more than 28 days to heal, he is medevaced by RAAF Hercules transport aircraft back to Australia. Then he is really alone and far removed from his mates who often never had the chance to say goodbye.

DEATH

In civilian terms, the loss of life in similar circumstances to battle is known as 'sudden death'. Because the event is not planned, nor is it expected or imagined as happening to any particular person, the sudden departure of a comrade forever can be devastating. People will often say, 'I was only talking to him this morning' or something along those lines to indicate that they were shocked by the death of the subject. Greg Gilbert had just such an experience:

> The saddest thing was from that same occasion [the battle at Nui Le 21 September 1971]. There was a Digger on the Company Headquarters whose nickname was 'Kiwi'; he was a New Zealander [Private K.M. Kingston-Powles]. I think it was just the day before it happened. He and I were sitting down having a cup of coffee or whatever and he had been telling me about these great plans he and his wife had for when he got back and the next day he was one of the blokes that got killed. I felt quite sad about that in terms of all the plans he had had for the future with his wife.[14]

Delta Four were obligated to leave three of their dead on the battlefield when they were forced into a fighting withdrawal on the afternoon of 21 September 1971. They were recovered the next day when a company of New Zealanders arrived to assist. Captain Peter Schuman was asked for his reaction to the decision to leave the dead behind:

> It happens, I had experienced it before. Sometimes you just can't do it. It does destroy guys if they know they are going to be left, because if the dead are left and the half wounded, where do you draw the line? And sometimes it's unavoidable. You have got to head for the ideal, but if the ideal is not achievable and there are too many baddies, then you can't risk lives. And I hate to say this, but it is foolish. Risking lives to save dead; to save corpses. That is just dumb soldiering.[15]

One man who was able to express his feelings at the death of his four comrades said:

> The deaths kind of hurt everyone. It was just the way we trained; the way we lived together; the way we had gone on leave together; all the blokes that had originally joined in Townsville—it was just like a huge family—it really was. And then of course, as soon as a family member dies . . . I don't think I would hurt any more now if my father was dying than the hurt of those blokes dying at that time—in all honesty.[16]

Those sentiments from Wally Burford indicate the strength of camaraderie and fellowship amongst platoon members. It should be acknowledged as a strength and remembered by those who have to deal with the grieving process. But, for everyone the dealing with this loss will be always a very personal thing. Everyone will handle it differently and in their own way depending on their own relationship with the man who has been killed.

Private Kevin Benson was a good mate of a fellow who was killed a week before he was due to return to Australia at the completion of his National Service obligation. He discusses the chain of events and emotions when his mate was taken back to the chopper pad after suffering a horrendous chest wound:

> I didn't know then at that stage just how badly he was wounded. I knew he was in a lot of pain. What worried me was his own sort of safety, cause he was sort of standing up and then Frankie [Private F. Wessing] grabbed him and he put him on his back and tried to get him out. It was afterwards when the word had come through that he didn't make it that it really shocked me. I remember having a bit of a cry.
>
> He was such a good mate to everyone. And he had everything going for him. He was nearly on his way home. He was going home to get married and I think he had a job teed up.

I suppose it was one time then when I wished, 'God I wish I wasn't here'. I suppose when I look at from then on I thought, 'I don't want to stay here'.[17]

The battle that Delta Four endured was a frightening experience as has been stated in several parts of this book. Private Grahame Tooth describes what he believes was the impact of the battle and the death of his mates:

Instead of being sort of happy go lucky, everyone was sad and upset for a while. I think it changed people, they just seemed *different*. They were different. They seemed to go from happy go lucky, naive sort of people and I think they were made mentally tougher. They grew up from being kids to mature adults who now realised the difference between life and death.[18]

The 'toughening' that Tooth describes is not necessarily a bad thing because soldiers will need all the armour they can muster when facing the bloody result of battle. Others saw the reactions to the battle differently and thought that there was almost a counter-balance to the grief and sorrow taking place:

Strangely enough, I thought they were all happy. I thought they were pretty buoyant you know. I wouldn't say happy. Actually there was a couple of funny incidents. There was a nasho, I remember his face but he was sort of joking around, I think a bullet hit his boot and it scored the heel of his boot and I think the stock on his rifle got shot to pieces. So, he was sort of laughing about it. Generally the atmosphere was quite good. I might add to that, I don't think in any way it was probably detracting [from the men who were killed], they weren't trying to make light of that, not for one minute. I think you could probably say that human nature sort of covers up in a sense just to keep you on top of the situation if you like. Sort of like a counter balance, and I think that's the way it was and I remember after the operations we used to have the booze ups and the cooks used to put on a really good feed for us—that sort of thing. I can't remember a great deal being said and I think the guys just accepted what had happened.[19]

It is important that soldiers come to terms with death and the accompanying grief. The difficulty in Vietnam lay with the fact that Diggers killed in action were taken back to the field hospital and their bodies flown back to Australia for burial or wherever their next of kin so decreed.[20]

GRIEF

Many Diggers have experienced some difficulty in dealing with their feelings of grief because when their mate died it usually occurred when they were still out on patrol. When they returned from their operation their mate had been flown back to Australia. When they themselves returned to Australia at the end of their tour of duty they were often many hundreds of kilometres away from their mate's final resting place—if they knew at all where it was. The battalion chaplains would conduct memorial services for the men who died on active service as they occurred, but it was often sometime after the event and the impact was lost. The normal grieving process was fragmented and incomplete. One of the platoon commanders, Graham Spinkston, discusses his emotions about one of his Diggers who was killed:

> Losing a soldier is probably the worst thing that can happen to you, and when I think back on it now I still recall those incidents and I always wonder if we had done something differently they might have survived. In fact I met [Private] Jim Duff's mum when they unveiled the Vietnam Memorial for the first time and to just sit there and talk to her was really good for me. I could actually talk to her about her son dying, and it was the first time I had really had a chance to talk to someone who had had a relationship with him other than his mates.[21]

This 'talking it out' is now considered part of the normal process when dealing with victims of trauma during stress counselling. Post traumatic stress was not dealt with in Vietnam, which underpins the current emphasis on the post traumatic stress disorder syndrome attributed to Vietnam war service.

LEFT OUT OF BATTLE

Back in Nui Dat there were about seven men, either on bunker picket or returning from R & R, who were summoned to the company headquarters by the company 2IC, Peter Schuman, in the late afternoon when word of the casualties suffered by Delta Four was filtering back on the Battalion Command radio net. One of those Diggers, Dean Cooke, who was back in base camp, recalls that moment:

> It was that evening, Captain [P.J.] Schuman, I remember him standing there and he read out the casualty list. I was almost stunned with disbelief that Nibby [Private R.J. Niblett] had got killed, and [Private K.M.] Kingston-Powles and the other guys, well, we didn't know them. Nobody knew them very well, so you know it really had no effect whatsoever on me. But as far as Nibby was concerned, he was really well liked in the platoon, a really nice guy and it was just a shock. I think the reality of war sort of came home to you. I remember later on I felt a lot of guilt over that because I sort of howled sometime later over that. I felt really guilty that I wasn't involved in that. I felt that I should have been there you know.[22]

RESPONSIBILITY AND GUILT

Dean Cooke mentioned that he felt guilt in not being out bush with his mates when they were in strife. There is also another guilt which occurs to the men who hold positions of responsibility. The company commander of Delta Four, the man who has overall command and control of his Diggers, saw it in this way:

> Probably the hardest part for a commander to accept is the
> responsibility he feels when he loses men under his com-
> mand in battle.[23]

I discussed these feelings with several other platoon commanders and leaders who lost men in contacts and everyone agreed
that at sometime they had thought, 'If only I had done this
or that', or 'I should have done something else and he would
still be with us'.

Naturally these doubts all flood in after one is off the field
of battle and safely ensconced with nothing but raw emotions
and free from pressure and out of danger. Major Jerry Taylor
was fairly pragmatic when he admitted:

> True, it was frequently physically and emotionally very
> demanding, often very frightening, and sometimes terribly
> sad. But we were infantrymen, and these things were part
> of the job.[24]

In 1995 I was contacted by one of the men from Delta
Four who had returned to Australia before the last major battle
involving Australians in Vietnam was fought by the company
in September 1971. He admitted quite candidly that for many
years he experienced extreme guilt and anguish over the fact
that he wasn't at the battle. Indeed, he blamed himself for the
deaths of some of the men from his section because his place
had been taken by a less experienced reinforcement who was
also killed. In his view he thought he was to blame—albeit
indirectly—for the loss of his mates. Mistaken as he was, he
truly believed that to be the case and it took some convincing
on my part to change his mind and allow him to understand
the reality of what had occurred.

BATTLE SHOCK—THE CRUCIBLE OF COMBAT

Casualties in battle are not always physical and can result from
battle shock caused by exposure to sights, sounds or smells
that absolutely horrify and terrify the casualty. These stressors,

combined with the intense, loud noise, chilling fear and a huge rush of adrenalin can create a deadly mental cocktail for the soldier unprepared for this onslaught. The Digger in battle is placed in a crucible which brings all of his emotions to boiling point and if he is unfit and unprepared for the heat generated in this tempest he will be hurt. Wally Burford explains what happened when one of his fellow soldiers broke down in the middle of a very intense fire fight:

> Well, I think you can be in the Army for 20 years, but until you first get in contact and you first have a battle you're never going to find out what a person is like anyway. You can't possibly train someone and know what they are going to do under fire with any certainty. We had one chap in our platoon who thought he was good enough until we hit that bunker system on the 21st [September 1971]. He was the section commander of the lead section there and he just went to pieces—he was just laying there gibbering, bawling, crying. So, no matter how much training you have had, you don't know if a bloke is going to react in that manner.[25]

Corporal Mick O'Sullivan saw several cases of battle shock during his time as a company medic. Battle shock was not always related to being wounded or seeing someone killed. He saw

> . . . a couple of times where death had been very close to individuals. I can't remember his name, but a bullet in fact hit the woodwork of his SLR and to see the after effects of that on a member was quite horrendous and in fact we casevaced him out. The easy answer, if viable, was to casevac them back out, give them a rest period and they would come back out again after one or two five–day breaks for a resup and then they seemed to fit back into the company all right. The expectation must be that they are going to return to the battle front again and the quicker you are able to do that no doubt it is the better plan.[26]

FRIENDLY FIRE

Probably the worst moment for a soldier is when his own forces kill their own men through accident on the battlefield. This type of accident happened to Delta Four when one platoon ran into another in very thick bush and were unaware of each other's presence. A forward scout fired at a target he thought was enemy—but without positively identifying his target. The tragic results were one dead and one wounded with only two shots fired. Major Jerry Taylor takes up the story of what happened:

I don't believe that there can be anything sadder, or more devastating to the morale of a rifle company than to have an accidental death, in this case caused by a friendly patrol clash. On the 18th of September, D Company took a resupply before the start of Operation Ivanhoe, which resulted in the Nui Le battle. Next morning we moved off, using our normal search formation, which was two platoons up, on this occasion 10 and 11 Platoons, separated laterally by a grid square; with CHQ in the centre and about a grid square in rear; and 12 Platoon in reserve, trailing CHQ. This formation gave us maximum ground coverage, and also the ability to concentrate rapidly in any direction. After we'd been going about 10 minutes I got an encoded message from Battalion Tac saying that a special agent report said we were within 500 metres of an enemy battalion. I halted the company and made a quick contingency plan with the platoon commanders. Then we started off again.

After about a further 20 minutes I got another encoded message, revising the first, and telling me that we were within 500 metres of two enemy battalions. I passed this to the platoon commanders, but made no other comment—it really needed nothing from me to emphasise the obvious. As you can imagine, everyone was very tightly wound, and moving with extreme caution. Given the circumstances, it's not hard to understand how the fact was missed that the track that 11 Platoon was paralleling was gradually converging with the one which 10 Platoon was on. Suddenly the leading scout of 11 Platoon saw a black figure moving about 75 metres ahead of him. Quite correctly in my view he opened fire, and a bullet from his SLR hit the figure in the back of the head, wounding him fatally. After a brief fire fight, during which another member of 10 Platoon was slightly wounded in the leg, it was realised that there had been a 'friendly clash', and both platoons ceased fire.

I don't think it's possible to convey what an appalling loss this was, and how badly it affected all of us in Delta Company. The leading scout who had fired first, a resourceful and dedicated young soldier, was devastated by the event. I had to point out to him very forcefully that he was in no way to blame; that he had done exactly what he'd been trained to do; and that under normal circumstances we would now be congratulating him for his resolute action and good shooting. Task Force Headquarters mounted an investigation into the incident, and the Task Force Commander concurred that it was one of those occasions when a series of adverse circumstances had come together at that particular time and place, and caused this terrible tragedy. Nevertheless, I was the senior commander on the ground. When things go right it's the commander on the ground who gets the credit. When things go wrong, it follows that he must also take the responsibility.[27]

It seems to all that it is a 'senseless waste' and that someone should take the blame. The reality is that these type of accidents occur because of many factors and usually not just a lack of care. It is important that the people involved are not shipped out of the unit. That would simply alienate the man or men, bring about a lack of confidence and very quickly destroy what morale was remaining in the unit involved. In the Delta Four incident, the soldier concerned was kept in the platoon, taken out of scouting until he regained his composure and showed that he was ready to scout again. The company medic, Corporal Mick O'Sullivan, was asked to keep an eye on the Digger who was showing signs of breaking down. He explains:

I can reflect back on that incident and yes, sometimes by confronting the stress that he was put under to cause that battle stress can be the answer and I think in that scenario it was. He stopped, he was with the rest of his troops who

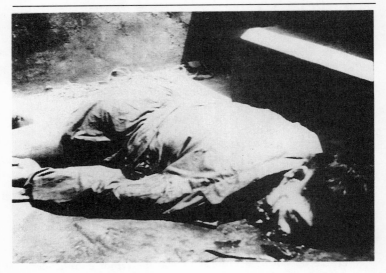

The carnage of war. A dead Viet Cong lies as mute testimony to the savagery of battle.

rallied around him, gave him the support that he needed and it was very quickly put behind him and forgotten. Which I think in that scenario was no doubt the ultimate answer.[28]

THE ENEMY DEAD

Soldiers will sooner or later be confronted with the sight of dead enemy. My experience has been that for most men it is a sobering moment and not one of mock bravado. Regardless of whether the dead person lying in front of you is enemy or friendly, it is still a sight filled with the awful reality that a living person has been extinguished—never to breathe again; never to laugh, cry or feel happy. Our Christian beliefs dictate that we have respect for the dead and Diggers are in that way no different to anyone else. Indeed, when I asked the enemy soldiers who I interviewed in Vietnam in 1993 why they respected the Australian soldier, the answers were usually that we buried their dead, took care of the enemy wounded and did not commit atrocities.[29]

One Digger who was tasked with burying some dead enemy recalls his first experience with handling a dead enemy:

> I must say it didn't sort of shake me up at all. Because that was it—he was the enemy. But it give me the creeps when I can remember grabbing him to bury him. That sort of put a cold shiver through me. But the gory part of it all didn't worry me. If I remember rightly he had the top of his scalp sort of lifted. That sort of didn't worry me a great deal.[30]

Kevin Benson had come to terms with the fact that the dead man he was handling was the enemy—a case not just of justifiable homicide but more one of 'better you than me' rationale. Another who thought in a similar way was the company medic, Corporal Mick O'Sullivan, who recalls his first sight of a dead enemy soldier. He said he had no thoughts

> other than to look down on a limp body and think that that was a human life some two hours ago, probably no other reflections other than perhaps that it is one less that can be firing or killing the rest of my company group.[31]

KILLING THE ENEMY

So, it comes down to the job of closing with and killing the enemy. That theme was well established in the interviews with the men from Delta Four. Killing is a very personal action and the memory of doing it stays with the man who pulls the trigger for the rest of his life. One of the riflemen from Delta Four who was drafted into the Army also adopted the philosophy that the enemy were targets as opposed to people. Private Bob Meehan thought:

I don't think we ever looked on them as the enemy, we just looked on them as they were something to be eradicated. I don't even think they were human, we looked on them as if they were targets. I never really gave them a second thought. They were just something that I had to go out there and find and eliminate.[32]

Another man who thought that the enemy were targets and not people as such was Wally Burford, who became emotive on the subject when questioned about what it is like to kill an enemy soldier:

Well at times he frightened shit out of me, but you know the whole thing was I wanted to see him; I wanted to kill him—in all honesty, that is what we had gone up there to do. Everyone talked about their first kill; and everyone thought about their first kill and what it would be like to kill them and that is what we wanted to do. At different times though, I noted when I saw the first body; the first bloke that [Private J.M] Johnny Lawton got, I saw him. Ten Platoon had already dug a hole by the time we got there after that contact and they had this bloody enemy in the bottom of the grave and I went for a walk and had a look at him, and I tried to feel a bit of compassion and I thought, oh, gee whiz. To me they were just . . . it's like bloody shooting dogs or cows or whatever. You didn't really assimilate them as being a human being—well I most certainly didn't anyway.[33]

This sentiment expressed by Wally Burford is interesting as he was a National Serviceman drafted to do the job which in its basest form he has told as bluntly and as honestly as possible. I suspect that infantrymen do not dwell on what the enemy is and where he comes from and his family and so on because it would involve him emotionally and possibly cloud his instincts and judgment, much the same way that hatred does. I experienced this after I was shot in the battle at Nui Le and walked into an adjoining ward at the 1st Australian Field Hospital at Vung Tau and there was a Viet Cong soldier laying in a bed with no legs below the waist. A range of emotions flooded through me as I had just lost four of my own men, but in the end I only felt sympathy for a fellow soldier who will suffer for the rest of his life.

Sergeant Daryl Jenkin offered the following comments on what emotions run through a person when they are confronted with killing and the effect it had on the men in his platoon at the time:

> I certainly never felt any remorse about it. Not seeing what they could do. It was a 'dog eat dog' situation I guess and I think the feeling of most people was you got him before he got you. You were quite happy to do it—that is what you had been trained to do.[34]

In all of the comments from the men who were asked about killing and hatred, there came through a very matter-of-fact attitude that was one more of acceptance and not once was there any false machismo about the job that they had to do. It is probably the realisation after the event that lives have been lost and that there is not much joy in ending another's life regardless of their politics. It was just a job that had to be done.

REINFORCEMENTS—FILLING THE GAP

Owing to the manner in which drafts of National Servicemen were brought into battalions deploying for duty in Vietnam every three months, there always came a time when about halfway through the tour sections and platoons would lose men who had spent almost two years either training for war or fighting in one. These departing nashos were a cruel blow to the men remaining in Vietnam. Not only were they losing expertise and teamwork from their unit, they were probably saying goodbye to their mates forever as they came from all over Australia and often not near where the battalions were based back home. Reinforcements also replaced those who were killed or who were wounded and unable to return to their platoon or company for some considerable time.

In 1993 I visited the battle site and spoke to an ex-North Vietnamese Army officer who had fought in the 21 September battle and he said that the Commanding Officer of the 3rd Battalion, 33rd NVA Regiment had been killed during the fighting and it was an awful blow to the unit which 'lost its way' for some time after his death.[35]

On arrival in country the men would be sent to the 1st Australian Reinforcement Unit (1 ARU) where they would undergo familiarisation and acclimatisation training before being allotted to units requiring reinforcements. The time spent in 1 ARU varied considerably depending on what was happening in the units and the Task Force at the time. It could be hard for reinforcements, or 'reos' as they were called, fitting into a tight knit platoon. Private Garry Sloane recalls his initial days on joining 12 Platoon early in the tour and describes the men and the greeting he received. He thought 12 Platoon was

> . . . very tight knit, close bunch of blokes. They accepted us but they were wary of us. They didn't turn their backs on you or anything like that, but when you stopped for a smoke or whatever, they would just sit and look at you to see what you were doing. It was a bit of an eerie feeling for a while.
>
> I think it was not very long after we got in there, I think it was only a couple of days after that, when a couple of enemy fired a few shots and we had to chase after them. And that was sort of when they really opened up because instead of going to ground, we just bolted and took off after them, the whole section, not just the new guys, and we didn't sort of falter or hang back and were up there with them. We didn't find the enemy of course, but that sort of broke the ice.[36]

The old hands of 12 Platoon were simply waiting to see what the new men were made of before becoming attached in any way to their new team members. This is fairly understandable because they have probably just said goodbye in one way or another to some old friends who they knew inside and out, and now they have been replaced by new faces, new temperaments and people who they know nothing about.

The reinforcements that came into Delta Four would have benefited greatly from attending the battalion's 'Lifesaver' exercises held between operations to pick up some of the finer points of working with the unit. There is much to be said for a battalion reinforcement unit despite the associated manpower and manning problems that go with that type of approach. But, in the long run it might save more lives.

The training and continuous movement from one unit to another was a feature of the reinforcement chain and there seems to have been very little continuity until a 'reo' reached his designated unit. Kevin O'Halloran tells of his feelings and experiences in this regard. He found that he was

> . . . continually, whether it was from Pucka to Singleton—
> then across to Nui Dat, and then even 1 ATF; to 4 RAR;
> continually changing over—meeting different personnel. I
> mean if you had have been with the battalion you would
> have known all the guys, gone across with them, known
> how they worked and lived, and what sort of personalities
> they are. But it was continually learning new training, new
> faces, just trying to be involved with people. You just never
> got time to settle down.[37]

In several cases reinforcements came out to the platoons from 1 ARU and straight into the field. This happened in 11 Platoon and three days later, three of the five reinforcements were dead. These men had barely time to get to know the man next to them and yet they were expected to fight with and protect each other. In the case of 11 Platoon the two reinforcements killed in action probably died from a simple lack of not appreciating basic battlecraft and failing to seek cover when they should have. They were unlucky to have to face intense battle on 21 September when raw arrivals would have been quite flustered at the intensity of combat. One soldier who had some thoughts on the reinforcement system offered these comments:

On the whole the reinforcements were not trained to the same degree we were. I think we had the unfortunate incident where we killed one of our own blokes and he was a reo; and I think that reflects on the sort of training. You know at that stage, our blokes, as soon as you had a contact the first thing you did was hit the deck and then worry about it later. Apparently he just dropped to one knee or stood where he was and got hit. There was another reo also got wounded that day and it seems rather coincidental out of all the blokes that were being shot at that day—by ourselves, the two people—one person dead and one wounded were both reinforcements.[38]

To emphasise this fact, 12 Platoon commander, Graham Spinkston, recalls that his platoon was reinforced in the field in September and two of the three reinforcements were wounded within several days of arriving in the platoon. This perhaps serves to indicate that they may have not been reacting with the same battle cunning that the rest of the platoon were at the time.

The tragic by-product of battle is either wounded or dead soldiers. They can be physically or mentally wounded and if they do survive, they can often be scarred in one way or another for the rest of their lives. It is important that soldiers understand and acknowledge the human cost of war and the associated destruction that accompanies it. Young men going into combat are seemingly blessed with a false belief of immortality and that bad luck or misfortune will not come their way and it will 'happen to someone else'. That youthful optimism is probably the main reason that men still enlist in today's armies around the globe.

This chapter has tried to demonstrate that not all casualties of war are physical and that there is an emotional price to pay for being exposed to the grimmer side of fighting. Men should never go into battle unprepared and their mental preparation is just as important as their physical training and battle drills for survival. Reinforcements should be weaned into their units slowly and not thrown into battle willy-nilly and if ever we have a draft system again, soldiers should be taken into the unit to serve a full tour of duty and not leave after only five months or so of active service. We worked very hard to achieve teamwork and slick battle drills in Vietnam and then threw it away when half the National Servicemen went home. Finally, I have hopefully shown that the grim reality of battle has an impact for greater than what is often portrayed in celluloid medium.

7

BACK TO REALITY

You had just spent 12 months in a war and you didn't want to be treated as a hero or anything, you just wanted to get home.

DARYL JENKIN
PLATOON SERGEANT

FOR A RIFLEMAN, SERVICE IN A COMBAT ZONE can be likened to running a car and, if the car is not serviced, checked for wear and tear, greased, had the oil changed and the tyres rotated, then things will start to go wrong. Soldiers in a war zone who face mortal danger through contact and fire fights with the enemy on a daily basis will be like the neglected and under-serviced car if they are not themselves taken out and given rest and recuperation. The Australian Army had two systems of rest during the Vietnam War. There was a system known as 'R & C', or rest and convalescence leave, which was given to the Diggers when they returned from arduous operations. Authority to grant the R & C was at the discretion of the CO of the unit if he believed that R & C was warranted to recharge the batteries of the Diggers. The other leave was a more formalised arrangement where a soldier was granted five days leave for R & R or rest and recreation

leave after he had been in country at least three months.
Qualification for the R & R was that your tour of duty had
to be for at least six months and to the war zone.

R & C

When a company came back into Nui Dat after a long patrol,
a series of well oiled drills would ensure that the soldiers were
divested of their dirty greens, re-issued with fresh clothing,
underwear and changed whatever webbing and equipment
needed replacing. Weapons, equipment and the Diggers were
checked by the platoon commanders, sergeants and medics.
Once the Digger was fully ready to deploy to the field again,
the sub-unit would Stand Down from duty and head for the
seaside town of Vung Tau. The troops would load onto trucks
with their basic webbing, ammunition and weapons and an
echelon bag with civilian clothing, swimming togs and a wallet
full of Military Payment Certificates to change into local
Vietnamese piastre once they hit town.

On arrival at the Peter Badcoe Club,[1] which was located
inside the sprawling 1st Australian Logistic Support Group (1
ALSG) camp at Vung Tau, the company was split up into
officers, SNCOs and Other Ranks and allocated their dormitory-style accommodation in comfortable wooden huts in very
pleasant surroundings close to the beach.

After settling into their huts, the Diggers would then hand
in their personal weapons to the CQMS. Then the company
would parade in civilian clothing and be briefed on the town,
its dangers, traps and pitfalls and given a general warning on
local traditions, customs and the 'White Mice' who were the
National Police and who tended to shoot first and ask questions (if at all) later. Soldiers were warned off certain areas as
'no go' or out of bounds areas—which were immediately
noted as being their first port of call when they got outside
the front gate.

A curfew existed in the town and anyone caught breaking
curfew was immediately jailed in the 1 ALSG detention
facility, affectionately known as the 'slammer' to the Diggers.

After their briefing, the soldiers were taken the five kilometres into town on a bus provided for the occasion and dropped off at a facility in town known as 'The Flags', which provided a bar and eating facilities for the Diggers and thus avoided the need for the troops to move backwards and forwards to the 1 ALSG complex and it also kept intoxicated Diggers more or less in one place.

The ironic part of this R & C leave was that once the Diggers hit town, there was very little rest *or* recuperation. Their main aim in life seemed to be to consume as much beer as they could fit into their shrunken bellies. This usually meant that Vung Tau was crowded with 'two pot screamers' after a very short while. Other soldiers sought pleasures of the flesh and for that pursuit there was no shortage of Vietnamese women to accommodate the virile young Australians. It was estimated that in 1971 there were 3000 bar girls plying their trade in Vung Tau, where not only Australians but American, Korean, Thai, Vietnamese and New Zealand soldiers came for R & C. It was also rumoured that the VC used Vung Tau for their own R & C but I have never been able to prove this.

The incidence of venereal disease was high unless soldiers took adequate precautions by using condoms and a Army issued antibiotic pill commonly called a 'no sweat' pill, which was alleged to ward off the disease provided it was taken before sexual intercourse. Some soldiers scared of contracting VD and the military punishment that came with being diagnosed as a 'dripper' took pills before and after the event just to make sure. Whatever they did worked because very few of the Diggers contracted VD whilst Delta Company was stationed at Nui Dat.

But catching venereal disease and being caught out of bounds were not the only dangers to the Australian Diggers seeking enjoyment and liquid refreshment in the town. Gangs of teenage Vietnamese youths roamed the town on Honda 50 cc motorcycles and would not hesitate to roll an unwary Digger who was alone or had lost his bearings late at night. These gangs were known as 'cowboys' and had perfected the art of driving past an unsuspecting pedestrian and removing his watch off his arm with a deft stroke using a piece of wire. They usually targeted Seiko-type watches with a flexible metal band popular amongst the soldiers and bought cheap from the Post Exchange (PX). Another favourite game was for kids to surround and press in on a Digger noisily begging for money or food while one of them neatly sliced his hip pocket with a scalpel and retrieved his laden wallet. There were other more sinister crimes in this gaudy town. Several servicemen were murdered when they got out of their depth and tried too hard to recover stolen goods or the like, or had a confrontation or misunderstanding with a pimp. On one occasion when Delta Four went to Vung Tau for R & C, it was not allowed into town because a woman, allegedly a whore, had been found murdered and an Australian or New Zealander was said to be responsible, so it was considered prudent that no leave be taken in town for that particular R & C.

The Peter Badcoe Club was well furnished with recreation facilities, such as an Olympic size swimming pool (unfortunately named the Harold Holt Memorial Pool prior to the Prime Minister's disappearance off Portsea beach), tennis courts, basketball court, gymnasium and concert hall. There was a bar, PX facility, tailor, barber shop and barbecue areas right on the beach. There were all manner of surfing and sailing craft, as well as power boats for water skiing.

The soldiers had the choice of staying at the Flags overnight if there was room or returning to the Badcoe Club. The officers were quartered in the Grand Hotel on the esplanade of the main beach in Vung Tau. The officers were quartered two to a room and the rooms became part of the 1 ALSG Officers' Mess Annexe and were permanently available to Australian military officers visiting Vung Tau. The chance to mix socially with one's fellow officers without the soldiers around was seen as a welcome respite after the continuous living cheek by jowl on patrol. The R & C leave was also a chance for the Diggers to be away from the eyes of their superiors and to be able to socialise with their mates who might be in other platoons or sections of the company. In all, it was a nice break away from work, the hierarchy and formal role playing associated with war fighting. Wally Burford saw his R & C breaks in this light:

> It's a pressure relief . . . you just virtually blew your self out of the water for a couple of days, you didn't worry about the war. All you worried about was getting it up and how many times and how much piss you could drink. You got away from the war for a short period of time even though in Vung Tau you were conscious of it. There's people with weapons and . . . you're on leave in a town that's been very heavily affected by a war, but at the same time, just the fact that you could drink and you could go to sleep and you didn't have to get up and do gun duties—just silly things like that, that just let you get away from war and that was extremely important.[2]

One thing that was evident was the physical condition of the men after two days 'rest' in Vung Tau. They were usually hungover and their stomachs fragile. It was a fairly common sight to see Diggers retching over the side of the trucks as they travelled back to Nui Dat through fishing villages where fish were being dried on racks. The smell of nuoc mam is quite potent and those with a poor disposition usually paid the price much to the delights of their mates who showed absolutely no sympathy at all. Drug abuse (apart from alcohol) did not seem to be a problem with the Australian Diggers and very few cases came to light. It was considered that everyone could get into enough trouble with beer let alone playing around with dubious drugs. The first day out on operations was usually a quiet one with not too many kilometres being covered as the men recovered from their overindulgences.

REST AND RECREATION

When Diggers went on R & R they had a choice of destinations. As the war progressed so did the venues where they could go for their five days of leave. Many American servicemen headed 'Down Under'.

Married men from the company usually went back home, which meant that they were often away for 10 days as their leave did not start until they reached the front door of their destination. Travel was always civil air and Qantas or Pan American airways were the servicing carriers. For others, there were exotic locations such as Bangkok, Taipei, Hong Kong or even Tokyo if one could wangle the trip through American friends. The R & R vacancies were allocated by the unit Adjutant on a pro-rata basis to the various companies in order to ensure that companies did not fall below a viable operating strength. The men sometimes spent their R & R by themselves but usually tried to travel with a mate or at least a fellow Digger from the same company. Time spent on R & R was cherished and usually spent in much the same way as R & C but at a slightly less frenetic pace and in cleaner, more expensive surroundings.

Not everyone went to the exotic locales offered for R & R. Corporal Warren Dowell who had a reputation as a 'player' came back to Australia. I asked him why and he replied:

> That's what I ask myself now. In fact the reason why was I wanted a break away from Asia and all things Asian. I wanted to go somewhere where I felt safe with round eyes, and I wanted a complete break away from Asia and the pressure. I wanted to come back and get on the grog back here with people that I knew and I knew that I would be safe. But having said that, in the years after, Asia became a second home (to me) and I love it. But by that stage (during the war) I had had enough.[3]

Indeed the men who were in positions of leadership, like section commander Warren Dowell, quite often stated that they felt they needed a break because

> . . . I think just the pressure that we were under all the time. Especially section commanders and anybody with added responsibility. You had to perform because if you didn't perform then someone was going to get hurt.[4]

Another who sought refuge from the war back in Australia was company medic, Corporal Mick O'Sullivan:

> You were back here knowing that you could completely relax and haven't got the problem of keeping one eye open all the time to see what is going on around you.[5]

Garry Heskett found that when he went to Hong Kong on his R & R, other emotions crept into the picture:

> Had a great time and . . . Spent a lot of money, wasted a lot of money but I don't care—I had a great time. But, I felt guilty because the rest of the platoon, some of them hadn't had R & R at that stage, I think our section was one of the last to go on R & R and you felt like you were letting the team down. It's that bonding. It was team spirit. It's like laying in hospital you know, you've got no right being there.[6]

These sentiments were echoed by several other men who assured me that they were most sincere in what they said. They did not want their message to sound trite or obviously sentimental.

A Digger on R & R could find himself on leave in a foreign country and could be fairly lonely and have a miserable time. The Diggers who were rotated through Nui Dat on bunker duty during operations felt this same loneliness when taken away from the teams that they lived with day in and day out for almost two years. Private Kevin Benson explained what happened when he was taken out of a patrol to 'have a rest' on bunker duty back in the 1 ATF base camp at Nui Dat:

> I know I got horribly drunk. I think it was just a bit of an unwind. Because it wasn't our first time out. But we had been out [bush] quite a while, I know. Yes, just to come back and sort of relax and unwind as much as you could. It was a very lonely place though when you come back like that.[7]

But, sooner or later the leave would be over and the men would return to their mates and try hard not to say how much of a good time they had had.

OPERATION SOUTHWARD

As part of the Australian military forces withdrawal from the Vietnam war zone in 1971 and 1972, the battalion vacated Nui Dat in October and November 1971 and spent the remainder of their tour in Vung Tau and its immediate surrounds. The battalion's main body was home by Christmas but Delta Four was chosen to form the thin 'red line' and protect the logistic elements packing up those stores, equipment and vehicles worth returning to Australia. It was a difficult time for the company because many of the original National Servicemen had departed as their time was up, so the company was inundated with reinforcements. The company commander, Major Jerry Taylor, felt the loss of the two-year conscripts:

> These were the people who had been with us right from the early days; and had been in all our battles, big and small. We felt their loss very keenly, not only because they were old friends, but also because they were battle hardened, and their knowledge and experience could not be replaced.[8]

The company was then reinforced and boosted with a formidable array of resources to give it mobility, communications and firepower.

The flood of reinforcements caused many headaches as the newly formed battle group struggled to attain some semblance of teamwork and *esprit de corps* that it enjoyed in the days before the move to Vung Tau. It didn't happen as all would have wished. The company 2IC, Captain Peter Schuman, recalls what he described as his most difficult time on this tour of duty:

> I didn't know whether we were going to get done over or that the Army of North Vietnam were going to stand on

the hills like Zulus and salute us as we left the shores. I never knew any day, and they could have taken us out any day because we were just a . . . I don't know whether some deal was struck with them or not, but we were certainly vulnerable and one company with a few APCs and 600 logisticians weren't very much match for old D445 if they wanted to have a swim one day. Oh, we would probably have put up a good show, I suppose, and had all the fire support that the American Army could muster for that particular battle. I don't know whether it was because we were very close to and locked up next to the town or not and the political climate just wasn't with it, but they [the enemy] certainly left us alone towards the end.[9]

Jerry Taylor also described this time of protecting the final stages of the withdrawal as his most troublesome and difficult, despite the tough battles that he had experienced earlier in the tour.

After many of our National Servicemen went home, the company was topped up by volunteers from the other companies, and not all of those volunteers were chosen with sufficient care. Under the conditions which prevailed at Vung Tau, some of them became a bloody nuisance. However, I don't believe that the company 'clicked' to the same degree during the withdrawal phase at Vung Tau, because there was not the same clear definition of task and objective, and that resulted in a much lower level of commitment. It also became obvious as the withdrawal progressed, that Delta Company was being used as a glorified work party, and I personally resented that very much. This was a pity, because I personally found the three months down in Vung Tau far more difficult to cope with than operations in Phuoc Tuy had been, and we needed all the help we could get. I felt far less comfortable with the environment, and I was very worried by the potential for disaster that Vung Tau and the surrounding Province presented.[10]

Why the enemy didn't have another crack at the Australians before they left Vietnam will probably never be known. However, it was discovered in 1993 that during the battle on 21 September 1971 the 33rd NVA Regiment was badly mauled and their commander killed in action. They were forced to withdraw and re-fit and this may have had some effect on the desire to take on the Australians so soon after the last battle. Jerry Taylor summed up the options open to the enemy:

> Our role in 1 ALSG was purportedly that of a ready reaction force, to provide trained, hard hitting muscle if the enemy decided to put in a final effort to send us home with a bloody nose. They could do this in one of three ways: sapper attacks against 1 ALSG, which I considered very likely, or a concerted ground attack against the base which I considered highly unlikely because of the difficulty of withdrawal from the peninsula afterwards. Or thirdly, by drawing Delta Company Group away from Vung Tau and back into the province, by using our AATTV people as the bait to get us into the sort of regimental ambush that B and D Companies had fought our way out of on the 21st of September, and where we could be taken out in detail. I considered this last to be the most likely option, because it was what I would have done if I'd been the enemy commander, and to this day I don't understand why they missed the opportunity.[11]

So, the time in Vung Tau passed fairly monotonously, apart from the shenanigans of those Diggers affected by alcohol and getting into the strife that all Diggers have done before, did then and still do today. But it was a tough time on those who were in positions of leadership and required them to adjust their styles to meet the new challenges that the change of circumstance had brought about. It came back again to the junior leaders exercising their authority by setting the example and insisting on high standards.

RETURN TO AUSTRALIA

Coming home from a tour of duty in Vietnam was described by one veteran to be like winning a lottery or a pools draw without the accompanying intense jubilation. Returning from a war zone where one has experienced combat means that you have personally won, because you are alive, and physically—and hopefully mentally—in one piece. But the total jubilation and euphoria is missing because you have lost some mates or seen them maimed. There is also the expectation of seeing one's loved ones again and enjoying the reunion of family and friends whose main link with you for the last year has been through letters or audio tapes.

Delta Four came home in March 1972 on the HMAS *Sydney*, which was departing Vung Tau harbour for the last time. It was a strange time for the men of the rifle company because they were leaving the war zone with the war still unfinished. Most believed that it would be lost eventually, once the Americans withdrew completely under the umbrella of 'Vietnamisation'. Some soldiers saw the withdrawal of the Allies as a 'sell out' but at the same time they could offer no solution other than tactical withdrawal for the small Australian force.

The Vietnam War was a divisive conflict from an Australian domestic perspective. At the beginning, there was much support for the intervention of the Allied forces to counter Hanoi's threat against the southern capitalist regime. As the years rolled on, the anti-war movement gained momentum in Australia as well as the US, dividing both nations internally. The popular songs on radio were heavily laden with anti-war messages and the living rooms of Mr and Mrs Citizen were bombarded nightly with graphic film footage (usually of American soldiers) showing the devastation, carnage and brutality of war. In addition, there was no 'good press' that came out of Vietnam. It was all bad news and that, associated with a lack of global allied strategy for fighting the war, meant that the war looked and sounded like a bottomless pit claiming young soldiers' lives for no realistic solution to the conflict.

So, by the time Delta Four was due to return to Australia in early 1972, the anti-war movement was at its zenith in Australia and trade unions, Labor politicians and university students were demonstrating and holding moratoriums on a regular basis. Some conscripts were bold enough to burn their draft cards and some, who went on to become children's television show hosts and producers, went to jail rather than complete their National Service obligation.

It has become a tradition in Australia that returning troops march through the city where they disembark. As all of our previous conflicts had been held on foreign soil, the Vietnam War seemed to be no different, but it was. Unlike returning troops from previous wars, the returning Vietnam Diggers faced considerable hostility despite the fact that they were doing their duty as their country had democratically agreed. That hostility was generated by those citizens who saw the war as unjust and not in Australia's interests. The arena for this display of political hostility and sometimes, aggression, was the welcome home parade. It became a very delicate matter and one which was never handled with any tact or aplomb by the politicians in power at the time. The Diggers became scapegoats for an unpopular war and one which saw Australia divided on the issue for decades. Unfortunately, even the Labor politicians at the time did not nothing to protect those servicemen who, after all, were only doing as their country demanded.

No one in Delta Four on board the *Sydney* expected to be given a hero's welcome because they had seen the increase in the anti-war movement protests and demonstrations, and some had even had their mail stopped because the postal workers union members had refused to deliver mail to soldiers serving overseas in Vietnam.

The trip back on the *Sydney* was about 10 days for those disembarking in Townsville and another three for those continuing on to Sydney for their post-tour leave. Compared to the trip up to Vietnam, where the soldier's days were crammed with training of every variety from sun-up until dark, the trip back was decidedly indolent. The men were free to do pretty much what they pleased and apart from minor administration and some mess duties, the trip home was a pleasure cruise in uniform. One soldier who returned on the *Sydney* recalled his most vivid impression:

> It was the first time I had seen real meat for about 12 months [laughs], or real food actually. The time we were over there you used to have all dehydrated stuff, you know

you just add water and you would have scrambled eggs and mashed potatoes and that, well, when we got on the *Sydney* it was back to real food. There was sausages—something you had never seen. It was a relaxing sort of experience I suppose, we didn't do much for 10 days. Just sort of laid around on the ship, saw movies; that was about it. Two big cans of beer a day, they used to ration you two big cans of beer a day.[12]

For many on board from Delta Four, the trip home by sea was a chance to unwind, reflect on what happened in the war zone and prepare for the enormous change back to civvy street. It was also a chance for men to talk together about what had happened and the incidents that took men's lives and saw them look death in the eye.

The battalion disembarked in Townsville, gathered at The Strand along the city's beach front and, when re-united with the advance party and some who had been evacuated back wounded, the battalion marched through the streets of this tropical provincial centre. There were no demonstrators or protesters hurling abuse, coloured paint or blood. It was a polite, if not restrained welcome, with many spectators on the footpaths being relatives or friends of those marching. Some of the unkind comments came from civilian football playing mates who made sarcastic comments about 'Charlie' being a bad shot and not being able to hit such a slow moving target. In all, it was a parade without much fuss and attended by Major General A.L. MacDonald and the very tall figure of the Leader of the Opposition, Gough Whitlam, who was grabbing as much political mileage as he could before the forthcoming general election which he went on to win in December 1972.

Those soldiers who were from southern states and taking discharge or leave south of Brisbane, continued on to Sydney where they were met by the Minister for the Army, Andrew Peacock, and several other dignitaries. Then it was time for the men to proceed on well earned leave. Some men returned on the ship with very little time left in their National Service

Mortarman Private Garry Heskett on return from Vietnam at Garden Island in Sydney with his sister and grandparents in March 1972. It was the last voyage to Vietnam for the converted troop ship. (*Photograph courtesy of Garry Heskett*)

obligation. One National Serviceman who came home on the ship recalled his discharge procedure in Sydney:

> It was a Friday or a Thursday or whatever, the ship berthed, I got all my gear; I was told to report to Watsons Bay, up on top of the hill there, at eight o'clock the next morning. That night I went with my parents, we went out and had a few beers. Next morning I got up to Watsons Bay, got interviewed, discharged, got a train ticket and came home. I might have spent two days at Watsons Bay, but it wasn't long. Some bloke there just interviewed you; I suppose I was pretty naive. He said, 'Do you want the system to give you a job?' and I said no, being pig-headed like I am [laughs]. 'What are you going to do?' and I said, 'I dunno, just go home and see what happens'. I just said no, yes, no

195

and that was it, probably if I would have said I want some assistance—I daresay I would have got it. So, you know it was just a couple of days and you were gone.[13]

Watsons Bay, located at South Head in Sydney, was the discharge cell for the Eastern Command Personnel Depot and there were similar depots in every capital city. The experience that Grahame Tooth had was also repeated for thousands of other National Servicemen who were in Phuoc Tuy Province one day and in George Street, Sydney, the next. This rapid transformation and returning to a hostile and unpopular environment—from the veteran's point of view—was not conducive to rapid or complete assimilation back into normal civilian life. Many returned soldiers chose not to mention their involvement in the war because it brought unpleasant reactions on many occasions. This 'hiding from the truth' became the base reason many Vietnam veterans found solace in each other's company when they came home because there was no-one else they believed they could talk to about their experiences and their feelings. When the deceit that was undertaken by the politicians to get Australia into the war for regional security reasons was uncovered much later, there came a feeling that they had taken part in a shameful and wrongful enterprise. It was no wonder that post traumatic stress disorder became a catch word for Vietnam veterans when they were not afforded the pleasure of feeling that they had served their country in a noble cause as their forefathers had done in previous military expeditions abroad.

Another National Serviceman, Kevin Benson, who returned to Victoria, was asked what he thought about protesters and his welcome back after a year in the war zone:

Actually they [the protesters] didn't worry me at all. Maybe a couple of times it sort of struck home, but I just let it flow over the top. When I lobbed back home [from Vietnam] my uncle said, 'Oh come on, let's go up the pub'. So, you know, he is as proud as punch of me and we go up the pub and he said to the barman, who he knew, 'This is my nephew, he is just home from Vietnam'. He says,

'Oh, yeah', and he walked away. And I thought, phuh, up yours! Because I was pretty proud of it too! That was one instance that sort of stays in my mind.[14]

Benson, who was discharged more or less at the same time as Grahame Tooth, returned to his home town of Geelong and the next Saturday went to Kardinia Park to watch his beloved Cats play in the Victoria Football League competition. Some of his civilian friends saw him a few rows back in the grandstand and yelled out wanting to know where he had been for so long. Kevin Benson chose to reply with something innocuous rather than risk ruining his day at the footy. It was not until an Anzac Day reunion in 1991 that Benson for the first time wore his medals. They were pinned onto his sports coat with a safety pin and the ribbons were back to front. I, his old platoon commander, accompanied him on the march that day 20 years after he had come home.

It was Army and probably enforced government policy at the time that servicemen should not wear their uniform in public, unless absolutely necessary, and especially if travelling on public transport. For a while officers and soldiers working in the Army Headquarters in Russell Offices in Canberra wore civilian clothes to work to avoid unpleasant incidents with those opposed to armed intervention in Vietnam.

There was no march through Sydney city because the battalion paraded in Townsville—and it was probably not politically wise to stir up more trouble before the forthcoming general election in December. Private Garry Sloane remembers when he disembarked:

If we had been given the opportunity to land in Sydney Harbour, as proud as we were to have been there and come home, if we had been allowed to march through the streets of town, and we got paint or eggs or spat on, and I reckon I can speak for every bloke in the company, irrespective of how hard [Major J.H.] Jerry Taylor said, 'don't break ranks', I think there would have been some blood spilt in the streets. I think every guy was proud of what he'd done and in fact we were told when we got off the ship to change out of uniform and get into civvy clothes and go home. I said well stuff you, and I stayed in greens and flew to Melbourne in uniform, and it was a good feeling. There was a lot of old fellows, obviously Second World War Diggers, saying 'Good on you, mate, good to see you home.'[15]

Others from Delta Four had varying experiences and found that the treatment they received caused all types of family problems as well. It was generally felt that the protests back in Australia had very little effect on the troops in the war zone, apart from the angst caused when the postmen refused to deliver mail. When asked, Kevin Byrne felt there was little effect:

No, I don't think it did. It was more of a disappointment and I think it may have had some lack of, well lessening of morale value, but I think it was a personal disappointment. It was huge disappointment when we got back, a huge disappointment. I remember, well it's a light hearted incident now, but at the time it had a really big effect on me. I remember getting back and I was a skinny bugger with short hair and my sister, Maureen, was being crowned Miss University in Brisbane when I first got back and I went along because we were very close. I had to leave [the function] because I ended up in about three fights and was taunted all night by these university students because I was a Vietnam veteran and I had just come back and they knew it. There was an element there—not all of them—but there was a fairly hard core anti-Vietnam element in the University of Queensland and I never saw my sister crowned that night. There was no point in staying as I was being harassed and I remember being belted and I got in a cab and went home. I remember my mother and father asking me what happened and I told them and I said, 'I'm really disappointed that I've come back to an Australia that treats its own this way after going to Vietnam and fulfilling an obligation that we had nothing to do with in the original decision making process.[16]

The reaction that Kevin Byrne recorded was repeated time and again for many men who returned from their tour of duty and felt as if they had done something wrong, when in fact

Second Lieutenant Kevin Byrne enjoying the South China seaside at the R & C Centre at Vung Tau. (*Photograph courtesy of Bob Hann*)

they had done almost everything right because they had made it back alive.

One of the Regular soldiers in Delta Four, Dean Cooke, felt very strongly about the protesters, who he thought should have aimed their message at the politicians. He was asked if the protesters affected him whilst he was in Vietnam:

> Not while I was over there, not one bit, no. I can't remember anything about the protesting while we were over there, it really didn't effect us. I think I felt more sorry for the Yanks because it must have been really demoralising to know that your own country people, your own people in your own country were against you being there and I think in that respect I get a hating for the protesters. And it's still in my mind today. I reckon some of them, I reckon Jane Fonda should have been taken out and tried for treason and shot—I really believe that, because of what she did up in North Vietnam. I reckon she betrayed the men in Vietnam, even though whether it's right or wrong, they were over there and probably the majority of them were draftees and there not because they wanted to be there, and I felt she just betrayed her country.[17]

On the other side of the country, a National Serviceman who was back home in Perth found a slightly different picture to that of the more rabid political style on the east coast:

I think when I came back, the anti-war movement, I never really run into anyone from there, but [it] probably comes from Perth's isolation to a degree. I think just the blasé way people treated you. You know, you have been up there; you have done a hard job. You live like mongrel dogs; we had fought; we had died. I thought myself I was going to die, and then, my mates that I came back to, blokes that I had been through school with and known—I just couldn't really relate to them when I came back. The last thing virtually before getting called up was I was in the State hockey team—that was going to be my . . . well that was my ambition at that stage to play for Australia. I still think I probably would have done so because that was my whole life, sport at that time. When I came back, that was just gone, I tried to play again, but I think I turned up at one training session and I thought this is not real, in comparison with the life that I had been living. I moved out of home, my folks were absolutely fantastic the way they accepted my idiosyncrasies at that stage. I did some strange things. I know the old man worked at the *West Australian* newspaper and he used to come home around two o'clock in the morning. At one stage he came in and he woke me up *under* the bed. I was under the bed, I was having a sly smoke under the bed! Just things like never remembering to flush the dunny; but I knew I was putting a strain on them. The old man would come home, there could be myself on my own passed out. I might not come home for days or I could come home with eight or nine blokes and they would all be bloody camped everywhere all through the house. My folks were absolutely fantastic, but I realised very quickly that you know, I couldn't put them through that sort of thing, so I moved into a flat with other army mates and spent 12 months there. And that to me was the de-winding period and that was the therapy for the four of us in that flat. We had regular get togethers; regular booze ups and alcohol became a big part of my way of life for the first year when we were living in the flat. But that was our way of winding down at that stage. There was no such thing as psychological counselling or any bloody thing like that at the time. I suppose we were all pretty nutsy, but we were nutsy because we were living in the environment that we couldn't relate to anyone else that we had known before we went to Vietnam.[18]

Given the rapid transformation that was required of National Servicemen from civilian to fighting warrior and then back again into civilian life with no allowance for re-adjustment or the ever-so-popular counselling that is given to people who witness a plane crash or bus accident today, then it is no wonder that some men became bitter about the way they were treated on their return to Australia.

Dean Cooke recalls one incident when he was adjusting back to civilian life in Brisbane not long after he took his discharge from the Regular Army in 1972:

My first, my initial contact with a protester was in Brisbane here. I used to drink at the Brunswick Hotel after I got out of the Army, and used to drink there quite often and there was a guy I knew and his name was 'Moose' for obvious reasons. He was a big bloke, he used to drive a big petrol tanker. Anyway it was Friday afternoon, we used to go down the pub and he was sitting there just about all night drinking and at this stage it was just on evening and I think the majority of the people, Friday afternoon of course, would probably have gone home for tea, and there was a good few of us still in there and we had these tables away from the bar. There was myself and there was another guy who had actually escorted the HMAS *Sydney* over to Vietnam, he was still in the Navy. But anyway, I was talking and I was just asking him what they got up to on the ship—just general talk about Vietnam and this other guy 'Moose' at the end of the table said, 'Oh, you're nothing but killers of women and kids'. I couldn't believe it, but anyway I must have retorted somehow, probably said something to him that annoyed him! (laughs) I went back to talking to this [Navy] guy and next thing he turned around and whack! I was sitting on the floor. He decked me, whacked me straight off the stool, so I jumped up and we had a bit of a battle if you could call it a battle—David and

Goliath and, but I let him know where I stood, I wasn't
going to take that rot and to this day I will not take anything
like that, although I think public opinion has changed. But
that was my initial contact with a protester if you like in a
sense. But I don't like what they did. I think for that reason
when the Gulf War was on, I know that was different
circumstances and that, but I was really wrapped when on
the news they showed you the American people actually
getting behind their soldiers, and I think that's an unbeatable
combination if you have got the support—the moral support
with the people behind you.[19]

Many of the men interviewed for this book had similar
stories. I had a similar incident to Dean Cooke. When I was
encased in plaster after surgery following multiple gun shot
wounds, a university student informed me that 'It served me
bloody well right' when I explained what had happened in
reply to his questioning at Ballymore rugby ground in 1972.
That sort of attitude tended to scare veterans away from
publicly showing they were a veteran and indeed many
veterans did not march in Anzac Day parades until after the
Welcome Home Parade held in Sydney in 1987, 15 years after
the last Australian troops left and in many veteran's eyes, 14
years too late.

The lesson learnt by the general public and our political
masters has since been realised and was demonstrated most
clearly when Australia sent troops off to the Gulf War in 1991.
Yet the reason for that involvement and Vietnam were not
that dissimilar. As one strategic studies professor once
remarked, 'If Kuwait grew bananas and not oil, would we still
have gone to war in the Gulf?' The answer is naturally an
emphatic 'no'. We went for other strategic reasons—once
again aligned to the USA and, on reflection, for reasons which
were in no way dissimilar to events in 1964 and 1965. Back
then there were other more recent conflicts such as
Konfrontasi with Indonesia, the Malayan Emergency and
Korean War which precipitated the ill-fated Allied intervention in south-east Asia.

The underlying theme that emerged from interviewing the men of Delta Four was the intense pride they felt in the job they had done. The Vietnam War may have been lost from a strategic perspective but they as individual soldiers and members of their company personally felt that they had not lost their war, they felt that they had done a good job in their military duties. Their record was not blemished in any way and they served with some distinction. Consequently, the manner in which they were treated by some sections of the public, whether it was consciously or not, did not sit well with the men. They felt then that their efforts were in vain.

8

THE ALLIES

I thought the Kiwis were pretty good as long as they didn't have a can of beer and a guitar in their hands.

PETER SCHUMAN
CAPTAIN, COMPANY 2IC

RIFLEMEN IN THE FIELD DO NOT OPERATE IN A COCOON, they cannot achieve half of what they want without support in some form or other. There were many agencies operating in support of the Delta Four riflemen and they were mainly the quarter master types and the cooks who were detached from the catering platoon to the rifle company. Coming back from operations was as slick an operation as any other event that needed to be organised. It was the time when the Company Quarter Master Sergeant, Bob Hann, would come into his own and ensure that all of the men who had been out 'in the weeds' were organised so that no time was lost in getting them de-kitted, deloused and ready for a cold beer. There would always be the post-op session when the chopper crews and APC crewmen would be invited down to the company boozer for a session of reminiscing or more widely known as 'telling lies'.

Because the riflemen spent most of their time out bush and saw very little of the echelon types, it was difficult for them to give me their impressions of the people that supported them most closely. A few comments were gleaned here and there but in the main they would only admit that 'the pogos' back in Nui Dat 'did all right'. Perhaps this is some form of warrior elitism or egalitarianism at play, I am not sure, but they were more forthcoming with those they met and worked with in the field when they were out on patrol.

The CQMS and his staff are often seen by Diggers as 'stingy' types who will not give anything out of their Q store unless they receive a blood oath to return it in better condition in which the Digger borrowed it. In fact, that is a myth and the CQs of this world are usually ex–riflemen with bad knees or backs who can no longer hack the pace in the rifle platoons. In fact, one quarter master type in a Brisbane based battalion had no knees at all, having lost his in a mine incident in Vietnam, but he was still able to serve the Corps in a reserve unit. Delta Four CQMS Bob Hann saw his job this way:

My job was to look after the logistic administration, if you like, of the company. Also, I felt fairly strongly that I had an obligation, a responsibility, to make that as simple as possible for the soldiers. To not fuck them around and to make things happen and to try and anticipate what was needed, and try to get it set up before it was needed. Often that meant that you fucked around like an old gin doing things that were never needed, but it was nice when you had everything organised and someone would say out of the blue that they needed this and you could say, 'Well, there it is'. I saw my job as to make life as comfortable as I could for the blokes. Christ Almighty, they spent six weeks at a time up to their balls in bloody mud and living on shit rations and doing it bloody hard. The last thing they wanted when they came back was to be fucked around and that was the job. When things went well there was a lot of satisfaction in it. When you could get a little bit extra for people. Because they all thought I was the meanest bastard in the world and I have never met a generous Q man yet.[1]

A relaxed CQMS Bob Hann at Vung Tau in early 1972 just before the final withdrawal of Australian troops from the war. (*Photograph courtesy of Bob Hann*)

The CQMS was also responsible for looking after the belongings of soldiers who had died. He tidied up the bits and pieces of administration that nobody wanted to do, especially those close to the man killed. Bob Hann had done this many times:

KIAs [killed in action] or WIAs [wounded in action], casevaced back to Australia or killed in a road accident when we were at Canungra—no difference. By then the emotion has gone. The emotion happens at the time when it has all happened. When you get their gear back it was bloody days later and it certainly wasn't a pleasant task, but it was not the sort of thing you would imagine it to be because the emotion has all been spent and you are more concerned that he might have something in his gear that he might not want his parents or his wife to see. Things like letters and stick books and things that you would take out. I used to check their gear pretty carefully. In fact it depends on what the circumstances were. If there were people from his platoon there, I would get them to go through it. Often there was stuff there that you didn't know whether it was his or whether they had borrowed it from somebody or whatever.[2]

The company commander of any rifle company relies implicitly on his CQMS to make sure that the store is well stocked, has the right number of things in it and that all the serial numbers of weapons and radios match the ones in the register. Jerry Taylor had this opinion of Bob Hann and his crew in the Q Store:

> Staff Sergeant Bob Hann was the CQMS, and an excellent one he was too. I've always tended to feel that 'being in the rear with the beer and the gear' is rather a depressing pastime and in fact as 2IC B Company, 2 RAR in 1967, I had flatly refused to be left out of battle, and threatened physical violence to my company commander if he even thought about it. So my sympathy lay very much with Bob, having to do one of the unglamorous but vital jobs that underpins the efficiency of a rifle company, and thence a battalion, in operations.[3]

The essential thing about the support from the echelon back in Nui Dat was that nothing was ever questioned and if a rifle platoon wanted a 9-volt battery with two alligator clips soldered onto the top—they got it. Support for the men in the field was the name of the game and Bob Hann and his crew did it well.

THE TRACKS

On several occasions Delta Four was taken to and from operations in armoured personnel carriers. Whilst not many people liked travelling in these '12-tonne steel coffins'—as one Digger described an APC—an uncomfortable ride was always better than a long walk with your pack on your back. On more than one occasion Lieutenant Chris Stephens, RAAC, a troop officer in A Squadron, 3 Cavalry Regiment, collected members of Delta Four and moved them from one AO to another. The types of jobs the APCs did were various as Chris Stephens explains:

> Time out would vary, you could be out on operations, outside the wire for days. I think the longest I did was about 33, 34 days, that we actually stayed outside the wire and did not come back. Unusual to a degree because you

APC Troop Officer Lieutenant Chris Stephens on patrol with his 'tracks' in Phuoc Tuy Province in 1971. (*Photograph courtesy of Chris Stephens*)

have to come back for servicing and a few other bits and pieces. It wasn't necessarily the bodies that had to come in, it was the vehicle that had to come back. But you would pull out of the Dat, usually with a company on board, redeploying them somewhere, taking them to a spot, dropping them off and then you would either remain in support of their battalion or move to another battalion, depending on what was going on or being given a TAOR of your own to go to and conduct some operations in. Could be a section ambush. Divide the troop up into an ambush of three, or an ambush of two groups depending on what you think the threat might be, and then sit tight. You could sit in an ambush in an APC for up to three days. I think that was the longest I actually sat in one place. After that, the routine—for me, certainly—got a bit uncomfortable. It was just too long in one place and noisy and one gets the uneasy feeling that instead of you watching somebody, somebody's probably watching you and it's time to pack up and go away. So, you would move around to some other particular area and start the same process again. Patrol some roads, just have a presence here and there; push into some areas that nobody else could easily go to; just again establish a presence and then come back out. Resupply occasionally, protect a fire support base—acting on information that somebody might have a problem that night. We used to carry SAS and sneak them into places under various guises and then go back and pick them up. That would always be an interesting little exercise, just trying to give them some cover. Once or twice, getting them out of trouble. There was no way you could get a helicopter to them to get out of there and they certainly couldn't walk out, so, there had to be some arrangement to get APCs in to meet them. But that's the broad routine.[4]

The relationship between the APC crewmen and the 'grunts' as the Diggers were affectionately called was good. On many occasions when the Diggers were picked up from a grid reference in the middle of the scrub, the APC crewmen would throw on a brew of hot tea or coffee which always seemed to be at hand and refresh the weary infantry. They might have spent a lot of their time together chiacking one another, but a common respect for each other's lot was usually the norm.

THE TANKIES

Delta Four had the unusual experience in Vietnam of participating in two full fledged company attacks but even more uniquely with armour—Centurion main battle tanks—in direct support in the assault. The deployment of tanks to Vietnam was one that was considered by some pundits as a waste of time because 'tanks can't fight in the jungle'. The men from C Squadron, 1 Armoured Regiment certainly proved there detractors wrong in the battle on the Suoi Ca in July 1971. Major Jerry Taylor describes his relationship with the armour:

There was always a lot of debate about the use of armour
in an operational environment like Vietnam. Unfortunately,
war seldom provides ideal operating conditions for everyone. The trick is to bend with the prevailing wind and
modify procedures and techniques so that you make the
best use of all available resources. Now, not unnaturally, the
Armoured Corps would prefer to operate over open rolling
plains where they can move from bound to bound at best
speed—that's the type of environment in which armour
operates best. But they very quickly adapted to the less than
ideal conditions in Vietnam, and learned to put them to
remarkably good use.

Delta Company quite often had the support of
armour—either APCs as a form of transport, right through
to tanks helping us to fight our way into a bunker system.
We relearned the old lessons that with determined leadership
and an acute awareness of the limitations and danger of
using armour in close country, there's no reason why APCs
and tanks can't be used to excellent effect, even in the
densest forest.[5]

There were several Diggers who thought that the tanks were
dreadful to work with but at the same time were quite glad
they were at the point of battle. Rifleman Wally Burford
recalls the battle on the Suoi Ca:

We were in a fair bit of bother but when the tanks came
I felt a huge wave of relief seeing those blokes—except for
the fact that they might run you over. You were always a
bit concerned about that. But, it was a hell of a relief seeing
them go through the lines and that saved the day for us.[6]

Working with the armour was not without its problems
as Burford explains:

Knowing exactly which way they are going to go and which
way they are going to be firing. It needs someone usually
to jump up and have a chat to them and by doing that they
are most certainly exposing themselves. There needs to be
some sort of communication link that you don't have to
jump up and bloody stand behind the tank to talk to

someone even though you think standing behind a tank,
you've got the tank in front of you—in jungle warfare it's
not like that. You know you could be standing up smack
bang in the middle of the bunker system, you're not too
sure where it is. I think that would be the main difficulty
in co-ordinating what they are doing compared with what
the ground troops are doing so you can have some sort of
unison. They can go forward and you can sweep behind
and you can support each other, because they are pretty
vulnerable in the jungle. An RPG can take one of them
out pretty quick so they do need infantry support as well.
They can only fire in one direction and while they are firing
in that one direction, they really need the infantry in close
support to be able to keep the nasties off their back.[7]

Wally Burford really hits the nail on the head when he talks
about infantry protection because without it, the tanks would
be sitting ducks. Again, it comes back to co-operation and
working as teams.

Another Digger, medic Corporal Mick O'Sullivan,
remembers when the tanks provided him with protection that
probably saved his life:

My surprise was in the ability of a machine that size and
such to operate so effectively, as they did in that particular
battle, that we had in close jungle areas and their ability to
manoeuvre and get in and sometimes knock down small
trees to get to exactly where the battle was. They moved
forward to where I was treating a wounded guy, [Private
J. M.] Johnny Lawton, in the forward position. We were
under heavy fire and I was able purely to give the hand
signals and the bloody tank came up and sort of traversed
directly in front of us, took all the fire on the side of the
vehicle; and the crewie was up the top with his 30 or 50
cal firing into this bunker system. But I was then able to
get Johnny Lawton out. I was amazed in the ability of those
bloody tanks to operate in such close country.[8]

The last word on the tanks is probably best left with
Corporal Warren Dowell, who didn't mix his words when
he said:

Forward Observer Lieutenant Greg Gilbert preparing his defensive fire tasks for Delta Four. Note the absence of rank, which was a common practice in the company. (*Photograph courtesy of Greg Gilbert*)

Anybody that says that tanks can't operate in the jungle just doesn't know what he is talking about. They did an excellent job and got in there and really sorted it out for us, and it was a sad day when we saw that they were being pulled back to Australia. They did a good job.[9]

THE GUNNERS

The other supporting arm that figured highly in day-to-day operations and was probably seen as part of Delta Four because of the very close working relationships that developed was 104 Battery, Royal Regiment of Australian Artillery, the 4 RAR Direct Support Battery. As indicated in Chapter 9, the artillery was one of the most feared weapons that the Australians had and underlines the need for infantry to always have artillery or indirect fire in intimate and close support, especially when working in the jungle.

The Forward Observer (FO), Lieutenant Greg Gilbert, saw his role when working with Delta Four as:

I think mostly it was to inflict casualties behind as opposed to right at the front; to inflict casualties and also to prevent their escape. To sort of hold them. You couldn't inflict casualties on the people that were causing damage to yourself because they were usually so close to your own people that you couldn't get it in that close.[10]

The company commander worked closely with the FO. Major Jerry Taylor reflects on his relationship with the FO:

Obviously I worked very closely with my FO, Greg Gilbert. Greg was a very good gunner; his advice was always excellent; and he got the fire down on the ground rapidly, and always in precisely the right place. Between us we worked out some very effective drills using the guns, that had to do with sealing off the enemy's rear and our flanks immediately on contact. These drills were to pay particular dividends on the 21st of September. I often say that the reason I'm still alive today is because of Greg and the guns. However not everyone I know sees that as much of a recommendation for artillery.[11]

The importance of the gunners knowing their trade is emphasised by Jerry Taylor:

The effect which his weapons, or the weapons which he controlled could have, were profound. An accidental discharge with a rifle can create one effect—but an artillery shell in the wrong place can have a profoundly different effect and I can recall particularly in the battle of the 29th of July and again on the 21st of September, where we used such a lot of artillery, and particularly on the 21st of September, when artillery was firing almost at maximum range, and we had very poor communications, that it was very nice to know that Greg was totally on top of his job and that there was never any likelihood—from his point of view at least—of there being an accident.[12]

Rounds will only land where you ask them to and consequently the FO himself saw his greatest responsibility as ensuring his FO Party were absolutely spot on with their navigation:

I think the emphasis that I placed was certainly that I wanted [Bombardier Russ] Pullen to be able to operate by himself as an Observer to be able to conduct artillery effectively; I also remember stressing the importance of good navigation. I spent a lot of time with them on map reading skills and being able to put ground to map and map to ground and all the rest of it to make sure that if they did call artillery in they were reasonably confident that they were not going to put it in the wrong place, like on top of them.

I would stress the importance between the team and the company commander or the unit commander and the sub-unit commander and the FO; that each has to know and respect what the other is doing, and work more as a partnership than a boss–subordinate type role and, as much as an FO can influence or control that, my advice would be to try and establish that working relationship.[13]

Naturally the men of Delta Four worked with several other supporting arms and organisations, such as the sappers from 1 Field Squadron who often provided splinter teams for operations where mines were expected or the aviators from 161 Independent Recce Squadron or the men from 9 Squadron RAAF who were only seen on occasions, such as resupply missions or casevac flights. A lot of the air support came from the American Army for helicopters and gunship support, the Marines for naval gunfire support or the American Air Force for fast air Fighter Ground Attack support. Unfortunately space precludes a more detailed discussion of these other support groups.

THE ALLIES

So, what did the riflemen think of those other Allies and those in support of the 1st Australian Task Force? On this issue there were plenty of comments and they have to be taken in the context that many of the Diggers did not know the organisation that supported the Allies in Phuoc Tuy Province in 1971. The Americans viewed the Australian Area of Operations as small fish indeed. The Americans concentrated their efforts more in the north in almost conventional war at battalion, brigade and division sized operations. The ARVN in Phuoc Tuy played a secondary role and most of the units in the area were in training for operations in the Delta or north toward the DMZ. The New Zealanders were under operational command of the Australian Task Force and were well integrated into units and the Headquarter organisation concerning SOPs and so on. If any comments were derogatory they were not meant to be. They probably only reflect the personal attitude of the infantrymen when comparing themselves with another organisation, undoubtedly revealing a cerrtain tribal bias.

THE AMERICANS

The Americans in Phuoc Tuy who worked closely with Delta Four were the occasional infantry company that was tasked to support a major operation such as Operation OVERLORD and a battery of 155 mm howitzers and 8" SP guns which seemed to drift around the province. There were American ground units in the area but contact with them was very limited and usually social. Major Jerry Taylor gives his impressions of the Americans that he dealt with:

> In 1967/68, 2 RAR worked often with the United States Army and the Air Force, but less so with the Navy. The line infantry units that I encountered tended to be rather patchy in quality, and I put this down to two factors—their training methods, and the trickle feed reinforcement system which they used.
>
> I believe I'm right in saying that their training was not nearly as prolonged and thorough as ours was. In addition, they tended to reinforce units on a trickle system, rather than putting in a complete unit at the start of a year and relieving it 12 months later. Consequently I don't believe that US line units had the same sense of 'family' that existed in good RAR battalions. My own observations led me to believe that there were also considerable disciplinary problems in some US units which I encountered, especially towards the end of the War. Some of these problems were drug related. Be that as it may, I always found US personnel

very willing to help. Their co-operation with us was excellent; and there was certainly nothing wrong with their physical courage.

On 21 September we had Lieutenant Rodriguez, a United States Navy pilot, overhead as a forward air controller in Jade 07, controlling almost continuous air support to us. He remained overhead all day and well into the night, returning to base only for more fuel and marker rockets. He was eventually ordered home at about 2130 hours, and I was told that on arrival several bullet holes were discovered in his wings. The interesting thing was that the holes were from the top down—he'd been flying so low that the 12.7mm heavy machine guns on Nui Le were firing down on him. I believe he received the Navy Cross for his work that day, a decoration heartily applauded by all of us in Delta Company.[14]

The platoon commander, Second Lieutenant Kevin Byrne, had a reasonable amount of contact with the Americans:

Some American units were first class. Some of the fly boys were, the pilots; I remember 'Jade 07'. Tremendous. The Jade FAC 07 was fantastic comfort. Some of the SEAL Teams; some of the artillery units were first class but there was a great disparity between them. There was a great gap between the best and the worst, unfortunately. I remember when—on one of our first operations—we were putting in that cordon for 3 RAR's push [Operation OVERLORD] and I remember marrying up with an American platoon on a river and they were just terrible. They really were. I got my platoon up and left at night. We had linked up but they had harboured up with us and I said, 'No, look you guys stay here and we will go and harbour up elsewhere', because they were just so noisy and they used spray for mosquitoes. And you know if you really wanted to telegraph to the Viet Cong where you were you just stayed with this unit—if you really wanted trouble.[15]

Private Dean Cooke found he could find little to recommend one particular unit he met up with when he came in to the battalion Fire Support Base when on a patrol:

I remember at Courtenay Hill, the American artillery guys down there. We came in one day, I think we had to do some ambushing; there was some VC located or sighted around there somewhere. I'll never forget them guys. There seemed to be a mob of negroes there had this open back truck, and the commander, the officer—a white bloke—I remember he called them up to the truck, they had to get on the truck and go on a patrol or something. And these guys, they would have had to be the slackest mob I have ever—I couldn't believe it! Half of them, because they used to have these helmets and flak jackets—different to us we used to have the shirts and the bush hats sort of thing. And these negroes they were just so slack and sloppy, I think he had to send a couple of them back to get their helmets, one guy forgot his helmet or his weapon or his jacket. I couldn't just get over the ill-disciplined and the lackadaisical attitude they had towards what they were doing. To me it was unbelievable.[16]

These views by Byrne and Cooke were supported by section commander Warren Dowell, who was also unimpressed by some of the American infantry units:

I can remember the Americans, actually working with them, when we were doing a blocking force for 3 RAR and a Brigade of Americans coming down from Long Khanh [Operation OVERLORD]. Delta Company and 11 Platoon were the easternmost part of the blocking force for the Battalion if I remember correctly, and we had to marry up with Americans. Everything you see on TV is unfortunately true about the way they were. No security, carrying gunliners and that sort of thing, chewing gum, smoking, and some of them had ear-plugs stuck in their ears—that sort of thing. They really didn't impress me. Then we had, off Courtenay Hill, a detachment of guns, 155s. That didn't really impress me either; it looked like whoever was the biggest bloke and had the biggest baseball hat was the one that was in command. But having said that, there must have been good American units either earlier on in the piece or further up North. But the ones I saw in Vung Tau and in the field really didn't impress me at all.[17]

Forward Observer Greg Gilbert saw a different side to the Americans through his role as artillery co-ordinator for the company. He recalls:

> At the artillery we had a thing called an NOGLO which was a US Marine Naval Offshore Gunfire Liaison Officer and there were two of them during my stint and I got on quite well with both of them. One, or both, I went up to Saigon with for a couple of days. Got a lift up and stayed in a BOQ [Bachelor Officers' Quarters] in Saigon and I went out onto a ship off the coast with one of them once. Flew out and landed on the ship and had a lovely breakfast of scrambled eggs that I can remember. So I got on well with them, and in fact am still in contact with both of them.[18]

While he doesn't comment upon their professionalism, it should be remembered that many American units that Australia worked with in Phuoc Tuy Province were high quality and should not all be judged the same. However, one man who had the opportunity to travel around and see a few American units was Lieutenant Chris Stephens from the APC Troop supporting 4 RAR. He recollected that he

> . . . saw them as gunners occasionally, a medium battery— the most untidy organisation one could have come across. [Lieutenant] Denzil Bourne, it's not my line it was his line, from this same battery, a big negro coming up, he had no shirt on and the whole place was looking like a shambles and saying, 'What have you killed today, man, besides time?' And that battery in itself was having problems with drugs. People had, I think they were inside our Fire Support Base, been offering grass and so forth around the place. Struck me as extraordinarily laid back battery and being that laid back, and it may be a cultural thing, therefore incompetent—and that may be an unfair criticism. They did fire a mission at some stage though it didn't fall around me. It fell short from those big guns [155mm] and it was a battery's worth about five rounds fell short amongst the troops—none of them went off. They didn't fuse them in the first place correctly, so not only did they miss the target,

but fortunately they had also stuffed it up and not fused them! That was a sort of an indication to me that things were not well in the world. I was struck by Armed Forces Radio and these advertisements that told American soldiers how to clean their M16 when they get up in the morning, you know, take Part A out, put oil here and it was something that they had to be told. That was something I couldn't grasp. That's not to criticise it in a sense because they had half a million men there at that stage, whatever it may be, and many of them perhaps didn't know how to do it, I don't know. When you're dealing with those sorts of numbers maybe that was an appropriate way for a Force of that size to do business. I found it to be fairly strange. American Air Force, excellent, very, very willing to get in there. Cobras [US Army gunships] and indeed other aircraft looking for targets and looking for jobs, they were so willing that they got in the way. They were very willing to get in and mix it to that extent.[19]

And they did love to 'mix it' as Chris Stephens says. They would often crowd the skies over a contact just to get the opportunity to unload some ordnance and complete a mission. Platoon commander Graham Spinkston backed up Chris Stephens with these remarks:

I had a lot of time for the American air support we got, in the sense that they had a 'can do' attitude, and whilst the RAAF were very professional and very good there were times when they wouldn't do things. Probably because they weren't allowed to and not in the sense that they were not prepared to do it for you and ultimately if your life was on the line they would do it. But the Americans would always have a go and they had less concern about equipment and things, so if they had to clear an LZ with the rotor blades they would because if didn't matter—they would just go away and get another helicopter—whereas the Australians couldn't do that. So I had a lot of time for them. I am not saying that they were particularly professional but they were always prepared to have a go.[20]

Captain Peter Schuman, Company 2IC, has these views of
the Americans that he came across on his tour of duty:

> The US guys, the 155s across the road, whoever they were,
> they certainly gave us some support every now and again.
> The US Air Force Phantoms and gun ships from Bien Hoa;
> always on time and on target and did the right thing. They
> were pretty professional. You can't beat the US firepower
> and the co-ordination—it was very good. It was just excel-
> lent. The only trouble is being able to use it, there just
> seems to be, in our terms, there's just so much at the one
> time for it to use. There is just not enough room on the
> battlefield to get it all in.[21]

Sergeant Daryl Jenkin holds a similar view to Jerry Taylor
and Peter Schuman about the size of their forces and the
employment of their force when he says:

> I think the problem was that their Army was so big that
> they had units from one end of the scale to the other, and
> we were so far south that I don't think we were looking
> at any of their top units. There seemed to be that many of
> them everywhere you went. There just seemed to be
> thousands of them. They all seemed like they were going
> everywhere and nobody was doing anything. The thought
> that stuck in my mind was our Army being so small. You
> seem to know everybody in the Army and then you come
> across their Army which was absolutely massive.[22]

There is no doubt that the Americans are good when it
comes to doing things on a big scale, but for the Australian
infantry in Phuoc Tuy it was a different approach to what
the Americans were used to and not within their thoughts
or parameters of operating against a guerilla Army. Their
philosophy was: big was powerful, therefore, big was good
and would win in the end. Wrong. Not in jungle fighting
against an insurgent guerilla with local support on his own
playing field.

THE NEW ZEALANDERS

Another ally who worked with the Australians in a very close relationship were the New Zealanders. In fact it was almost a sponsorship as the New Zealand units were integrated with the Australian units in almost every sphere. There were exchange personnel at almost every level and the battalions 2, 4 and 6 were known as ANZAC battalions because one rifle company was totally New Zealander. This company would be known by the prefix of Whisky or Victor Company depending on which unit it was attached to at the time. It was easy to integrate with the 'Kiwis', as they were affectionately known, because they used very similar SOPs to the Australians.

Major Jerry Taylor offered these opinions on the men from the Land of The Long White Cloud:

We also worked with the New Zealanders. Both 2 RAR in 1967/68 and 4 RAR in 1971 were ANZAC battalions, which meant that each battalion had one or two RNZIR companies and some specialists, under operational command. In my view, the fighting qualities of the New Zealand soldier were exceptional; and the quality of their officers was outstanding. I can only guess at the morale effect on the enemy when confronted by an angry Maori infantryman, but it must have been devastating. They were splendid examples of what a warrior race should be. However, I still feel that the 'ANZAC Spirit' as we knew it in Vietnam may have been more perceived than real, and that it was, in fact, rather a thin veneer. I place no blame on either side for this, and it had no visible effect on the cohesiveness of operations. In any case, it's only my own gut feeling.[23]

Platoon commander Kevin Byrne had his thoughts on the New Zealanders and was not afraid to ruffle a few feathers on what he had to say:

I always thought the New Zealanders, and this will probably create some sort of controversy, were over-rated. The New Zealanders were in a minority, they did their job, don't get me wrong, but they were always trying to one-up you. The

Kiwis were always trying to be better than the Australians, whoever it was, because they were in a minority, and I found that is a normal course of events with Kiwis in any case. I found them competent, obviously there was no problem working with them.[24]

Section commander Warren Dowell had plenty to say about the Kiwis and thought they were warriors in the truest sense:

Kiwis—they could play harder in town than we could, but having said that, when we got into trouble with the 3rd of the 33rd they were the company reacted to come and assist us. I think one of the other Companies was reacted, I think it might have been D Company 3 RAR, was reacted as cut-off but the Kiwis were actually reacted to come and assist us. When they arrived, they really looked the part. They looked like they meant business, and the thing I liked about them was that even though they were made up of Maoris and Pakehas—they were us. New Zealand/Australians, Australians/New Zealanders. They were trained under the same system as we were and I had nothing but confidence in their ability.[25]

CQMS Staff Sergeant Bob Hann had a different opinion because of the way in which the New Zealanders carry on socially. A few other Diggers had similar views. Bob Hann explains:

I hated Victor Company because we used to follow them on R & C, and they used to get down to Vung Tau and wreck the joint and we would come in and they would close the bloody town down. The second time it happened, Jerry Taylor went to the Mayor and said to open this bloody town old son or there is going to be hell to pay. The place was under curfew—I think they put a six o'clock curfew on. After they lifted the curfew everything was opened again but they used to give me the shits. The poofters used to get down there and drink themselves senseless and go and wreck the town. And then we would miss out.

They would love to fight. I went to a couple of the 'do's' they had, the big do you have when the company comes in from the scrub. They were strange people. The

CSM was a Maori and the CQMS was a big bloke and he was the bloke that ran the company and kept the peace, because they had people who were higher caste than the CSM, Maori princes and all that sort of shit. The sort of stuff that you run into in New Guinea but you certainly don't run into it in Australia. You get to one of these end-of-operation BBQs and every bloody time it would finish up in one gigantic fight. The bastards would fight just for the hell of fighting. They were bloody crazy. They had this thing that when they were down in Vung Tau they had to beat the record of the previous company that had been down in the amount of piss that they drank before they got to town. No wonder they wrecked the joint.[26]

Bob Hann was obviously still smarting from missing out on his R & C when he was thinking of the Kiwis, so I asked another soldier for his views and Sergeant Daryl Jenkin offered these remarks:

I worked with New Zealanders fairly closely. They were certainly different. Their training was different. There was a strong rivalry with the Kiwis, having the Kiwis in the battalion. I think a lot of it was sort of hearsay and the Australian/New Zealand thing there was always the rivalry. But if you look at the end results they were pretty good because the runs were on the board.[27]

And that was the bottom line, what really mattered was how they performed in the bush.

The New Zealanders were obviously capable and competent in the bush and apparently something to be avoided when on leave unless a good singer or pugilist.

THE ARMY OF THE REPUBLIC OF VIETNAM

The comments offered in this section must be weighed against the fact that many units in the Province were under training or re-fitting and sometimes the units may have been Regional

Force or Popular Force soldiers who were little more than reservists with very little training background or combat experience. Some men like Forward Observer Greg Gilbert had mixed emotions about the ARVN they met:

> We had an interpreter attached to us on our first operation and I decided that I could only improve things by learning a bit of Vietnamese, so I got him to sit down with me each day for about an hour or so in the afternoon. I would ask him how you would say this and that and I would write it down and then practise it by the next day, so after six weeks of an hour a day of Vietnamese I could make myself understood. I thought of him as my mate but he ended up doing me wrong because I left my pistol in my tent when I went to Vung Tau on R & C and he went and pinched it. I then got in deep trouble because I had lost my pistol.[28]

Sergeant Daryl Jenkin philosophises on why his opinion of the ARVN was very high:

> I thought they were nothing but a great shower of shit and bloody hopeless. But when you think back now as to why they were like that, it was quite obvious—they had been fighting since they were kids and more, fighting a losing battle. We were only there for 12 months and then we came home. They were there forever. I think, you look back on it now [and] it is quite easy to see—poor training, poorly equipped, fighting a losing situation. It is quite easy to see why they were like they were. Whereas, we can train for 12 months before we went, go for twelve months and then come home again.[29]

Jenkin makes a very good point about the ARVN being battle weary, but it probably follows that the Viet Cong must have been the same. It probably comes down to believing in your cause and good leadership. The Americans had a lot to do with the tactics the ARVN employed, in fact they dictated what and how operations would be carried out, principally because they were supplying the equipment, the communications and the advisers to many of their units.

Lieutenant Chris Stephens recalls the ARVN working with his APC troop:

> We helped them out every now and again. We were tasked to carry them from here and there, we would visit them sometimes in their areas. It was the only time I ever had weapons go off on a vehicle that wasn't meant to go off—a machine gun rattling around the place. That point drove me to put them on top which we were not supposed to do, but it was better that they fired the M60 *outside* rather than *inside* the vehicle, if it was to go off. And I would have to say, to be absolutely honest, [that] there was a stealing problem which we didn't have with our own infantry, or very rarely. If they were inside then you would find rations or water or medical kit or ammunition or your radio, whatever it may be—would be gone when they got off. So, that always gave us cause for concern.[30]

Not everyone was so willing to condemn or damn the Vietnamese soldiers. Captain Peter Schuman had sympathy for the ARVN:

> I felt very sorry for them. Mislead; conscript; fighting a long way from some of their villages, for a cause that was corrupt that they didn't believe in, and we just held it all together, hoping for a miracle that didn't happen.[31]

Second Lieutenant Graham Spinkston also reflected on his original opinion of the ARVN and now thinks:

> At the time I didn't have much respect for the ARVN—we didn't work with them on operations, and I never had any dealings with them even at the end. But thinking about it now, after the event and talking to other people, when we got there they had been fighting the war for 20 years and they had to live with it, so I think that coloured the way they performed in many respects. They always had to have an eye on what might happen, and as it turned out what did happen. But I know from talking with people that some of their units were exceptionally good and some were quite bad, but that happens everywhere.[32]

Regardless, the ARVN were not in good shape in 1971 when all was said and done. Delta Four had an interpreter called Hai attached and he was also used as a local guide on occasion. Corporal Warren Dowell recalls one event, that if it had been carried through, would have caused an international incident. It was after the 21 September battle and five men from Delta Four had been killed in action and, as so often happened when Delta Four got into a big contact, Sergeant Hai was never around. Dowell explains:

In fact I was in the boozer the night they tried to hang him. I think it was only though [Lance Corporal L.J.] 'Blue' Roulston who cut him down that he was got out of trouble. He had a bad habit of coming to the briefings prior to the operations and must have known what was going on. Because if he thought it was a bad op, he used to disappear, and then we knew it was going to be a bad time too. Then the night we had the big barbeque and piss up at Nui Dat after everything had finished he turned up and was drinking our grog. I can't remember who started it but somebody got hold of him with a toggle rope, and I am sure it was bloody Blue Roulston who had to come in and sort it out and cut him down and tell us all to sit down and shut up. Hai hit the toe after that and we didn't see him again. I wasn't impressed with him at all. If the op seemed to be in a bad area—he seemed to disappear on us. He must have known what was going on.[33]

Platoon commander, Second Lieutenant Kevin Byrne, probably hit the nail on the head with the ARVN when he said:

I can understand why they really got belted. Mind you, we saw the worst I guess in the end because they were pretty well shattered by the time we got there.[34]

The Australian view of his allies in Phuoc Tuy Province varied from admiration to contempt, and what must be remembered is that there were all types of soldiers operating in the province, which in real terms was a side-show to the 'real' war raging up near the DMZ in 1971. However,

Australian soldiers do compare well with our allies and stood fairly high on a rating scale when it comes to their professionalism in the field. But, they were a small, very well trained army using a group reinforcement system which allowed good teamwork and leadership to prosper and develop—the two essentials for success in battle.

9

THE CONG

Just as tall trees are known by their shadows, so are good men known by their enemies.

OLD CHINESE PROVERB

IN SEPTEMBER 1993 I RETURNED TO VIETNAM for the first time with 18 men from Delta Four and four other veterans who were from other companies or units. Several wives and children accompanied the group. Whilst in Vietnam I was introduced to several former enemy who fought against Delta Four in 1971. They told me of their impressions of the Diggers.

There were several themes that were pursued in asking the men from Delta Four about the enemy. They were along the lines of what did they think of them as fighters, did they hate them, how did they feel about killing the enemy, or did they feel sorry for them.

THE ENEMY AS A FIGHTER

There is no doubt that the enemy that the Australians in Delta Four faced were a mixed bunch. Contacts with the enemy varied from irregulars whose main task seemed to be supporting the Main Force Viet Cong units to caretakers in camp sites to porter parties collecting and dumping supplies in caches. In July 1971, Delta Four hit their first real Main Force unit, 274 VC Main Force (Dong Nai) Regiment and later in September several contacts were made with North Vietnamese Army (NVA) units from battalions of the 33rd NVA Regiment culminating in the battle at Nui Le on 21 September 1971.

The men of Delta Four were well briefed on what and who the enemy were before they left for Vietnam. Every exercise they participated in had an 'exercise enemy' usually from a sister battalion that had just returned from the war zone. But until one actually sees an enemy 'in the flesh', so to speak, a contact will undoubtedly feel just like another exercise until real rounds start hitting home or people start getting wounded and killed. Platoon Commander of 12 Platoon, Graham Spinkston, gave his views of the enemy:

I don't think I ever underestimated them. They fought under incredibly difficult circumstances. They didn't have all the support we had. I think we always had their measure if we fought each other on equal footing—but it would have been touch and go. I think particularly the NVA, and some of the better Viet Cong regiments, were good but I think we always could have held our own against them. The NVA certainly were pretty tough and professional and they proved that, and I think some of the VC units were good. Some of the local units, I don't think we had a great deal of respect for and I don't think they were very effective, but by the time we left the province they had disappeared anyway. D445 [Battalion] had practically ceased to exist by the time we had finished and it really was then an NVA war. Given the difficulties and the hardships that they fought under, I have a fair degree of admiration for them because they could see no end to what they were doing. Many of them were a long way from home without all the good things we had.[1]

Platoon commander of 10 Platoon, Second Lieutenant Kevin Byrne, was forthright in his summary of the enemy as warriors:

A mixed bag. The old Chau Duc District Company were grist to the mill and of course they weren't well trained. 274 VC Main Force [Dong Nai] Regiment were pretty good, pretty good; they were pretty solid, but that 3rd of the 33rd [NVA]—very good, very good. Very efficient fighting unit given the wherewithal that they had; given the fact that they fought without artillery and fought just with mortars that they carried around; fought without air power. I thought that they were excellent, excellent.[2]

The theme that the enemy did reasonably well given their paucity of supporting arms and air power was evident in the interviews and well recognised by the men of Delta Four who enjoyed air and artillery superiority. Delta Four had tangled with larger enemy units on two occasions when they had the advantage in numbers and being dug in. The Diggers saw at first hand the enemy's fighting ability in close quarter battle where the engagements were at grenade-throwing range.

Major Jerry Taylor thought that

. . . anyone who didn't respect the enemy in Vietnam was a bloody fool. And let's be absolutely clear about it—they won. I had no time for their politics, nor for the butchery that they sometimes inflicted on elements of the civilian population, but before we start breast beating about that one, perhaps we should recall My Lai. I personally very much respected all of them as an enemy. They were fighting in their country, *for* their country, as indeed they had been for centuries. They were relentless, ruthless, cunning, and courageous; and I often wonder how long the war would have lasted if they had had the lavish scales of supply and support that we enjoyed. The truth was that the enemy were extremely competent and well motivated soldiers—as could be expected of those who are fighting on their home soil. Certainly we in Delta Company respected them—I can't recall ever hearing anyone in the company calling them 'noggies', 'gooks' or similar insults used usually by people who had never come into real contact with them. We referred to them as 'nasties' or simply the 'enemy'. Having encountered them on several occasions, we had a healthy respect for their fighting qualities.[3]

The riflemen who struggled to gain superiority and victory over their elusive foe in the jungle had a lot of respect for the fighting qualities of the enemy, as Private Garry Sloane remarked:

> The NVA—very professional. A man who wouldn't give ground. He would stand and go toe-to-toe. Not scared to fight but I think that is part of any Asian-type person. The life thereafter is better than the life you are in and you get in and do the job. They certainly won't back off. Even though we had to tactically withdraw for a short period of time, he was right up our hammer.[4]

The incident that Sloane refers to is the evening of 21 September when Delta Four were forced to withdraw and consolidate in an all round defence for the night. The enemy clung desperately close throughout the withdrawal because of the close artillery support that was crashing in on their positions. They waited until the artillery eased later that evening before withdrawing themselves.

Private Dean Cooke didn't mix his words when asked what he thought about the enemy:

> My personal belief, I always thought, probably incorrectly, that they were shit sort of thing, to put it bluntly. And I always felt we were better, that's probably because of our indoctrination. But I think you really have got to have a lot of respect for them. Just taking their situation and taking our situation, we had air superiority, we had the superiority of technology at that stage, and given what they had, and what they were up against, I think you have got to have tremendous respect for them.[5]

National Serviceman Wally Burford from 12 Platoon offers these thoughts about the enemy, especially the NVA, who often were as much a 'conscript' as he was himself:

> I think though someways they did it tough in that when we went up there we knew we were going up there for a maximum of 12 months. When they came down from the

north, most of them came down and it was virtually a life
sentence for a lot of them and to be able to accept that sort
of situation, you have got to be tough.[6]

The last word on what the men from Delta Four thought of
the enemy is reserved for Captain Peter Schuman, the Company 2IC, who saw a considerable amount of the enemy at
close hand, especially on his first tour of duty:

> Local guerillas; they were an embarrassment I think to their
> Army and nuisance value to ours. They were probably good
> outside their village area knowing the track system and being
> able to control caches and things of that nature and also
> with a little bit of village support, when it was needed, for
> units coming through. The Regular North Vietnamese units
> I thought they were pretty good. I had been into positions
> where I had been able to observe their forward scouts and
> section commanders in battle. They used very similar drills
> to ours, such as machine guns to the right and high ground.
> In fact very similar section commanders' commands with
> their field signals. Once you took the section commanders
> out of the battle, or the scouts, there was a definite pause
> in their battle drills until they got things moving again. It
> was almost that the platoon commander had to come up or
> the next leader had to come up to get them going. There
> was a leader and there was no natural progression within
> that first echelon to take the initiative. And I only say this
> through observation that I had been in a lot of contacts
> where I have knocked the guiding lights out in that forward
> element and it's really delayed any further action or follow
> up.[7]

Schuman also espoused his theory on why the enemy may
have been so determined to fight when confronting the
Australians:

> Well I have got two theories. You could say, 'Gee, that
> guy was pretty good, he stood and fought and died'. The
> other theory, or the other speculation I suppose is, what
> else do you do when you have got a wall of artillery falling
> behind you; 130 angry Australians in front of you and

surrounding you. There's only two ways to go. Either fight to the death or put your hands up. And a lot of times we were so quick in our contact drills and bringing our firepower down, that that's the way we caught them. There was nothing else for them left to do and they weren't going to surrender. We knew that.[8]

The enemy from the VC Main Force and NVA units were dogged and determined fighters and were an enemy to be respected. They expected and gave no quarter and fought hard when they thought they had a chance of winning. Their tactics seemed to be driven by their immediate resources and when they failed in assaults it was apparent that a lack of communications was the main reason. They manoeuvred when they had to and on one occasion in mid-September 1971, both 11 Platoon and the enemy put a 'hook' on each other and almost went full circle in the attempt to outflank each other. There was never any doubting the courage of the enemy and on more than one occasion Diggers were heard remarking on the bravery that they had witnessed when VC soldiers recovered their fallen comrades under fire.

HATRED OF THE ENEMY

This emotion is difficult to sustain because it is so mentally enervating. Hatred demands much of a person. It clouds reason and can cause more trouble than the original motive for the hatred. For a warrior there are degrees of hatred toward the enemy and they seem to be aligned to personal loss and the intervention of time. One man who had good reason to hate the enemy was Lance Corporal 'Jethro' Hannah, whose best mate was killed in action:

I really never hated until after the 21st of September and then I did hate what they stood for and what they had done. As I say, in my experience after they had killed somebody that I knew very well, hatred was there. And hatred was there until I came home.[9]

Hannah had a severe reaction at the time to the death of his close mate and the hatred he experienced affected his judgment as his emotions burst forth. All he wanted to do was to go forward into battle and kill anything that moved. However, he quickly regained his composure and got back to the business of fighting in the calculated way that would ensure his survival. His hatred of the enemy has since dissipated to simply being 'just the enemy'. Other men found that they didn't hate the enemy *per se*, they were simply the enemy that had to be eliminated in one way or another. Second Lieutenant Graham Spinkston thought that he didn't 'hate' the enemy:

> I don't think so. I wasn't one of these raving anti-communists who believed the only good reds were dead ones. I think they were good soldiers and I respected them for what they were doing. They were doing what their government told them to do as we were.[10]

Private Grahame Tooth was unsure of whether he hated the enemy and opted instead for this explanation of his personal feelings toward the enemy:

> I don't know, I don't know. Probably just there to be shot, I suppose would be the best way to explain it. I suppose that's a good way of summing it up. I don't think that I really hated them, I mean they were doing a job that their government believed in on the day, and I suppose we were doing the job that our government told us to do, and that's how I think now. But, at the time I don't know if I hated them or not.[11]

The company medic, Corporal Mick O'Sullivan, found that his hate was confined to a certain situation:

> When I was confronted with the death of our own individuals within our company—yes. A very strong hate, very strong hate, but other than that, probably not so.[12]

National Serviceman Wally Burford found that even the death of a friend didn't bring out the real 'hate' in him:

> I don't think hate—I think just wanted to see them dead. No, I didn't hate them, even when Ralph [Private R.J. Niblett] was dead you know, I suppose if you actually saw the bloke that shot Ralph, you would probably hate that individual—but I didn't see that sort of thing. You just want to see them dead and not for hatred, just because you're there to kill them and you wanted to see them dead.[13]

The absence of hatred could well be aligned to the fact that we as Australians were fighting in someone else's country for a cause that was less than perfectly clear. It is probably just as well that the hate was not a motive for killing the enemy. As has been witnessed in other conflicts, hatred can reduce the already mad environment of war into wholesale bloodshed and slaughter of innocents sometimes under the dubious cover of 'ethnic cleansing'.

SYMPATHY FOR THE ENEMY

Given that war is a contest with no second prizes and the enemy Delta Four faced lacked many of the niceties, such as field artillery and air power, it was appropriate to see if any of the Australians had sympathy for the enemy. Second Lieutenant Kevin Byrne was adamant on the question of feeling sorry for the enemy:

> No, no. I genuinely believed that we were there for the right cause and they were there for the wrong cause. So, no, I didn't feel sorry for them. On a personal level after contact and you saw enemy dead, I felt sorry for them individually but I knew in a fire fight that it was either them or us, or he or me, and so, no I didn't feel sorry for them.[14]

Some, like Major Jerry Taylor, found that there was some room for sympathy in certain circumstances:

I found it difficult not to feel sympathy for them as soldiers. Poorly equipped, with only the minimum of support, scratching for every meal, and with rudimentary arrangements and facilities when they were wounded, they still fought bravely and relentlessly.

We always searched bodies and equipment for intelligence purposes. The majority of enemy soldiers seemed to keep diaries. Often the handwriting and illustrations were of remarkable beauty. Often, too, there was a photograph of a girl or a wife and children. It was not unusual to discover that some of these men had not returned home for three or four years. I suppose I relearned the old lesson—just below the surface, all soldiers are pretty much the same.[15]

Captain Peter Schuman, a Catholic but not a 'fervent follower of the faith', albeit he attends church regularly, considers his feelings this way:

Yes, I did as a Christian I suppose. When we were searching the bodies and you came across rosary beads and holy pictures and things like that and they were Catholics from the North fighting for whatever their philosophy was. Here we were Catholics from Australia killing our own religious types and yes, that saddened me a bit.[16]

On the other hand some soldiers took a very pragmatic approach. Private Garry Sloane summed up his feelings in this manner:

No. He was there to do a job, in fact he probably had more right to be doing the job than what we did as Australians. We were sent there to do a job and he was there doing his job. They had their cause to fight for, we had ours.[17]

Another Digger was also adamant that sympathy had no place when he considered the enemy:

> No, not one bit of compassion for them. Even dead bodies I have seen, I was more worried about my mates who were wounded or killed or who had died.[18]

That sentiment is understandable if fairly shallow, but it depends on where the respondent is coming from when he answers the question. It will always be a very personal response depending on what has happened to the person answering the question and their own personal beliefs and values.

Quite a few of the interviewees felt sympathy for the enemy was a short lived emotion, easily obliterated by the loss of one's own comrades. Section Commander Warren Dowell offered these thoughts:

> No, when you saw them killed it inspired that little bit of bravado in you. It made you feel better knowing that they could be bumped off. I never felt sorry for the enemy. I felt sorry for the country, but not for the enemy.[19]

Another Digger, Private Kevin Benson, thought along similar lines to Warren Dowell:

> I can't say I ever felt sorry, not really. No. If anything I felt sorry for the innocent people that were there. I think I felt sorry for the young kids. This is all right for us, we can go back to Nui Dat and there would be some papers that someone had sent over and you would go through them and catch up on the news. Like these people knew nothing about what the outside world was doing. And as far as they were concerned that was just their little egg and it was always a war, and that's the way they lived. I felt sorry for them. They knew nothing else.[20]

In any war there will always be people who are not protagonists who will be killed simply because they were caught in the cross-fire of war. They might be accidentally bombed, strafed or blown up by a land mine. In the soldier's Memorial Hall in Long Phuoc there are several honour rolls in the Vietnamese equivalent of an RSL Hall. One of the boards contains the names of the two hundred villagers from Long Phuoc who were killed in one way or another during the war, which from the Viet Cong perspective lasted from 1947 until 1975. This same village was relocated during the war because of its pro-Viet Cong sympathies and no doubt some of the villagers were caught in the cross-fire but probably on unarmed support duties and thus exposed to danger more often than one would normally expect.

THE ENEMY'S PERSPECTIVE

When the project for this book was started, it was a desire of mine to find out what the enemy thought of the Australian Digger, the rifleman as a warrior. Australian indoctrination at places like Canungra and the Infantry School has always extolled the virtues and qualities of the Anzac. But what was he like in the eyes of the enemy? My interpreter in Vietnam in 1993 was given the task of tracking down enemy soldiers who had met with Delta Four in combat. It was almost 'Mission Impossible' and took almost a year before I had four men who were prepared to be interviewed for this book.

On the reunion trip back to Vietnam in 1993, I visited these former enemy soldiers and asked them a range of questions. Unfortunately the man who I most wanted to interview, who was an officer in 3rd Battalion, 33rd NVA Regiment, was prevented from being interviewed by order of the District People's Committee in Bien Hoa, most probably on order from the central government. I have been unable to discover why I was not allowed to interview him at his house as we were turned away most apologetically by the subject stating that he was not allowed to proceed with our interview. He did, however, make some comments to my guide to which I will refer but will not accredit personally in order to protect the individual concerned.

So, what did these enemy soldiers think of the men from Delta Four? What were their impressions of these foreigners fighting in their war of nationalism? What did they think were our strengths and our weaknesses?

Tran Tan Huy, an ex-commander of D445 Battalion and now the Chairman of the District People's Committee of Long Dat District in Long Dien, poses for a photograph after his interview with the author in 1993. (*Photograph by Jerry Taylor*)

AN ENEMY'S PERSPECTIVE

Fighting qualities of the Diggers

An ex-commander of D445 Battalion, Battle of Long Tan veteran and now the People's Committee Chairman of Long Dat District in Dong Nai Province, Tran Tan Huy spent from 1960 until 1975 in combat and is very proud of his time as a soldier. He offered these comments during our interview:

> During the war times I served with many units in the Long Dat District, especially I took part in many battles to fight against the Australian Forces. Australian soldiers like to fight in the jungle, fight very hard and very bravely and to fight against us. Hard tactics to fight against. The strengths of Australians were to always use artillery and planes. They fought as the same as like our guerillas against our guerillas, especially the Australian soldiers, they were industrious and hard, fight hard.[21]

I also asked Tran Tan Huy the question who were the hardest soldiers to fight against as he had fought Americans,

ARVN and Australians. At this time Tran Tan Huy became quite excited, almost animated, and his body language indicated that he felt very strongly about what he was saying:

> We fight against many troops, many armies from other countries and each country we have special tactics to fight against. Especially the Australian soldiers cause a lot of difficulty, that means, they used guerilla tactics.[22]

I asked him if he had ever encountered the Special Air Service (SAS) squadrons called ma rung in David Horner's book on the SAS, *Phantoms of The Jungle,* but referred to as biet kich by Tran Tan Huy which is Vietnamese for commando or ranger, and he replied:

> Yes, we fight against the biet kich and they're always hard to fight against the biet kich special force. Biet kich use Claymore mines and they blow up lots of mines and with shots and then withdraw because they only have a small group of soldiers.[23]

An amusing sidelight to this conversation was that Tran Tan Huy thought the biet kich (SAS) fought unfairly; when I enquired why, he said, with a straight face, because they fought like guerillas. When I responded and said that he was a guerilla fighter, he simply said, 'But that was different' and we could all only but laugh how one's viewpoint rests entirely where one stands at the time.

I asked Huy what was the hardest thing about fighting in the jungle; his reply indicates that living off the land was no hard chore:

> Yes, because we always live in the jungle, so that we fight in the jungle we have no difficulty. Yes, when we fight we have only one pack on our shoulder. We can live everywhere, any area and we can fight anywhere.[24]

But when it came to battle, Huy was more circumspect and admitted that the Fire Support Base policy that the Australian

Forces followed, where no major patrols (less the SAS) were out of artillery range, was a very sound policy indeed:

> The strongest part of the Australians was the artillery. Always artillery is can stop our attack, no means of . . . no other means cannot stop your artillery. So we want to destroy artillery of the Australians. [You are] the strongest when we are in contact with you and you fire the guns.[25]

As a veteran of the Long Tan battle in August 1966, it is easy to see why Huy takes this viewpoint as his unit was almost wiped out by the Australian and New Zealand and to a lesser extent American artillery fires that fired in support of Delta Company 6 RAR. What was mentioned in other parts of the interview was the difficulty in attending to the enemy wounded and getting drugs to treat their various wounds, illnesses and disease.

Another enemy soldier, and a veteran of the Battle at Long Tan, former major and deputy commander of D445, Nguyen Sinh, admitted during the course of an informal interview over lunch at his house that the thing that his unit found hardest to combat when fighting Australians was the use of their field artillery. He stated that air support was not as much a problem as the artillery because it could not stay on target for as long and was often blinded. However, the artillery was always a problem because it was used so effectively once an engagement commenced.[26]

Fighting qualities of the Americans

All of the enemy interviewed did not hold a very high opinion of the Americans they encountered, with the exception of a Special Forces unit. Their comments were usually derogatory and after a while became politically oriented, so in the interests of a balanced viewpoint they are not repeated in full. One such enemy warrior was Pham Van Canh, who was a corporal in the 33rd Regiment, an NVA Regiment which operated in the regions around Phuoc Tuy.[27] He was born in 1948 and he basically fought in the southern part of Vietnam, principally in the Dong Nai area of Long Khanh, Long Binh, Phuoc Tuy

Pham Van Canh describing the strengths of the Australian Diggers and the NVA tactics to overcome the Australians. Canh was a former corporal of 33 NVA Regiment who fought against Delta Four. Today, Canh is the Chief of Immigration in Vung Tau. (*Photograph by Jerry Taylor*)

and Vung Tau Special Zone from 1966 until 1975. The worst part of his time as a fighter was between 1968 and 1971 when American operations including food denial, chemical spraying and sickness took a heavy toll on his Regiment:

> The American fighter he is not very intelligent, because he have huge weapons and patrols very slowly. When he comes to an obstacle he only uses one line. When the Revolution Forces shoot at him and he dies, he cries and everything. He is not very good. Until 1970 American they understand their experiences of fighting in Vietnam but not after that. Especially the Division 199 of Americans, their Special Forces.[28]

This enemy soldier also said his unit had many difficulties between 1968 and 1971 which were basically caused by the raising of the American 199th Special Division, which had gained a lot of experience in fighting against the Vietnamese and were able to attack his unit and weaken it on many occasions. Canh added that chemical spraying, US attacks,

ARVN attacks and a lack of food hampered his unit and made operations extremely difficult.

Fighting qualities of the ARVN

The Army of The Republic of Vietnam (ARVN) were seen by the former enemy soldiers as merely puppets of the Americans and they didn't fight very well because of their tactics:

> Republic of Vietnam Army as fighters were very weak because almost all of them were forced to join the army and they rely on the strengths of the Americans knowledge and weapons of American knowledge.[29]

The 'knowledge' that Huy refers to is the American minor tactics that were taught to the ARVN. Because the Americans used a system of advisers with the ARVN units under training, there was a heavy reliance on American procedure which naturally went downhill once the Americans withdrew before the eventual end of the war. The policy of 'Vietnamisation' failed because it was too hasty, too late and not followed through to ensure that the ARVN could stand on their own two feet. Political expediency ruled and many lives were lost as a result.

Australian weaknesses

I asked all the enemy soldiers what our weaknesses were as soldiers; what did the Liberation Army try to target against Australians? The theme in all of the answers was much the same from all of the respondents. Our weakness was according to Tran Tan Huy from D445 Provincial Battalion:

> The weakness of the Australian soldiers were they did not know clearly the geography of this area. And that is not very good for the Australian soldier [because he has] to work hard (chuckles). So that as a target you want to find that it is not correct, not exact.[30]

The formal interpretation of 'geography' in Huy's answer relates not only to the ground over which the Australians moved but also the culture of the Vietnamese people. I tried to explain the rationale behind 'no go' areas, free fire zones and limited access areas that were enforced as part of the Allied strategy in the province, but as it had no bearing on what he did as a soldier, it was difficult for him to see how the Australians at times were hamstrung on where they could operate. He could not see why civil regulations should restrict military operations or manoeuvre and was unable to accept the problems that Australian soldiers faced in dealing with civilians in Phuoc Tuy Province.

The enemy's strengths

The former enemy thought that their strength lay in the fact that they were fighting for the right cause and that they would win in the end. There is no doubt that any soldier fighting for what he believes in, especially on his home soil, will always be a difficult adversary—witness the terrible casualties the Russians suffered when taking Berlin when the might of the German Third Reich had all but been crushed. The former enemy believed that their knowledge of the terrain was a good advantage, and their experience in battle. After all, most of the men I interviewed had a minimum of 15 years *combat* experience, which makes many actions second nature and provides a vast pool of instructional capability. They also felt that they were more mobile in battle despite the fact that they thought that mobility in general was weakness. As one who humped a 45-kilogram plus pack around and often encountered enemy only carrying five to six kilos of weight in ammunition and food and only one water bottle, the enemy obviously had some advantage in the way they could maintain physical freshness by not carrying huge weights to sustain long operations.

Difficulties for the enemy

I asked Pham Van Canh the question: what is the most difficult part about fighting in the jungle. Canh replied, obtaining food

The author (*left*) discussing Viet Cong tactics and clashes that Diggers had with D445 Battalion with ex-deputy commander of the Mobile Force battalion, Major Nguyen Sinh at his home in Long Phuoc. (*Photograph by Jerry Taylor*)

from local sources, ground movement (because his Regiment was basically barefooted a lot of the time), and the distances and hard work in the jungle. He mentioned that he found breathing very difficult and was probably an asthmatic. Sickness was another major obstacle that his regiment had to overcome to maintain efficiency. As a corporal he looked after a platoon. He said it should have normally been 32 men, but often it was only 16 new and under strength most of the time. His military training was conducted basically as on-the-job training in the jungle. It was very difficult during war time to find time and places to train, and he reiterated the need for constant rehearsal and daily training in shooting and grenade skills for his regiment.[31]

Another local D445 Battalion officer, Nguyen Sinh, who now runs a small tourist operation through old tunnels in Long Phuoc in Dong Nai Province, agreed to an informal interview without a tape recorder on 22 September 1993 at his home. He stated that the thing he feared most were the search and destroy operations launched by the Australians because his unit always lost men or equipment in such operations. He thought the Americans were easy prey because they were so noisy when they patrolled but the Australians were silent, good at patrolling and aggressive in contact.[32]

Respect for the Diggers and Uc Da Loi

I asked the former enemy what they admired about the Australians as soldiers and all of the men replied in a similar vein. The reply revolved around several issues. First, the Australians buried the enemy dead and treated them with some respect and dignity. It was Australian policy to bury the enemy dead if at all possible and the only time that it was not done in Delta Four's tour was when we were forced off the battlefield or after an ambush when the exact location of the enemy was unknown.

Second, we took care of their wounded. They also intimated that they themselves may not have been able to offer such treatment to the Australians if captured wounded. Australian soldiers may very well have been shot as they could not treat or care for enemy wounded.

Third, Australians did not commit atrocities, and My Lai was used as an example to highlight their answer. In the War Atrocities Museum in Ho Chi Minh City, the Museum is located—with a lovely touch of irony—in the former American Ambassador's residence and is referred to as the US War Atrocities Museum. There are no pictures of Australians committing atrocities but they are referred to as Allied puppets of the American Capitalist Regime.

The reason why Australians, especially veterans, are treated so well when they return today to Vietnam is because of the Civil Affairs program. The Vietnamese people have expressed time and again the value to their village or town of Australian

Civil Affairs projects undertaken in the late 1960s and early 1970s. There were always some derisive remarks during the war about winning hearts and minds associated with CA projects, but the bottom line is that today in Vietnam the projects are still highly valued, whether it be a school or water reticulation system or the orphanages that were supported by the Australians when they were in Vietnam. These sentiments were echoed most strongly by the principal of one of the local schools at Long Hai in Dong Nai Province, a former VC soldier, Pham Kim Luu. Despite the fact that the Australians were the enemy, the fact that they attempted to assist the Vietnamese people was very much appreciated.[33] In a letter Luu wrote in his capacity as the Chief of the Parent and Teacher Association he stated:

> Our people took part in the resistance against foreign enemy during the war to keep our independence and our freedom. Because of the complicated political situation at that we and you, Australians have been compulsorily fighting together. Everything is over now the war has ended. We have more friends than enemies . . . the Australians is the most sincere of all . . . Long time ago the Australian Task Force have made us much difficult, because you soldiers have fought very well and have a good military discipline, but in addition to that, the Australian soldiers never stole the innocent civilian property or hurt them and had made lots of social facilities.[34]

During all of these interviews I was accompanied by my own former company commander from Delta Four. He was invited along to record photographic details of the trip back and to photograph the former enemy subjects. I asked him what he thought of the genuineness of the answers to my questions during the interviews. He replied:

> I thought perhaps at first they might say what we wanted or what they thought we wanted to hear rather than what was the truth. But listening to them talk and watching them talk more importantly, I believed that they were saying exactly what they felt and the overriding point that they

made was that Australian soldiers were aggressive, courageous, that they fought very hard indeed, that they fought fair and that at the end of the day the Viet Cong or North Vietnamese units knew that any of their people who were wounded and left on the battlefield to be picked up by the Australians would be treated with the same care and compassion as we treated our own people. And that came across very strongly to me. I think it's possible to say if anything, we, the Australians are admired certainly in and around Phuoc Tuy Province.[35]

So, what is the bottom line on the enemy? In summary I think it is fair to say that there exists a feeling of mutual respect. If Vietnam was a 'dirty' war, as it is so often referred to by political commentators, then the Australian and former Viet Cong and NVA protagonists did not treat it in that fashion. The Australian Diggers from Delta Four had and still hold considerable respect for the better trained and equipped Viet Cong Main Force and North Vietnamese regular soldier than the irregular local guerilla. There was no doubting the fighting abilities or courage of the enemy that Delta Four encountered. The Diggers also admired their determination, cunning and dedication to their cause. I could find no deep seated hatred of the enemy, but neither could I discover any real compassion for the enemy—other than for their plight as humans.

From the enemy perspective, the Diggers were respected for their tenacity, their military qualities and discipline in and out of battle. They thought we were good at patrolling and were hard to counter. The former enemy believed that we fought hard but fair. The tactics that Australians used with Fire Support Bases providing quick and deadly supporting fire, and the strategy of winning hearts and minds through a pro-active Civil Affairs program, are the basis to the way we are seen today.

10

AFTER THE BLOOD COOLS

Life is a campaign, not a battle, and has its defeats as well as its victories.

DON PIATT
THE LONE GRAVE OF THE SHENANDOAH

WHAT IS IT LIKE TO LOOK BACK ON one's war time experiences and to actually meet the former enemy? What things actually go through a warrior's mind when the blood cools from the heady, exciting, personally challenging and sometimes almost barbaric times of war? Do soldiers have regrets about their role in killing their enemy, or in the case of Delta Four soldiers, actually participating in the Vietnam War? These questions were not easy for the men to answer and made some feel very uncomfortable because they felt that they could not do justice to such a large subject. Regardless, they spoke openly and honestly and from their heart.

WAS IT WORTH IT?

The men were asked whether our involvement was worth the lives we lost. It is undoubtedly a difficult question which will draw many emotions. One Digger, Grahame Tooth, drafted into the war, answers in this way:

> Well, I suppose no war is ever worth the involvement is it? But, that's a decision that the politicians made—not us. People have lost their lives . . . I don't think they were wasted, because, forget about the Vietnam war—think of any war—it would probably go to prove that we could stand up in any other war and be counted and really make our presence felt. I suppose I really shouldn't say that; it's a bit callous isn't it? I don't know if they were or they weren't. I don't think they were.[1]

Tooth's mixed emotions and thoughts reflect the wide range of answers from the men of Delta Four. One Regular soldier, 'Jethro' Hannah, who also lost a close friend in battle, had similar reservations because there was no direct resolution to the conflict—we withdrew, we were not defeated outright:

> I personally think, looking back at what we did as Australians and I think that if the Americans would have tactically done what we did and that was to patrol, it may have been a different situation. I believe it was worthwhile. Probably the most unfortunate thing about the whole thing is that the 500 odd dead, when you look at it now it is finished—they did die for nothing in a sense. However at the end, their deaths meant nothing because we didn't finish it off.[2]

National Serviceman Kevin Benson is just as perplexed when handling this difficult question:

> Was it worth it? I don't know, when you look at it and they say, 'Well we have got to stop the Communists coming down', but whether they would have come any further or not—I don't know. I think from the Army side of it, for the Australian Army, it was probably a great experience type of thing, a lot of experience gained. Like we lost 500 blokes, but maybe that in the long run might save bloody thousands on the experience that was gained.[3]

Another National Serviceman, Wally Burford, considers the involvement and its 'worth' like this:

> Well at the time, we did it without putting a lot of thought into the worth of it. We were told we were going to fight communists. It was made quite clear to us that it wasn't a civil war, it was communist insurgency that we were fighting. And I still think, the old 'Domino Theory' that they reckon has been shot in the arse since Vietnam, that was the worry at the time. Communism was on the march through South-East Asia. And I still think to a degree the involvement in Vietnam helped stop it. They say now it probably wouldn't have happened, but you go to places like Malaya, Borneo, Singapore where there was most certainly a fair degree of communist agitation at that time. They gave those places longer to build up their own governments; to make sure there couldn't be a threat because virtually Russia, China and virtually the whole of communism in South-East Asia had to put all their bickies in one barrel—and that barrel was Vietnam. And I think without Vietnam I think there could have been a lot higher degrees of conflict in South-East Asia. So, in that degree yes, I think we possibly did accomplish something. The end result of course, you pull out and leave the South Vietnamese there. They didn't last, oh they lasted as long as anyone expected them to. No one really admired them or respected them while we were up there. In that sort of form it makes blokes like Ralph [Niblett] and . . . I just can't myself believe that those blokes were just wasted for no bloody reason, I really can't. I like to think that by being in Vietnam we did help them stem the expansion of communism at that time.[4]

Wally Burford covered a lot of ground in his answer, including the popular rationale of the time that communism needed to be stopped in South-East Asia. This seemed to be a creditable platform upon which to build the strategy—the little that did exist—surrounding the war.

Platoon sergeant Daryl Jenkin was in his third campaign fighting counter-guerilla warfare and he supported Burford's answer when answering the question of the war being worth it:

Yes. I do. I am a firm believer in the 'Domino Theory'. Not probably to the extent that it was laid out originally, but I still believe our threat is going to come from up there, and closer. Even later, when I think of this training [that] we are involved in now here in Australia, I sometimes wonder about it. I always believed our Army should be trained at CRW [Counter Revoluntionary Warfare] because if you can get him trained in CRW—he can fight anywhere. A well-trained soldier can do anything. He can fight anywhere under any conditions.[5]

Jenkin's views do raise an interesting point on the type of training Australia should be concentrating on. Captain Peter Schuman took a similar view to Daryl Jenkin because he sees the need to maintain skills and expertise as a price that must be paid for in some way and war is the best training ground for future warriors and trainers.[6]

One man who has been exposed to politics and public life since he left the Army and who has run as a Federal and State Parliament candidate and been mayor of Cairns, is Platoon Commander Kevin Byrne:

A lot of people have asked me that [question], they ask me that more and more now and I guess it is because as time passes, people look back and wonder whether it was worth it. Incredible isn't it—nearly 25 years. And here [Cairns] we celebrated the 50th Anniversary of the Coral Sea and we weren't that far behind—Second World War. Yes, I think it was. Look it was part of the time; it was part of the foreign policy; it was part of the world then and obviously it was worth it at the time. The same question could be asked about, look at Japan's dominance here in Cairns, in terms of finance. Was it worth going to war with Japan, and at the time my word it was, and at the time I think Vietnam was worth it.[7]

A counter view is held by ex-Regular Digger, Dean Cooke. He sees the war as being commercially exploitive and that the treatment of the returned servicemen, including their unfriendly reception, caused a lot more damage than the casualties suffered in the war:

I don't think so, probably not. I have tried to work it out
and I think there are blokes still probably trying to work it
out. I know one guy actually, he is the pastor at my church
I belong to, he was over there with 2 RAR and he came
back and he ended up a heroin addict and drank heaps and
was into heroin and dope and stuff like that. He actually
threw his medals overboard coming back, he was a National
Serviceman. He's getting counselling now. He's not freaked
or anything like that, it's just some little things I suppose
he's working through—dealing with. Personally, no, I don't
think so. I think as far as the Americans were concerned, I
think the big multi-nationals or the big companies made
mega bucks out of it. I think there was the influence there
I think, probably a lot of influence from business and stuff.
You know, the ones who stood to make millions of dollars
and no doubt they did, especially through the American
system.[8]

The Forward Observer, Lieutenant Greg Gilbert, agreed and
also took a more pragmatic view on what the involvement
was all about and if the Australian involvement was worth
504 lives lost:

On 20/20 hindsight you would probably say no. At the
time I suppose the government was losing its British ally
and looking to get the Americans in, and the way to get
the Americans in was to support the Americans in Vietnam.
At the time I remember thinking that it was a bit problem-
atic and our main concern was to cement our relationship
with the Americans more than any concern about the
Vietnamese.[9]

One Regular soldier who has the advantage of having been
back to Vietnam several times since the end of the war
conducting tours for mainly Vietnam veterans answered the
question on the 'worth' of the Australian involvement in this
way:

The way it ended, possibly not. We were achieving our
goals, our aims. We did a lot of good for the people over
there building roads and hospitals, setting up windmills, and

253

farms and schools and that sort of thing. The people over there really appreciated it, including the ex-enemy. The Australian soldier is very, very well-respected there and I think everything we did was what we were told to do, what we were expected to do. I don't know how the outcome would have been if we had stayed there. It still could be even going on today because they are an ingenuous little enemy—they can make anything out of anything. I don't think it was wasted. What we did during the period of time we were there was for the good of the people that we were looking after at the time.[10]

So, there are mixed views about the 'worth' of the war. Peace activists will no doubt hold the view that no war is worth the loss of human lives. In fact, I have not met too many men who have been in war who believe that war is anything other than a job to be done, and that there is no value to the combatant who survives other than the experience of 'having been there and done that'. Often the only positive aspect is the fact that those experiences may well save his and others' lives later on when facing combat in another situation or theatre of war.

REGRETS

But do soldiers and especially those from Delta Four have any regrets about their involvement in the Vietnam war? This was a poignant question to ask because of the enormous controversy that surrounded Australia's involvement in the war. The situation was also muddled by the fact that conscription became a big issue and a philosophical debate raged over the deployment of conscripts in a foreign war which did not directly threaten the country. However, 'Jethro' Hannah had no difficulty in answering this question:

No. No. I have no regrets. Once I was told that 4 RAR was going I accepted that, and by that time through our training we knew what we were going to do when we got there and I do not regret going to Vietnam.[11]

Company medic, Corporal Mick O'Sullivan, who went on to become a Warrant Officer Class One and a Regimental Sergeant Major of a unit and brigade, saw his involvement as being part of a soldier's career and necessary for gaining the right experience:

> Oh no. It was a chapter in my life. I don't reflect or like to reflect back on it a lot now. But, no doubt it definitely enhanced my ability and my learning to effectively perform in other areas, which again helped my career progression in the Army.
>
> I can only say that for half of my life that I spent in the Army, I enjoyed that immensely, but by far my greatest posting ever was to have served in 4 RAR and in particular, Delta Company 4 RAR, which will remain, even with its pitfalls and its downfalls and some of the bad times, one of the greatest memories of my life and my 20 years in the Army.[12]

So for the regular soldiers it was taken more as part of their professional development to serve in a war zone and they were committed to the event and whatever came with it. For those who were only serving as ordered by their government, there is a different viewpoint. National Serviceman Wally Burford expressed his regrets:

> Oh, the obvious regret is the blokes we had killed up there, you know, what sort of people they could have been. Blokes like Bernie [Pengilly], bloody Ralph [Niblett]. That to me is the regrettable part. We were lucky we didn't have any mine incidents with blokes with legs or anything blown off. So, no, most of the wounded I have heard about have recuperated to different degrees. I had the experience of meeting Ralph's folks the last time I went over to Canberra last October [1992]. They were just sitting there with another mate [Private M.J.] Mick Gilpin who was in 10 Platoon and company headquarters up there and we were just sitting in the RSL there having a drink and Mick saw a woman walk past with 'Niblett' [indicates a name tag]. He said, 'That's Ralph's mum', and I just broke down on the spot. You know, I really did. Anyway I followed them

up and oh, that got to me. It was something that I wanted to do for a long, long time. I chased up Bernie's dad and had a chat to him, but Ralph's folks I had always wanted to meet and that gave me the opportunity to say, yes . . . That was immense for myself that day.[13]

Burford's feeling that his grieving was incomplete is shared by many of the men. There was no common war cemetery for the fallen from Vietnam and unless they are reasonably local they can never say 'goodbye' to their mates or console the next-of-kin. Private Kevin Benson had no regrets despite having a rough time on his return to Australia as a Vietnam veteran:

No. It was an experience. I would hate my kids to do it. I always said that if war broke out I would take them bush. I would hate to go through now what my father went through. Because I can remember when I came home he just cried like a baby. And that shook me up. No, the whole experience of it was good, but see I enjoyed that life too, the Army lifestyle. I think that if I had have really sat down and looked at it in a mature frame, when I got home, you know I could have re-enlisted and been quite happy. You know I enjoyed it, yes.[14]

There were a few men who served in Delta Four as National Servicemen who expressed this desire to serve on and several thought it was because of their 'positive' experience of war. Grahame Tooth agreed with Benson:

Yes, I have a couple of regrets, I have got a couple of things that I'm sorry now that I didn't do. I have got no regrets about going in the Army, I thought that it was a fabulous time. Irrespective of going to Vietnam or not. I think this government should make everyone have some sort of training, still in this day and age, even if it was six months. The biggest regret I have got was getting out when I did. One of the things when I got interviewed when I got out, it was probably too rushed and if I'd thought about it for a week or a couple of weeks and then talked to some other blokes, I would have stayed in the Army. But, now I suppose speaking to other blokes that stayed in or had a bit longer time to serve, they went back to Townsville with the battalion for whatever, and I would have liked to have still been in that environment with them in Australia for probably six months and if I would have done, I probably wouldn't have been here today. So, I've got regrets, probably that I would have liked to stay in there a bit longer.[15]

Bob Meehan was heavily involved in raising money for the Vietnam War Memorial erected and unveiled in Canberra on Memorial Drive in 1992. He personally raised several hundred thousand dollars for the memorial and yet only served in the Army for two years and I needed to find out why he felt the way he did.

To be honest I have sat down day after day, year after year and thought why the hell I do it. I was involved with the initial stages of setting up the Welcome Home Parade, I was on the committee that looked after the Regiment and mainly generated around 4 RAR and mainly around Delta Company and Support Company and then I got involved in the national memorial and was Director of the network and fund raising and raised $960,000 through my group and I was one of the five veterans to choose the design and then once we knew that we had the money, then they set up the mobile [NAMBUS] museum and it slowly dawned on me. Delta 4 RAR/NZ was my life, my family and I'm still trying to look after them—I guess I always will. It was the highlight of my life. We were a family, Delta Four.[16]

Meehan sums up what it is that keeps the men from Delta Four in constant contact with one another and why the Back to Vietnam reunion trip in 1993 came from a groundswell of support from the soldiers and was not placed upon them by their senior officers or sergeants.

Another interesting observation was made by one National Service Digger who came to Delta Four after all the action was over. His answer to the question of regrets was most interesting:

No, only that I never got into contact.

I had gone into the Army and been trained, and I think that is one of the things about the training, is that they really did instil in you a sort of fierceness. You were trained to be aggressive and it took a lot of time; probably took about two or three years to get that aggressiveness out of me—even when I got out of the Army. You had to react to certain situations. Trained for eight months, even while I was over there and patrolling, I was still learning . . . they taught you, you were built up for it, you were ready for it, and you never knew.[17]

THE POLITICIANS

During the interviews, the politicians came in for a lot of stick as being irresponsible or not meeting their responsibilities and taking the flak off the Diggers who were 'just doing their job'. During the Vietnam war there was a protest movement that started slowly in Australia, much like a rivulet in the highlands, and as international recognition of the movement grew, it slowly became a tidal wave which eventually swamped Australian politics. The anti-war movement did not start until well after the Australian Task Force was established and probably gained support after the abortive Tet Offensive launched by the communists in 1968. Whilst the Tet Offensive failed militarily it claimed world-wide recognition owing to the horrendous casualties taken by all sides. In effect it was the beginning of the end for the Allied cause because it served to underline the communist resolve without any form of winning strategy being declared by the Americans or Vietnamese apart from restricting bombing and tying their own hands behind their backs to appease those opposed to the war.

Lieutenant Greg Gilbert, the Forward Observer attached to Delta Four, agreed with many others interviewed that the anti-war movement was mis-directed by the protesters especially when physically carrying out their protests:

I think like everybody else, that by blaming the military was misdirecting it. They would take out their protest on the military whereas in fact the military were at the behest of the politicians, although they did go to the politicians in terms of throwing paint and whatnot on returning servicemen, and not even wanting to acknowledge the servicemen because they disagreed with the war. I thought it was unfortunate and unfair.[18]

THE EXPERIENCE OF WAR

When soldiers experience war they often say that they left as boys and returned as men. It may sound 'macho' but in reality the soldier is saying that the experiences have changed him in some way. Regular soldier Private Dean Cooke explains:

> I definitely didn't feel any different. I think I was a bit older. Not so much in years but . . . My sister commented on a few things on how I had changed, and I'm sure that everybody had changed. I don't think you can go through something like that and not change you know.[19]

Most of the men interviewed were asked what is was that they had learnt and what was the most important thing they had gained from their war experience. Captain Peter Schuman was adamant on his thoughts:

> The value of hard training, the value of getting a team together as fast as possible, the value of getting rid of weak links around the place. You have got to get rid of them, there is no value in having whingers, bitchers or people who just won't play the game as part of your team. Get rid of them. If they're not . . . if someone says, 'I don't believe we should be in Somalia', get rid of them ASAP, out of the unit. Just don't tolerate them, don't let them, don't give them a second chance to say, 'I'm sorry, what I really meant was . . .'. Everyone has got to be committed from that day, everything you do as a leader from that day onwards, whether it be company commander right down through your platoon commanders is directed internally towards the company. You receive things from on high, but the company is as far as people think. You might let them think

then about the battalion, but that is as far as the world is—that's the world. Everything lives, dies and is born within that. You keep the focus within there. Yes, or when something happens outside you can say, 'Don't worry about what happened over there, it will never happen here, that's not our style.'[20]

Schuman believes very strongly in the commitment to the cause to carry the team forward and to overcome problems and obstacles placed in the way of the team. The rifle company is about as high as he thinks the men want to relate to on a fighting level because of the manner in which the war was fought by Australians in the jungles of Phuoc Tuy Province. Private Kevin Benson sees what he gained from his war experience as being more personal:

You learn to respect your mates, I think that is what comes out of it most of all. You have got this something between all your mates that you were there with that is hard to explain. It is just that feeling. You have been through something together that will just stick forever.[21]

These sentiments were echoed by Private Garry Sloane, who went on to serve for another 20 years after his time in Vietnam:

Mateship, friendship, camaraderie between soldiers. I have only been out of the Army a couple of years and I have seen a slide down from probably the time when National Service finished. Like our guys—if one guy was going into town, the company would go into town and you would knock around together.[22]

What Sloane says is probably true because the training for war drew the men together and the way in which they lived in dormitory-style accommodation, with very few cars and other assets to split the groups, reinforced the team togetherness. Today almost every Digger has his own car and they have their own room and can be somewhat isolated if they are not drawn into the team.

Garry Sloane, a former soldier, checks his maps at the Horseshoe where he spent time protecting a semi-permanent Fire Support Base and patrolling the area behind him. Sloane now conducts regular trips back to Vietnam as a tour leader. (*Photograph by Jerry Taylor*)

For some men simply staying alive was the most important thing; for others, especially those in positions of responsibility, it was professionalism. Platoon Commander Kevin Byrne comments:

> The most important thing to me was to be thoroughly professional at my job, and this sounds trite doesn't it? Being thoroughly professional at my job, to ensure that we would all live another day and that we would see our time out and do our job to the best of our ability. I wanted to bring all the people home that I went with and still do our job to 110 per cent capacity. Now that goes back to [Major] Jerry Taylor's sobering comments about you can't make an omelette without breaking an egg and obviously in that process we lost some people.[23]

Almost every section commander and platoon commander up to the company commander felt exactly the same way as Byrne.

Wally Burford had to think long and hard on the question and his reply seems to be fairly typical of the Diggers:

Gee, tough one. I think most certainly it changed me, I think most certainly emotionally, I think you build a cocoon because of the blokes that die up there. I think you build a cocoon over your feelings to a fair degree. I think as far as life is concerned, you know that's taught me that. That people die and how to cope with it and why and when that sort of thing does happen. I think the meaning of team spirit. I think when we went back to Sydney for the Welcome Home Parade [1987]—it was like going back in a time warp. You forget about the camaraderie, you kind of build it up in your mind and you don't know whether it still exists but you see those blokes. Some of those blokes I hadn't seen for 20 years and it was just like I had seen them yesterday. You learnt how to live as a member of a team of people that are just stuck together for a particular reason. That to me would be probably the highlight of the Army—that you can see blokes 20 years later and it was just like yesterday, it was just a fantastic feeling I think if people haven't been in that position they can never understand what I am talking about.[24]

Responsibility extends down to every man because men depend on each other and that responsibility is what forces men into behaving in a wiser and more controlled manner. Some of the section commanders and platoon commanders were younger than their charges, so it is only natural that they suddenly had to 'grow up' and take responsibility or men's lives would be lost.

A Private soldier reflected on his 'lessons learnt' in this way:

I think it made me grow up, to change from being a . . . I may as well say it, as a young lout into a grown man. It made me learn that you can see life in a different manner. It made me learn a hell of a lot of discipline in which rightly or wrongly I carry that out in my work, which a lot of people regret—but I still do it. I try to discipline my kids in the same way, which maybe I shouldn't. I think I discipline them too hard, but it taught me bloody discipline probably at the highest level. I had a couple of years in my life which were fantastic. I met a lot of good mates that I regretted not contacting years ago. I only started getting in touch with them since 1987, before that I never ever saw them or bothered about them. Now, I have got back in touch with a lot of them and seen how they live and how they have been through stuff. I think that one thing I got out of it—being in the Army—was to meet these bloody great blokes you would never meet anywhere else. I spent 18 months there, and I have spent 20 years on the Council, and I think more of those blokes that I spent 18 months with than what I think about these blokes that I have worked with for 20 years.[25]

The man with the most responsibility was the company commander, Jerry Taylor, and he had this to say to my query:

In answering this question, I can do no better than to quote in part from *Duty First*, the history of the Royal Australian Regiment, and it says:

'The Regiment's involvement in the Vietnam War demonstrated yet again, if such is necessary, that the brunt of the battle falls on the infantryman. It proved, too, that while techniques and weapons change, the basic skills do not. Physical and emotional fitness and toughness are of fundamental importance; so is the ability to handle weapons swiftly, instinctively, and with maximum effect under all conditions. As is always the case, it demonstrated the need for decisive and resolute leadership at all levels; plans and orders that are clear and unambiguous; and the determination, ability, and offensive optimism of everyone concerned to carry those orders through to a successful conclusion.'

I also believe personally and passionately that, in the end, battles are won or lost at section and platoon level. It's the initiative and leadership of junior commanders, and the aggressive optimism and determination of the soldiers, which make even an indifferent plan work. And finally, it proved yet again that the Australian soldier, properly led, is among the best in the world.[26]

After being pressed for a more personal response to my question, Jerry Taylor went on to add:

> I suppose in a profoundly dangerous situation such as we faced on the 25th of July and to a greater degree on the 21st [of September 1971], you get to know that all the theories—and they are all fairly simple and basic theories that are learnt in peacetime—do actually work in wartime, and I don't really believe there is any difference between the sort of operations that we confronted in Vietnam or the sort of operations that were confronted for example in the Falklands. It was the basic skills which came into play and which won the day. From a personal point of view, I guess that my own perceptions about what leadership with all that that means; courage in personal preparation had also been vindicated. Inevitably, if I had the time again there would be a number of things that I would do differently—but at the time one acted on what one's instincts told one was right and using the principles and the lessons and the experience which you picked up in 'x' number of years soldiering.[27]

ON WAR

Most of the men were asked what was their reaction to war in general and how they felt when Saigon fell in 1975. One National Serviceman reflected on how sad he felt:

> Well, my reaction then was probably two or three things. One, when I saw the bloke on TV getting into the helicopter on top of the Australian Embassy, I realised that I stood there where the helicopter took off from. I actually used to walk around that perimeter of a night time. And I was probably, I don't know if I was sad or whatever but I . . . it dawned on me that the North Vietnamese had finally got what they set out to achieve. They were fighting for their independence to take over the country as the communists and it took them that long to get it. Maybe it could have been achieved a lot quicker if other people

A pensive Warren Dowell remembers his mates who did not return from the Vietnam War after a ceremony at Nui Le Battle site in September 1993. (*Photograph by Jerry Taylor*)

didn't get involved with it. If we hadn't have interfered, well they could have probably achieved it a lot easier.[28]

Warren Dowell became quite philosophical about the war:

I wasn't fighting for kangaroos, meat pies or Holden cars or anything like that. We were doing it for the other people in the section and the other people in the platoon. There was no flag waving or any of that stuff. It was for the people that you had around you because you knew that you had to do it well because they were doing it for you. That flag-waving and all that—nothing in that way at all.[29]

And that's what it comes down to in the end. Soldiers definitely do not die for flag, country or anything remotely nationalistic. They might enlist for some patriotic cause but on the field of battle they put their lives on the line for their mates, their fellow soldiers, who they know will do the same for them. But do they carry out acts of bravery for glory, for pieces of metal to bedeck their chests? I asked some of the subjects how important medals including honours and awards were to them. Greg Gilbert gave this answer:

I don't think they are really important to soldiers. I don't think that they do anything with Honours and Awards in mind, and I don't think, not in my experience anyway, that it influenced the way people act. They didn't act in particular ways with an eye on an Honour or Award. I think, retrospectively, that in some cases that when people did some things that were 'above and beyond' type thing, that it was gratifying in some cases to see an Honour or Award [bestowed] in that it showed some sort of recognition of the situation in which that person had placed themselves.[30]

Captain Peter Schuman, awarded a Military Cross for his actions as a troop commander on a patrol with the SAS on a previous tour of Vietnam, believes:

They are very important. They are like the colours, they are like the regimental badge, they are part of the trappings of being a soldier. I don't know about a quota system, but I certainly had a hand in nominating people and not all of them got up. For what reasons I don't know. I never worked in the honours and awards area and I wouldn't really know what gets up and what doesn't get up. But they are important, yes. People that have served the regiment well should be given a pat on the head.[31]

The 'quota system' that Peter Schuman refers to was a theory that was held by many who served in Vietnam and who saw many a brave or gallant action go unrecognised after the person had been nominated. There is no doubt in my mind that some sort of 'quota' system did exist, as the Australian Army was operating under an Imperial honours and awards type of scheme at that time. There were several men who were nominated for acts of bravery and lesser awards were handed out.

The company commander, Jerry Taylor, was quite specific on what he thought happened during the Vietnam war in regard to medals for bravery:

The Delta Four reunion tour group pose for a group photo outside the Soldiers' Memorial Hall in Long Phuoc. Most of the Vietnamese men in the photograph were ex-members of D445 Battalion, including ex-commander of the unit Nguyen Hoang Lam in uniform with soft cap. Note his badly injured right arm. Lam was wounded on five separate occasions during his fifteen years of combat. (*Photograph by Jerry Taylor*)

During Vietnam, the Australian system of awards was based on the British—which is to say, there was a specific number of decorations allotted to the campaign, and thence a specific number to each unit. Now that probably meant that there were too few to go round, and as a consequence someone who deserved an award—or possibly a higher level of award—did not necessarily get it. Presumably under this system only those considered most deserving eventually got them, so I suppose that kept the intrinsic worth of each decoration high.[32]

What is interesting is the ratio of medals that were handed out to those who served in the RAAF compared to those who closed with and killed the enemy. The number of awards handed out to fliers and crewmen is unbelievably high.

A sombre veterans' tour group immediately after a remembrance ceremony in which 4 RAR lost five killed and 26 wounded at Nui Le in September 1971. The brother of one of the soldiers killed in action is standing third from the right in the rear rank. (*Photograph by Jerry Taylor*)

GOING BACK—CONFRONTATION WITH THE ENEMY

In 1992 a groundswell of support started for a Delta Four reunion in Vietnam to coincide with the September battle. The idea was that men from the company would gather in Darwin and then set off for Saigon or Ho Chi Minh City and visit the areas where the men served and fought. The culmination would be a visit to the Nui Le battle site on 21 September and a memorial service to commemorate the event. The trip back was momentous for the men concerned, especially the visit to Nui Le which was jungle in 1971 and is now cultivated rubber plantation. One day later on a visit to the Long Phuoc tunnels, a meeting with our former foes was floated as an idea with an ex-member of D445 Battalion. He agreed and after obtaining clearance from the Local People's Committee, it was arranged for the Delta Four veterans to meet their former enemy at the Soldiers' Memorial Hall in Long Phuoc. The Memorial Hall is similar to an Australian RSL hall with space for honour rolls and a small shrine. As each veteran entered he was asked to place a joss stick in the

Ex-commander of D445 Viet Cong Mobile Force Battalion
Nguyen Hoang Lam and the author compare bullet wounds
after a lunch for the Delta Four veterans hosted by their former
enemy. (*Photograph by Jerry Taylor*)

joss stick bowls at the foot of a Bhudda and a bell was rung
once for each veteran placing a stick.

What followed then was most remarkable. Over 20 former
Viet Cong had gathered with no less than three ex-command-
ing officers of D445 present; the senior and most lively
character was one Nguyen Hoang Lam. Lam had been
wounded on at least five separate occasions and was the
spokesman for the enemy group. He spoke through our
interpreter, Nguyen Trung Hieu, and warmly welcomed the
18 Australian veterans. This welcome was unique because it
is very rare indeed that foreigners are allowed into Soldier's
Memorial Halls in Vietnam. Lunch was a typical Vietnamese
banquet and our hosts plied us with Vietnamese beer liberally
cooled with chunks of ice. After lunch Nguyen Hoang Lam

insisted on a series of toasts to each other, fallen comrades and the future of our peoples and this was drunk with a home-made rice wine of considerable potency which had a numbing effect on one's mouth after several drinks.

The function soon warmed up and there was much joking and gesticulating as each group attempted to communicate through only two interpreters and sign language. I asked Jerry Taylor what he thought of the whole affair, considering we had been remembering our fallen only several days before.

> I think it highlights yet again that if you keep politicians and diplomats away from the really important affairs, that the people who were *really* concerned with them will get to grips with the problems and put them in their right perspective. And I think that Australians had nothing to be ashamed of in their operations in and around Phuoc Tuy. They showed yet again they are soldiers of the first order and I believe that *that* fact was recognised by our old enemies—and as we now describe them—as our new friends—and they as soldiers saw us as what we are—which were soldiers. And because both sides were good soldiers according to their own lights, there was no requirement for any animosity or recriminations, and I think *that* point, of all the points that came out in Vietnam, was the thing that reinforced my respect for soldiers of whatever nationality.[33]

It comes back to the mutual respect discussed in the previous chapter on the enemy and it was demonstrated physically and emotionally by both sides during the lunch at Long Phuoc.

One amusing incident occurred when the group boarded their bus and Nguyen Hoang Lam, who has a terribly crippled and permanently dislocated right arm and who had drunk at least a bottle of 'rocket fuel', was about to get on his push bike and pedal eight kilometres back to Baria when Suzanne Heskett (wife of Garry Heskett) looked at Lam in his Viet Cong uniform and remarked, 'No wonder they won the war with tough buggers like that on their side!'

There was no obvious anger, angst or animosity on either side. Both sides respected each other for what they were and that was simply soldiers doing the job that their governments asked of them.

This book has been an attempt to capture how, what, where and why Australian riflemen went about their business and the way in which they did it in Delta Company during their tour of duty between April 1971 and March 1972. I have tried to capture their experiences and draw out lessons that these men learnt so that they may be a legacy to tomorrow's warriors of the Infantry Corps and the Australian Army in general. There were many hard learnt lessons drawn from the experiences of the riflemen who made up Delta Four and they should not be forgotten. Finally, I hope that I have drawn out the ethos of the Australian warrior in some form, by allowing them through this oral history approach to have their say. After all they were there and did it, and did it well.

APPENDIX

THE RIFLEMEN

Major Jerry Taylor, MC

Jeremy Hepworth Taylor was born in the United Kingdom and after commissioning from the Royal Military Academy, Sandhurst served as a platoon commander in the 22nd (Cheshire) Regiment during the period 1959–65. In the British Army he saw service in Singapore, Northern Ireland, Germany and active service in Cyprus before migrating to Australia and joining the Australian Army in late 1965. He saw active service in South Vietnam with 2 RAR in 1967–68. In 1970 he was posted to 4 RAR NZ/ANZAC Battalion for a second tour of duty and was appointed OC Administration Company. After only two months of duty in South Vietnam he succeeded Major Franz Kudnig as OC Delta Company.

On return to Australia he remained with 4 RAR as Battalion Operations Officer. Jerry Taylor was awarded a Military Cross for his outstanding leadership and gallantry during his second tour and particularly on two occasions when his rifle company was involved in set piece company attacks against Viet Cong Main Force and North Vietnamese Army forces. After 32 years of military service in both the British and Australian armies, Jerry Taylor retired as a lieutenant colonel from the Regular Army in 1986 and the Reserves in 1989. He was made a member of the Order of Australia in 1981 for his services as the Chief Instructor, Infantry Centre, Singleton.

Today he lives with his second wife Anna at Batemans Bay on the south coast of New South Wales and is self employed as a photographer.

Captain Peter Schuman, MC

Peter John Schuman was born in 1942 and enlisted as a soldier into the Regular Army for six years in 1961. He served in 1 RAR and 1 SAS Company, RAR before he applied for entry to the Officer Cadet School, Portsea in Victoria. He served in 1 RAR for a short time before he returned to the SASR as a troop commander. He completed a tour of Borneo between February and August 1965 and then South Vietnam as a troop commander between May and December 1966 in Three Squadron of the Special Air Service Regiment. During this tour of duty in Vietnam he was awarded a Military Cross for his courage and gallantry. After postings in OCS Portsea and 28 RWAR, he was posted to 4 RAR for a second tour of duty as company second in command of Delta Company. During his tour he acted as company commander when the incumbent officer commanding was repatriated to Australia for medical reasons.

After his tour of duty Peter Schuman saw a succession of postings in various regimental, training and staff appointments culminating in his promotion to lieutenant colonel in 1981. He served as Chief Instructor to the OCS of the PNGDF in Lae before postings in HQ 5 MD, 7 Brigade and HQ 7 MD. In Darwin he served as Chief of Staff, Land Component, Northern Command. In 1992, after 27 years of service, Peter Schuman folded up his kit and retired to take up an appointment as the Executive Director of the Fremantle Chamber of Commerce in Perth, Western Australia. Peter and his wife Robin now live in Fremantle and spend their leisure moments enjoying the company of their three grandchildren.

Second Lieutenant Kevin Byrne, MID

Born on Manus Island in Papua New Guinea in 1949 and then brought to Australia as a young boy, Kevin Michael Byrne entered the Army as a direct entry officer cadet through the Officer Cadet School, Portsea in January 1969. This gregarious, talented sportsman was soon recognised as a leader and graduated as Battalion Sergeant Major and was awarded the Sword of Honour for his achievements at Portsea. He was posted to 4 RAR as a rifle platoon commander and assumed command of 10 Platoon Delta Company. During his tour of duty, Kevin Byrne was Mentioned in Dispatches for his actions during the company attack against 274 VC Main Force regiment near the Suoi Ca river in July 1971. He spent his entire tour as the platoon commander of 10 Platoon. After tours of duty in Singapore and Papua New Guinea he served in a variety of regimental and training appointments before he separated from the Service in 1988.

Kevin worked for the Queensland State Public Service as Manager of the Cairns and Northern Region Development Board and Regional Manager of the Queensland Confederation of Industry. He dallied in federal politics, being nearly elected to the seat of Leichhardt in 1990. In 1992 he was elected Mayor of Cairns. Today Kevin and his second wife Amanda live in Port Moresby, Papua New Guinea where Kevin is Manager of PNG Tourism.

Second Lieutenant Graham Spinkston

Graham David Spinkston was a univesity student in civilian life in Adelaide, South Australia when he decided to attend the Officer Cadet School, Portsea in 1968. After graduating to infantry corps, 'Spingo' moved north to Townsville and joined the 4th Battalion as Assistant Adjutant. In 1970 he was moved across to command 12 Platoon in Delta Company. During his tour of duty Graham Spinkston was unlucky to be wounded but lucky enough to be carrying a thick book which stopped an AK-47 bullet from damaging him even further.

After returning to Australia he completed a tour of duty in Singapore and had the normal range of postings typical of an infantry officer. He commanded a rifle company in the 3rd Battalion RAR (Parachute) and served in several staff postings after graduating from Command and Staff College at Fort Queenscliff in Victoria.

Graham retired from the Army as a lieutenant colonel in Adelaide to set up his own company which conducts adventurous training and team building for business corporations. Graham and his second wife Jane were unable to return to Vietnam as part of this project as they were expecting their first child at the time of the reunion trip.

Warrant Officer, Class Two, Noel Huish

After the experience of school cadets and then the three month National Service Scheme in 1956, Noel Huish enlisted from that training as a six year enlistee and determined from the outset to be a career soldier. Initially a soldier in the Royal Australian Signals Corps as a result of his National Service, he was transferred to the Infantry Corps as a corporal in 1962. He then earnt his qualifications in the infantry while serving as an instructor at the 1 RTB at Kapooka.

In late January 1964 he became a foundation member of the newly raised 4th Battalion. He was posted as a section commander in 12 Platoon, Delta Company. He was promoted to sergeant the next year and moved to 6 Platoon, Bravo Company and saw active service in Borneo and Malaya in that capacity. In 1967 he was moved to the position of battalion 'Sheriff' as Regimental Police Sergeant and served his first tour of South Vietnam in that job. He served a short, but as he admits, an enjoyable stint as CQMS, B Company before being promoted to Warrant Officer Class Two in January 1970 and moved to re-raise Delta Company for their second tour of Vietnam.

Noel Huish returned from South Vietnam in March 1972 and after several training postings he was promoted to Warrant Officer Class One and served as RSM of the 4th Military District in Adelaide, the Adelaide University Regiment and then the 3rd Battalion, RAR. His final posting was as RSM of the 1st Military District in 1984 after 28 years of soldiering—of which the greater proportion was spent either leading or training soldiers. He is one of the principal stalwarts of the 4th Battalion RAR Association and is the catalyst behind most if not all of the Brisbane based Association activities. This professional soldier and career bachelor now lives in Ferny Hills, a suburb of Brisbane, and spends most of his time organising the Association activities and serving on the State Council for the Vietnam Veterans Association of Australia.

Staff Sergeant Bob Hann

Bob Hann joined the Army in 1959 at 17 years of age after a couple of jobs as a farm labourer in rural Western Australia. He served in 2 RAR and 3 RAR as a rifleman before he decided to become a storeman in the infantry corps. By the time he was a sergeant and serving in the 1st Battalion Pacific Islands Regiment in Papua New Guinea in 1967 he was concerned that the war in South Vietnam was going to end before he could earn his spurs in a combat zone.

South Vietnam was Bob Hann's first war as a soldier, which was somewhat unusual for an infantry senior NCO at that period of time given the campaigns since the Second World War in Korea, Malaya and Borneo. After writing to the Director of Infantry and asking for a posting to Vietnam he was posted as a platoon sergeant to Charlie Company, 4 RAR in 1969 and then moved across at the Commanding Officer's insistence to be the Company Quarter Master Sergeant of Delta Company as they were reforming in 1970. Bob deployed to South Vietnam and spent his entire tour as the CQMS of Delta Company.

After Vietnam, Bob served on for another eight years before taking his discharge in Brisbane where he was working as the RQMS of HQ 1st Military District. After 21 years of military service he joined the Public Service in the Bureau of Statistics where he works today. Bob and his wife Desley live in Ferny Grove, a leafy suburb of Brisbane, and spend much of their leisure time at their local bowls club.

Sergeant Daryl Jenkin, MID

One of four boys who joined the Regular Army, Daryl Kenneth Jenkin spent the greater proportion of his Army service in 4 RAR. He enlisted the day he turned 18 and worked hard at becoming an infantryman. He served in Delta Company on an operational tour of Borneo in 1965, his first tour of South Vietnam as a section commander with the same platoon and company in 1968 and in 1971 returned for his second tour as the newly promoted Platoon Sergeant of that same platoon—11 Platoon.

He was my platoon sergeant during his second tour and was wounded during his tour of duty in late September 1971. His platoon was engaged in a company attack on a bunker system which was the last major engagement by Australian troops in the war. For his actions during that same battle he was Mentioned in Dispatches. After his beloved 4th Battalion linked with 2 RAR in 1973 he moved on and served in several instructional postings including the Royal Military College, Duntroon before he took his discharge in 1984 after 21 years of regimental service.

For several years he ran his own landscape gardening business in Townsville. Today Daryl is a dog handler with the Queensland Corrective Services and is settling into a newly built house in the suburb of Annandale in Townsville opposite Lavarack Barracks with his wife Trish.

Corporal Warren Dowell

Warren William Dowell enlisted at the age of 18 in January 1969 and as the Regular Army rapidly expanded he quickly rose through the ranks to become a rifle section commander only 18 months after joining the Army. At the age of 19 he was a section commander leading his men on operations against the Viet Cong. He is a short, nuggetty man who played rugby way above his weight and with a passion, which often saw him at the epicentre of trouble.

A strong personality combined with his gregarious nature saw him commanding a rifle section for the first part of his tour with Delta Company and then he spent several months leading the rifle company's Support Section from August until November. As a result of an incident where his strong personal feelings overcame his better judgment he was reduced in rank to Private. He bounced back after this misdemeanour and continued to serve in 11 Platoon until he returned to Australia.

After returning from his tour of duty he stayed in the Army and served in postings which saw him in training and regimental postings, including a stint as a small arms instructor with the Malaysian Army at Kota Tinggi in Western Malaysia. He was promoted to sergeant in 1980 and he took his discharge in 1989 after 20 years duty as an infantryman.

Today Warren Dowell is the By Laws Officer for the City of the Gold Coast Council at Surfers Paradise on Queensland's Gold Coast and he and his wife of 15 years, Julie, live in Nerang. He spends his leisure time playing Golden Oldies rugby and golf.

Private Kevin Benson

Kevin James Benson was born and raised in Victoria where he was working as a labourer in an abattoir before he was drafted in July 1970. After graduating from Recruit Training at Puckapunyal, he was allotted to infantry and completed his infantry Initial Employment Training with the 4th Battalion at Lavarack Barracks in Townsville. After six months in the Army he was posted as a rifleman to Delta Company and joined 11 Platoon.

He served as a rifleman during his tour with 11 Platoon and completed his tour of duty in South Vietnam in March 1972. On return to civilian life at the completion of his National Service obligation, Kevin Benson went back to Geelong where he worked as a butcher. In 1992 he bought his own butchery business in Highton, a suburb of Geelong City, and he and his wife Maree live in nearby Grovedale. Kevin and Maree have three boys and spend their free time attending Australian Rules games to watch their Geelong AFL team and taking the boys to their local competitions.

Private Wally Burford

Walter Alfred Burford stands 172 cm and has a build which belies his true stature as a soldier and an athlete. Known simply as 'Wally' to all who knew him in Delta Company, and a man who doesn't blow his own trumpet. Few men in Delta Company would have known that he was a State representative in field hockey for Western Australia and a player knocking on the door to represent his country at the sport.

Wally was 20 years old when he was drafted from his Public Service job into National Service in July 1970, completed his recruit training at Puckapunyal and, like Kevin Benson, completed his Initial Employment Training as a rifleman with 4 RAR in Townsville. After less than 10 months in the Army, Private Burford would be on operational service with 12 Platoon, Delta Company in South Vietnam.

After only two months he was acting as a section 2IC, and after four months he was promoted to lance corporal rank. Private Burford had completed several years as a soldier in the Citizen Military Forces (CMF) prior to his enlistment as a National Serviceman and this combined with his attendance on an Assault Pioneer Course saw him as a valuable member of his platoon—especially when it came to siting and setting Claymore mines.

Wally Burford returned to his home State after his stint in Vietnam finished when his two year obligation ran out in November 1971. He went back to the Public Service but not to hockey as he had found that his two year absence in uniform had taken away his competitive edge. He married in 1976 and he and his wife have a son and a daughter in their early teens.

Private Dean Cooke

An unhappy home life and an unexciting job as a sugar bag maker pushed Dean Frederick Cooke into military service in Brisbane in 1970 at 18 years of age. After a stint at Kapooka for his recruit training, he soon found himself in Ingleburn learning the trade of an infantryman. After completing his initial employment training he was posted to 4 RAR where he prepared for active service with Delta Company as a rifleman before deploying in April 1971. Dean Cooke was barely 19 when he sailed off for war. During his tour of duty he spent a short time as a rifleman in his section and then completed the bulk of his tour as a section 2IC as a lance corporal.

He took his discharge a year after he returned from Vietnam and worked in several jobs around Queensland as a truck driver and labourer. Twelve years ago he decided to be a Christian and he became interested in becoming a minister for the Episcopalian Church. He worked as an ordained minister for half a year before he fell out with his Church's hierarchy and moved to Brisbane. He is currently a bus driver in Brisbane and is studying for the Ministry in the Pentecostal Church. He was married in 1976 to Kate and has four sons ranging in age from eight to 20.

Private Geoffrey 'Jethro' Hannah

The son of a coal miner in the Cessnock region in the Hunter Valley, Geoffrey 'Jethro' Hannah enlisted in the Regular Army for six years in 1969. By the time Jethro Hannah was 19, he had completed his recruit training—where he was awarded the prize for best rifle shot—and had passed his Infantry Corps training at Ingleburn. He moved to Enoggera where he joined a fragmenting 4 RAR which had just returned from its first tour of duty in South Vietnam. By the beginning of 1971 he had been allocated to 11 Platoon, Delta Company and was one of the senior soldiers—if not the oldest. His Section Commander, Corporal (later Sergeant) Daryl Jenkin, trained him as a forward scout.

During his tour of South Vietnam, Jethro Hannah acted as a rifleman, forward scout, radio operator and part-time machine gunner. After his tour of duty he served in a variety of regimental and training appointments.

Today he is a Warrant Officer Class Two and the head of the NCO Section in Careers Wing at the School of Infantry at Singleton. He is often referred to by his colleagues as 'The CSM of The Army' because of his long-standing association with the Infantry Centre and his refusal to attend an RSM's Course, having been an instructor on the course for many years.

He is married with two teenage children.

Private Garry Heskett

Born in Lismore, New South Wales and raised in the bush, Garry Robert Heskett left school at a young age and worked for the Post Master General's Department, as it was then known, in Granville, a suburb of Sydney. He joined the Army at 17 years of age in 1969 with the aim of attaining trade qualifications. Garry Heskett found himself allocated to Infantry Corps and then sent to 4 RAR, which was working up for a second tour of duty in Vietnam.

In 1970 he qualified as a mortarman for the Mortar Platoon in Support Company and he spent the majority of his tour providing indirect fire support to the platoons of the battalion from either fixed Fire Support Base positions or from APC mortar tracks on mobile operations. When the bulk of 4 RAR left for Australia at the end of 1971, Garry Heskett volunteered to remain as part of the beefed-up Delta Four to provide intimate indirect fire support as part of the Delta Company Group with the attached Mortar Section.

After six years Army service Garry Heskett left to pursue a career with the New South Wales Police Force. Today he is the Chief of Detectives for the Liverpool area and has the rank of Detective Sergeant.

Garry is married to Suzanne and they have been together for 20 years and have three children. Suzanne accompanied Garry back to Vietnam in 1993 and was acknowledged as being the person who most assisted others who had trouble coping with some of the more emotional aspects of the tour.

Garry lives on a property outside Sydney at Bringelly where he has plenty of space for his kids and horses. He is heavily involved in the Fourth Battalion Association and is an active honorary member of the Officer's Mess of the newly reraised Fourth Battalion, The Royal Australian Regiment.

Private Bob Meehan

Bob Meehan was drafted from his job as a upholsterer in October 1969 where he was quite content. He accepted his conscription happily enough, safe in the knowledge that the law required his employer to reinstate him once his National Service obligation was completed.

After completing his initial recruit training, Bob Meehan had shown he was infantry material and he was selected to attend his Infantry Corps training with the Special Air Service Regiment in Western Australia instead of normal Corps Training at the Infantry Centre, Ingleburn. This training was normally offered to those men who had shown that they were fit enough and may be willing to make the Army a career.

He had almost completed his SASR course when he injured his knee and was reallocated back to another infantry unit. At 21 years of age he was now in 4 RAR and allotted to Delta Four as a rifleman. He showed a penchant for the machine gun and carried the GPMG M60 throughout his tour of duty in Vietnam with 12 Platoon. He completed his two-year National Service obligation and left Vietnam before 4 RAR finished its tour of duty.

Bob Meehan enjoyed his time with the Army and especially with Delta Four, which he considers his 'other family'. He has been a very active member of the Fourth Battalion Association and was on the organising committee for the 1987 'Welcome Home Parade' and instigated the famous 'Nambus', which was a mobile museum used to raise money for the Vietnam War Memorial. Bob Meehan, his bus and his mates raised $960 000 for the Memorial, well over half of what the rest of the country raised.

Today, a divorced Bob Meehan lives in Moorebank in Sydney and works as a furniture fabric sales representative and is still actively involved in Vietnam Veterans activities. He has two adult children, one of whom is a trooper in the cavalry in the Regular Army, and his daughter is married to a sapper in the RAE.

Private Kevin O'Halloran

Kevin Francis O'Halloran was drafted into the Army in January 1971 and after recruit training at Puckapunyal he was allotted to the Infantry Corps and trained at the 3rd Training Battalion at Singleton. After only seven months as a soldier he was posted to the 1st Australian Reinforcement Unit (1 ARU) in Nui Dat where he spent several weeks and served with the Defence and Employment Platoon of the 1st Australian Task Force (1 ATF).

In September of 1971, Kevin O'Halloran was posted to the 4th Battalion and allotted to Delta Company. He joined the company as a reinforcement after its heavy involvement with the enemy and became a section rifleman.

Because of the reduction of Australian involvement in South Vietnam, Kevin was only required to serve 18 months as a National Serviceman and he was discharged of his military obligation in July 1972 having spent seven months of his service overseas.

Today, Kevin is the Manager/Secretary of the Wonthaggi-Inverloch Water Board in south-west Victoria and he and his wife Margaret live in the seaside town of Inverloch with their two sons. Kevin is a keen sailboard rider who enjoys the outdoor lifestyle whenever he can.

Private Garry Sloane

The influence of a cousin in 5 RAR and secure employment had Garry McIntyre Sloane considering a career in the Regular Army when he was a lad of 17 years. The move from Tasmania in 1968 saw him attend recruit training at Kapooka and after his choices of 'Infantry, Infantry and Infantry' were considered, he got what he wanted and served with 4 RAR in Malaya before departing for South Vietnam in 1971.

Garry Sloane was a member of 12 Platoon and as is often the case with the more experienced Diggers, found himself a forward scout on many occasions when on patrol. After a safe tour of duty he returned to Australia in March 1972.

In 1974 he left the Infantry Corps and joined the Ordnance Corps. He served another 20 odd years in the Army before retiring in 1991 with the rank of Warrant Officer Class Two.

In 1992 Garry Sloane began his task of drawing together the Vietnam reunion tour to Vietnam for Delta Four and was the driving force behind that successful event. He has been back to Vietnam many times and is now conducting tours back to Vietnam for veterans and their families.

Garry Sloane lives in Darwin where he earns a living as a printer (in between trips back to Vietnam) and is separated with three teenage children.

Private Greg Stuchberry

Gregory Mark Stuchberry enlisted as a Regular soldier for an initial engagement of six years in 1968. After recruit training he was allotted to the now defunct Royal Australian Army Service Corps as a clerk. After displaying a lack of talent in this field—which had been chosen for him—he served for a time as a clerk in the general and pay streams.

In 1970 he asked for and was granted a transfer to the Infantry Corps and was posted to the 1st Reinforcement Holding Unit (1 RHU) at Ingleburn outside Sydney in New South Wales. After several weeks he was sent to the Jungle Training Centre (JTC) at Canungra, some 20 kilometres inland from the Gold Coast in sub-tropical rainforest, and attended a four week Battle Efficiency (BE) Course.

In December 1970 he was posted as a reinforcement to 1 ARU for three weeks and was then sent to the Amenities Unit in Saigon for about five weeks. He wanted to serve in a battalion and left the safe environment of a clerical job and this soldier—who had never been formally trained as an infantryman—was posted to the 2nd Battalion, RAR and completed that unit's final three months in country in 6 Platoon of Bravo Company. He spent all of those months as a rifleman on patrol. His teachers were his section commander and his fellow soldiers in 6 Platoon.

After the 2nd Battalion returned to Australia, Greg Stuchberry was reassigned and joined the 3rd Battalion, RAR as a rifleman in Charlie Company. He served for about three months in 3 RAR and when 3 RAR completed their tour of duty in September 1971, he was posted to the 4th Battalion, RAR. He was allotted to 11 Platoon of Delta Company and joined the platoon which had just lost four men killed in action.

He stayed with Delta Company after the remainder of the 4th Battalion went home in December 1971, and he returned with the last Australian rifle company to serve in Vietnam in March 1972. He took his discharge after five years service and became a bricklayer. Irreverent, honest and open, he called a spade a bloody shovel. Sadly, Greg committed suicide in late 1995, unable to cope with the stresses of life.

Private Grahame Tooth

Grahame Arthur Tooth was born and raised in the rural countryside of southern New South Wales in the quite and peaceful town of Bundanoon at the foothills to the Great Dividing Range. Grahame Tooth was drafted into the Army in 1970. After his recruit training at 1RTB at Kapooka, he was allotted to the Infantry Corps and sent to the Reinforcement Holding Unit at Ingleburn, just outside Sydney.

Grahame Tooth then spent five months waiting to be sent to Vietnam as a reinforcement during which time he attended the Battle Efficiency Course at the Jungle Training Centre, Canungra with other members of the RHU. In June 1971, 21-year-old Grahame Tooth left for a tour of duty in South Vietnam.

On arrival in country he spent one month of his time training and settling in with 1st Australian Reinforcement Unit (1 ARU), and then a month with the Defence and Employment Platoon in Saigon on guard duties. In August 1971 he joined Delta Four as a reinforcement and was posted to 12 Platoon where he initially spent his time as a rifleman and then carried the machine gun. He survived the Battle of Nui Le and came home with Delta Four on the HMAS *Sydney*.

Grahame Tooth has been married to Paula for 22 years and they have two teenage children. Grahame lives in Bundanoon and works as an overseer with the Wingecarribee Shire

Council. He returned to Vietnam with his wife and daughter in 1993 and found it a memorable experience.

ATTACHMENTS AND DETACHMENTS

These are always referred to as simply 'atts and dets'. Examples are artillery forward observer parties, RAAMC medics from either the Battalion Medical Platoon or a Field Ambulance/Field Medical Company. Sappers from 1 Field Squadron, which was permanently assigned to Vietnam, were often attached to rifle companies as 'splinter teams' or 'mini-teams'. The sappers' job was to provide expert mine warfare assistance to the rifle companies and assist in demolitions or tunnel/bunker searching. The men from the APC Squadron would often be included as atts for either the duration of an operation or to provide the mobility to insert patrols into their area of operation (AO).

Lieutenant Greg Gilbert, 104 Battery, 12 Field Regiment

A Duntroon graduate in December 1968. He was allotted to the Royal Regiment of Australian Artillery and after passing his Young Officers' Course at North Head in Sydney he was posted to his Regiment in Townsville, North Queensland. This 183 cm, dark curly-haired artilleryman was posted to 104 Battery of 12 Field Regiment which had been 4 RAR's Direct Support (DS) battery for the Battalion's first tour of South Vietnam.

After being allocated to 104 Battery as a Forward Observer (FO), Greg began to gather together the men he wanted to form his FO Party. This five man group consisted of Greg, a bombardier and three gunners, who were assistants to the bombardier, and himself and carried the two radios for the party. More often than not the bombardier was allotted to one of the platoons and known as the FO Ack or FO's assistant.

Gilbert was mostly found in Company Headquarters when in the field and was the company commander's adviser on matters concerning indirect fire and air support. During his tour with 104 Battery in South Vietnam Greg was always allotted to Delta Company. His FO Ack was often allotted to 11 Platoon.

After his tour of duty in South Vietnam, Greg Gilbert served on for another 14 years, serving a total of 21 years in the Army and reaching the rank of lieutenant colonel before he changed careers and became a merchant banker for five years. Today he works for the National Australia Bank in Melbourne. He has been married for 22 years and has two teenage children.

Lieutenant Chris Stephens, Troop Commander, A Squadron, 3rd Cavalry Regiment

Chris Stephens attended Reserve Officer Commissioning Training after five years service as a trooper, rising to the rank of sergeant and after attending an ROBC graduated as a lieutenant into Armoured Corps in 1969. After completing and becoming dux of his Young Officers' Course at the Armoured Centre at Puckapunyal, he was allotted for duty with A Squadron 2 Cavalry Regiment as grounding and preparation for his eventual transfer to a unit heading for Vietnam. In 1970 he arrived in Townsville and was posted to 2 Troop of A Squadron, 3rd Cavalry Regiment.

Chris Stephens was a troop commander and had 30 or so troopers and normally 13 carriers under his command. Together with 1 Troop from A Squadron, commanded by Sergeant Levy, DCM, they provided the battalion with its APC mobility and firepower during operations from April 1971 until March 1972.

After returning from South Vietnam, Chris Stephens served in a variety of staff and regimental appointments, including overseas service with the United Nations with UNTSO in the Middle East. He commanded the 2/14th Light Horse (Queensland Mounted Infantry), then an APC Regiment, from 1988 to 1990. In 1993 he was promoted to Brigadier and today serves in Canberra. He is married to Adrienne and has two teenage children.

Corporal Mick O'Sullivan, MM

Michael John O'Sullivan joined the Regular Army in 1968 for a six-year engagement in Perth and after recruit training was allotted to the Royal Australian Medical Corps. After successfully completing training at the School of Army Health at Healesville in Victoria, he was posted to the 3rd Casualty Clearing Station and the 1st Military Hospital at Yeronga in Brisbane. During his postings in Brisbane he was sent to Papua New Guinea for six weeks to assist with an influenza epidemic. In September 1970 he was posted to the 4th Battalion as a medic and joined Administration Company. As was the case in 4 RAR, medics tended to be semi-permanently attached to a rifle company for reasons of continuity and teamwork, and Mick O'Sullivan was assigned to Delta Company.

During his tour of duty he spent almost all of his time in the field with Delta Company and is credited with saving my life when I was severely wounded in September 1971. For his actions during the Delta Company action on 21 September 1971, where he displayed courage and bravery in the course of his duty, he was awarded the Military Medal.

His subsequent career saw him rise through the ranks in RAAMC serving in RAPs, Medical Centres and General Hospitals. He rose to the rank of Warrant Officer Class One in 1984 and he was appointed the Regimental Sergeant Major of 1 Field Ambulance in Sydney in 1985 and RSM of 7 Field Ambulance in Perth from 1986–88. The culminating point of his career was when he was posted as the RSM of 13 Brigade in Perth, becoming the first ever RAAMC WO1 to be granted an appointment as RSM of a Brigade.

After 22 years service, Mick retired to take up an appointment with Christ's Church Grammar School in Claremont, a suburb of Perth in Western Australia. Mick and his wife divorced in 1990 and he now lives in Palmyra. He is still an active member of the Army Reserve in Western Australia.

GLOSSARY

1 ALSG	1st Australian Logistic Support Group (Vung Tau)
1 ARU	1st Australian Reinforcement Unit (Nui Dat)
1 ATF	1st Australian Task Force (Nui Dat)
1 RHU	1st Reinforcement Holding Unit (Ingleburn NSW)
1 RTB	1st Recruit Training Battalion, Kapooka, NSW
2IC	second-in-command
3TB	3rd Training Battalion, Singleton, NSW
AATTV	Australian Army Training Team Vietnam
ammo	ammunition
ANZAC	Australian and New Zealand Army Corps
AO	area of operations
APC	armoured personnel carrier (M113 tracked vehicle)
arty	artillery
ARVN	Army of the Republic of Vietnam
BE	Battle Efficiency (Course); conducted prior to deployment overseas at the Jungle Training Centre
bund	an earth work formed to protect vehicles from direct fire or blast; the raised pathways between paddy fields
casevac	casualty evacuation
Charlie	Viet Cong, from phonetic spelling of VC, 'Victor Charlie'

Chicom	Chinese communist
chopper	helicopter
CMF	Citizen Military Forces
CIA	United States' Central Intelligence Agency
click	slang for kilometre
CQMS	Company Quarter Master Sergeant, a staff sergeant
CRW	counter revolutionary warfare
CSM	Company Sergeant Major, a warrant officer, class two
D & E	Defence and Employment (Platoon)
DF	defensive fire, a registered artillery target
Digger	nickname for the Australian soldier, a legacy of WW1 trench warfare
Dustoff	acronym—'Dedicated untiring service to our fighting forces'—a helicopter for casualty evacuation
FAC	forward air controller
FGA	fighter ground attack aircraft
FO	forward observer for artillery and mortar fire
FUP	Forming up place, an assembly area for an attack
grunt	an infantryman
HE	High explosive ordnance
HMAS	Her Majesty's Australian Ship
HMG	Heavy machine gun, .50 calibre, 12.7 mm and above
hootch, hootchie	nickname for personal shelter or lodgings
HQ	headquarters
IA	Immedaite Action (drill)
JTC	Jungle Training Centre, Canungra, Queensland
KIA	killed in action
Kiwi	nickname for New Zealanders
kg	kilogram
klick, km	kilometre
LZ	landing zone, an area where several helicopters can land and insert troops
maintdem	maintenance demand for stores or equipment
MC	Military Cross, a decoration for gallantry for officers, unable to be awarded posthumously
medevac	medical evacuation, the Hercules aircraft flight returning to Australia

MID	Mentioned In Despatches, an award for outstanding service and is an oak leaf attached to the campaign medal ribbon
mm	millimetre (calibre)
nasho	a National Serviceman
NCO	Non Commissioned Officer
NDP	Night Defensive Position
NVA	North Vietnamese Army
OC	Officer Commanding
OCS	Officer Cadet School, Portsea, which conducted 12 month commissioning courses for the Army
OR	Other Ranks, privates and corporals
pad	a helicopter landing point or area
PF	Popular Forces; South Vietnamese militia trained to a lesser level than the RF
pit	entrenched fighting position for ground troops
pogo	anyone serving in a base installation
PX	Post Exchange, an American Services duty free store
RAAF	Royal Australian Air Force
RAN	Royal Australian Navy
RAP	Regimental Aid Post
RAR	Royal Australian Regiment
R & C	rest and convalescence leave, earned after injury, illness or arduous duty and taken locally
R & R	rest and recreation leave, earned after six months on operations in South Vietnam and usually taken outside the country
recce/recon	reconnaissance
RF	Regional Forces; South Vietnamese militia
RSL	Returned Services League of Australia
RSM	Regimental Sergeant Major, a warrant officer class one
SAS	Special Air Services (Regiment)
sign	indication of movement such as foot or boot marks
SOP(s)	Standard Operating Procedures
SP	self-propelled (guns)
SVN	South Vietnam
TAOR	Tactical Area of Operations
tracks	nickname for tracked vehicles, usually APCs
TsOET	Test(s) Of Elementary Training

US	United States of America
VC	Viet Cong
VHF	very high frequency (radio band)
Yank	American

Weapons

AK-47	Russian 7.62 mm assault rifle
Claymore mine	anti-personnel directional above ground mine
GPMG M60	general purpose machine gun, 7.62 mm
M14 mine	an anti-personnel mine with a danger radius of about one metre
M16 mine	an anti-personnel mine which was the deadliest AP mine in Vietnam, a lethal danger radius of several metres. Often called the 'jumping jack' mine
M16	5.56 mm Armalite assault rifle (US)
M26	high explosive fragmentation grenade
M79	40 mm grenade launcher or more affectionately, the 'wombat gun'
MG	machine gun
RPG	rocket propelled grenade, the weapon called B-40 or RPG-2 and larger RPG-7
SLR	7.62 mm self loading rifle, standard rifle carried by riflemen in South Vietnam and affectionately called the 'elephant gun' because of its loud discharge and hard hitting power
XM203	the experimental forerunner to the M203 which is a 5.56 mm M16 rifle with the M79 grenade launcher fitted below the barrel, also known as the 'under and over'

Aircraft

Bronco	aircraft used by forward air controllers (US)
B52	strategic jet bomber (US)
Caribou	A Canadian designed STOL transport aircraft
Cobra	assault helicopter
C130	Hercules transport aircraft
F4 Phantom	jet bomber

Vietnamese terms

Biet kich	ranger or commando
Dong Nai	North Vietnamese military region encompassing Phuoc Tuy and Long Khanh provinces
Nui	hill, mountain
Song	river
Suoi	stream

ENDNOTES

Chapter 1

1. Interview with Wally Burford, Glen Forest, Perth, Western Australia, 28 March, 1993.
2. ibid.
3. Interview with Dean Cooke, Kallangur, Brisbane, Queensland, 21 March 1993.
4. Interview with Bob Hann, Ferny Grove, Brisbane, Queensland, 20 March 1993.
5. Interview with Jerry Taylor, Bateman's Bay, New South Wales, 16 October 1993.
6. Interview with Geoffrey Hannah, Singleton, New South Wales, 12 July 1993.
7. Interview with Noel Huish, Brisbane, Queensland, 20 March 1993.
8. ibid.
9. Interview with Kevin Byrne, Cairns, Queensland, 6 March 1993.
10. ibid.
11. Interview with Grahame Tooth, Bundanoon, New South Wales, 31 July 1993.
12. op. cit. Interview with Wally Burford.
13. ibid.
14. Interview with Daryl Jenkin, Townsville, Queensland, 6 March 1993.
15. Dwyer was speaking to the Royal Military College Rugby Club at a coaching and training seminar conducted in Canberra at the RMC in early May 1984.
16. Interview with Graham Spinkston, Canberra, Australian Capital Territory, 13 November 1993.

17. Interview with Bob Meehan, Moorebank, Sydney, New South Wales, 15 May 1993.
18. Interview with Warren Dowell, Merrimac, Queensland, 16 June 1993.
19. Interview with Peter Schuman, Fremantle, Perth, Western Australia, 27 March 1993.
20. ibid.
21. op. cit. Interview with Dean Cooke.
22. op. cit. Interview with Warren Dowell.
23. ibid.
24. op. cit. Interview with Jerry Taylor.

Chapter 2

1. Interview with Garry Heskett, Bringelly, New South Wales, 15 May 1993.
2. For a more detailed description of the journey aboard the HMAS *Sydney,* see Gary McKay's *Vietnam Fragments,* Allen & Unwin, 1992; Chapter Three, Deploying to Vietnam.
3. Interview with Garry Heskett.
4. Letter, Brian Vickery, a platoon commander with 9 RAR, dated 16 June 1995. As recorded in *Reflections of a Platoon Commander*, by Brian Vickery, unpublished.
5. Interview with Geoffrey 'Jethro' Hannah, Singleton, New South Wales, 12 July 1993.
6. Interview with Daryl Jenkin, Townsville, Queensland, 6 March 1993.
7. Interview with Dean Cooke, Kallangur, Brisbane, Queensland, 21 March 1993.
8. ibid.
9. Interview with Jerry Taylor, Batemans Bay, New South Wales, 16 October 1993.
10. Interview with Grahame Tooth, Bundanoon, New South Wales, 31 July 1993.
11. For a comprehensive account of the battle see Lex McAulay's *The Battle of Long Tan,* Century Hutchinson, 1986.
12. Interview with Greg Gilbert, Windsor, Victoria, 22 May 1993.
13. ibid.

Chapter 3

1. Interview with Geoffrey 'Jethro' Hannah, Singleton, New South Wales, 12 July 1993.
2. Interview with Daryl Jenkin, Townsville, Queensland, 6 March 1993.
3. Interview with Dean Cooke, Kallangur, Brisbane, Queensland, 21 March 1993.

4. Interview with Warren Dowell, Merrimac, Queensland, 16 June 1993.
5. ibid.
6. Interview with Wally Burford, Glen Forest, Perth, Western Australia, 28 March 1993.
7. ibid.
8. For a full account see Gary McKay's *Vietnam Fragments, An Oral History Of Australians at War*, Allen & Unwin, 1992.
9. op. cit. Interview with Geoffrey 'Jethro' Hannah.
10. The Rules of Engagement that applied to the Australians in South Vietnam in 1971 were that soldiers could engage a target if:

> They are positively identified as enemy.
> They open fire first and are not obviously friendly.
> They fail to stop when challenged and are not obviously friendly.
> By night they approach a position and are not obviously friendly.
> If in doubt—do not shoot.

Every Company Q Store in 4 RAR had the Rules of Engagement above the door where soldiers would see it constantly and remind them of their obligations.
11. Interview with Garry Sloane, Darwin, Northern Territory, 10 September 1993.
12. ibid.
13. Almost everyone called the rifle grenade launcher by this name ('XM' for Experimental Model) but in fact it was the MX 148 which was a forerunner to the Colt Industries M203 which became a standard issue weapon in the US and Australian Armies (Brassey's *Infantry Weapons of the World*, 1950–1975, p. 235).
14. The 40 mm grenade arms itself by spinning and after travelling 17 metres is armed and will detonate on impact. Owing to the close distances between scout and enemy it was felt that the employment of HE grenades from the M203 would be impractical.
15. op. cit. Interview with Garry Sloane.
16. op. cit. Interview with Warren Dowell.
17. ibid.
18. Interview with Bob Meehan, Moorebank, Sydney, New South Wales, 15 May 1993.
19. ibid.
20. ibid.
21. op. cit. Interview with Warren Dowell.
22. op. cit. Interview with Wally Burford.
23. op. cit. Interview with Dean Cooke.
24. Interview with Kevin O'Halloran, Inverloch, Victoria, 4 January 1993.
25. ibid.

26. Interview with Graham Spinkston, Canberra, Australian Capital Territory, 13 November 1993.
27. Interview with Kevin Byrne, Cairns, Queensland, 6 March 1993.
28. op. cit. Interview with Daryl Jenkin.
29. ibid.
30. ibid.
31. Interview with Jerry Taylor, Batemans Bay, New South Wales, 16 October 1993.
32. ibid.
33. ibid.
34. Interview with Peter Schuman, Fremantle, Perth, Western Australia, 27 March 1993.
35. Interview with Noel Huish, Brisbane, Queensland, 20 March 1993.
36. op. cit. Interview with Peter Schuman.
37. op. cit. Interview with Jerry Taylor.
38. ibid.
39. op. cit. Interview with Wally Burford.
40. op. cit. Interview with Warren Dowell.
41. Interview with Dr Sue Gould, MO Defence Centre—Brisbane, 27 July 1995.
42. op. cit. Interview with Warren Dowell.
43. op. cit. Interview with Jerry Taylor.
44. ibid.
45. ibid.
46. op. cit. Interview with Kevin Byrne.
47. op. cit. Interview with Peter Schuman.
48. op. cit. Interview with Geoffrey 'Jethro' Hannah.
49. op. cit. Interview with Wally Burford.
50. op. cit. Interview with Kevin O'Halloran.
51. op. cit. *The Grey Eight in Vietnam*, Eighth Battalion RAR, 1970.
52. Sergeant Chad Sherrin ambushed an estimated 50–60 enemy and killed 19 enemy and captured 10 VC, and for his efforts was awarded the Military Medal.
53. op. cit. Interview with Dean Cooke.

Chapter 4

1. Interview with Bob Meehan, Moorebank, Sydney, New South Wales, 15 May 1993.
2. Interview with Warren Dowell, Merrimac, Queensland, 16 June 1993.
3. ibid.
4. Extract from *In Good Company,* by Gary McKay, Allen & Unwin 1987.
5. Article written for *Australian Defender* magazine, 1995.

6. Interview with Wally Burford, Glen Forest, Perth, Western Australia, 28 March 1993.
7. Interview with Geoffrey 'Jethro' Hannah, Singleton, New South Wales, 12 July 1993.
8. Interview with Greg Gilbert, Windsor, Victoria, 22 May 1993.
9. Interview with Graham Spinkston, Canberra, Australian Capital Territory, 13 November 1993.
10. Interview with Kevin Benson, Ocean Grove, Victoria, 17 December 1992.
11. Interview with Garry Sloane, Darwin, Northern Territory, 10 September 1993.
12. ibid.
13. op. cit. Interview with Geoffrey 'Jethro' Hannah.
14. Interview with Jerry Taylor, Batemans Bay, New South Wales, 16 October 1993.
15. op. cit. Interview with Geoffrey 'Jethro' Hannah.
16. ibid.
17. op. cit. Interview with Greg Gilbert.
18. ibid.
19. op. cit. Interview with Garry Sloane.
20. op. cit. Interview with Jerry Taylor.
21. Full details of this action were recorded in a diary by McDaniel and the details are recorded in *Vietnam Fragments—An Oral History of Australians at War,* Gary McKay, Allen & Unwin, 1992.
22. op. cit. Interview with Jerry Taylor.

Chapter 5

1. Interview with Kevin Byrne, Cairns, Queensland, 6 March 1993.
2. Interview with Geoffrey 'Jethro' Hannah, Singleton, New South Wales, 12 July 1993.
3. Interview with Jerry Taylor, Batemans Bay, New South Wales, 16 October 1993.
4. Interview with Chris Stephens, Canberra, Australian Capital Territory, 29 November 1993.
5. Interview with Greg Gilbert, Windsor, Victoria, 22 May 1993.
6. Interview with Warren Dowell, Merrimac, Queensland, 16 June 1993.
7. Interview with Wally Burford, Glen Forest, Perth, Western Australia, 28 March 1993.
8. For his actions during this battle and a previous encounter in July 1971, Major J. H. Taylor was awarded the Military Cross for his gallantry.
9. op. cit. Interview with Jerry Taylor.

10. Interview with Peter Schuman, Fremantle, Perth, Western Australia, 27 March 1993.
11. ibid.
12. op. cit. Interview with Chris Stephens.
13. op. cit. Interview with Kevin Byrne.
14. op. cit. Interview with Wally Burford.
15. op cit. Interview with Jerry Taylor.
16. For his actions on 21 September 1971, Casson was strongly recommended for the award of the Military Medal but was Mentioned In Despatches (MID).
17. op. cit. Interview with Warren Dowell.
18. op. cit. Interview with Peter Schuman.
19. op. cit. Interview with Jerry Taylor.
20. Interview with Greg Stuchberry, Cairns, Queensland, 7 March 1993.
21. op. cit. Interview with Greg Gilbert.
22. op. cit. Interview with Peter Schuman.
23. Interview with Daryl Jenkin, Townsville, Queensland, 6 March 1993.
24. Interview with Kevin Benson, Ocean Grove, Victoria, 17 December 1992.
25. op. cit. Interview with Peter Schuman.
26. op. cit. Interview with Daryl Jenkin.
27. ibid.
28. Interview with Dean Cooke, Kallangur, Brisbane, Queensland, 21 March 1993.
29. Interview with Kevin O'Halloran, Inverloch, Victoria, 4 January 1993.
30. op. cit. Interview with Chris Stephens.
31. Interview with Garry Heskett, Bringelly, New South Wales, 15 May 1993.
32. op. cit. Interview with Jerry Taylor.
33. op. cit. Interview with Warren Dowell.
34. op. cit. Interview with Peter Schuman.
35. op. cit. Interview with Geoffrey 'Jethro' Hannah.
36. op. cit. Interview with Kevin Byrne.
37. op. cit. Interview with Warren Dowell.
38. Interview with Noel Huish, Brisbane, Queensland, 20 March 1993.
39. Interview with Graham Spinkston, Canberra, Australian Capital Territory, 13 November 1993.
40. ibid.
41. op. cit. Interview with Dean Cooke.
42. Interview with Garry Sloane, Darwin, Northern Territory, 10 September 1993.
43. op. cit. Interview with Kevin O'Halloran.
44. Interview with Bob Meehan, Moorebank, Sydney, New South Wales, 15 May 1993.

45. op. cit. Interview with Garry Sloane.
46. op. cit. Interview with Wally Burford.
47. Interview with Grahame Tooth, Bundanoon, New South Wales, 31 July 1993.
48. op. cit. Interview with Greg Gilbert.
49. op. cit. Interview with Bob Meehan.
50. op. cit. Interview with Garry Sloane.
51. op. cit. Interview with Kevin Byrne.
52. John Keegan, *The Face of Battle,* Johnathon Cape, 1976, p. 263.

Chapter 6

1. For a good read on Neil Davis and his work, see Tim Bowden's *One Crowded Hour*, Collins, Australia, 1987.
2. Interview with Mick O'Sullivan, Fremantle, Perth, Western Australia, 27 March 1993.
3. Interview with Peter Schuman, Fremantle, Perth, Western Australia, 27 March 1993.
4. op cit. Interview with Mick O'Sullivan.
5. ibid.
6. ibid.
7. Casevac usually refers to the evacuation of a casualty from the field and 'medevac' usually refers to the evacuation for reason other than being wounded, viz., some men contracted exotic diseases such as leptospirosis and had to be evacuated back to Australia. The weekly flights out of Vietnam back to Australia were also called medevac flights.
8. Interview with Warren Dowell, Merrimac, Queensland, 16 June 1993.
9. Interview with Wally Burford, Glen Forest, Perth, Western Australia, 28 March 1993.
10. Interview with Daryl Jenkin, Townsville, Queensland, 6 March 1993.
11. Interview with Garry Sloane, Darwin, Northern Territory, 10 September 1993.
12. ibid.
13. op cit. Interview with Wally Burford.
14. Interview with Greg Gilbert, Windsor, Victoria, 22 May 1993.
15. op cit. Interview with Peter Schuman.
16. op cit. Interview with Wally Burford.
17. Interview with Kevin Benson, Ocean Grove, Victoria, 17 December 1992.
18. Interview with Grahame Tooth, Bundanoon, New South Wales, 31 July 1993.
19. Interview with Dean Cooke, Kallangur, Brisbane, Queensland, 21 March 1993.

20. The vast majority of Australian servicemen killed in Vietnam were buried in or near their home towns with only a couple of dozen interred in cemeteries in Western Malaysia in or near Terendak Camp.

21. Interview with Graham Spinkston, Canberra, Australian Capital Territory, 13 November 1993.

22. op cit. Interview with Dean Cooke.

23. Interview with Jerry Taylor, Batemans Bay, New South Wales, 16 October 1993.

24. ibid.

25. op cit. Interview with Wally Burford.

26. op cit. Interview with Mick O'Sullivan.

27. op cit. Interview with Jerry Taylor.

28. op cit. Interview with Mick O'Sullivan.

29. Taken from interviews with Phan Van Canh, Vung Tau, Dong Nai Province SRV, 20 September 1993 and Tran Tan Huy, Long Dien, Dong Nai Province SRV, 23 September 1993.

30. op cit. Interview with Kevin Benson.

31. op cit. Interview with Mick O'Sullivan.

32. Interview with Bob Meehan, Moorebank, Sydney, New South Wales, 15 May 1993.

33. op cit. Interview with Wally Burford.

34. op cit. Interview with Daryl Jenkin.

35. Interview with Nguyen Van Phoang, Vung Tau, Socialist Republic of Vietnam, 20 September 1993, confirmed by an informal discussion with Thanh (family name unknown) who wanted to remain anonymous. An interview with Thanh was refused by SRV Government authorities for reasons not explained.

36. op cit. Interview with Garry Sloane.

37. Interview with Kevin O'Halloran, Inverloch, Victoria, 4 January 1993.

38. op cit. Interview with Wally Burford.

Chapter 7

1. Named after Major Peter Badcoe, VC, killed in action serving with the Australian Army Training Team Vietnam.

2. Interview with Wally Burford, Glen Forest, Perth, Western Australia, 28 March 1993.

3. Interview with Warren Dowell, Merrimac, Queensland, 16 June 1993.

4. ibid.

5. Interview with Mick O'Sullivan, Perth, Western Australia, 27 March 1993.

6. Interview with Garry Heskett, Bringelly, New South Wales, 15 May 1993.

7. Interview with Kevin Benson, Ocean Grove, Victoria, 17 December 1992.
8. Interview with Jerry Taylor, Batemans Bay, New South Wales, 16 October 1993.
9. Interview with Peter Schuman, Perth, Western Australia, 27 March 1993.
10. op cit. Interview with Jerry Taylor.
11. ibid.
12. Interview with Grahame Tooth, Bundanoon, New South Wales, 31 July 1993.
13. ibid.
14. Interview with Kevin Benson, Ocean Grove, Victoria, 17 December 1992.
15. Interview with Garry Sloane, Darwin, Northern Territory, 10 September 1993.
16. Interview with Kevin Byrne, Cairns, Queensland, 6 March 1993.
17. Interview with Dean Cooke, Kallangur, Queensland, 21 March 1993.
18. Interview with Wally Burford, Glen Forest, Perth, Western Australia, 28 March 1993.
19. op cit. Interview with Dean Cooke.

Chapter 8

1. Interview with Bob Hann, Ferny Grove, Queensland, 20 March 1993.
2. ibid.
3. Interview with Jerry Taylor, Batemans Bay, New South Wales, 16 October 1993.
4. Interview with Chris Stephens, Canberra, Australian Capital Territory, 29 November 1993.
5. op cit. Interview with Jerry Taylor.
6. Interview with Wally Burford, Glen Forest, Perth, Western Australia, 28 March 1993.
7. ibid.
8. Interview with Mick O'Sullivan, Fremantle, Perth, Western Australia, 27 March 1993.
9. Interview with Warren Dowell, Merrimac, Queensland, 16 June 1993.
10. Interview with Greg Gilbert, Windsor, Victoria, 22 May 1993.
11. op cit. Interview with Jerry Taylor.
12. ibid.
13. op cit. Interview with Greg Gilbert.
14. op cit. Interview with Jerry Taylor.
15. Interview with Kevin Byrne, Cairns, Queensland, 6 March 1993.
16. Interview with Dean Cooke, Kallangur, Brisbane, Queensland, 21 March 1993.

17. op cit. Interview with Warren Dowell.
18. op cit. Interview with Greg Gilbert.
19. op cit. Interview with Chris Stephens.
20. Interview with Graham Spinkston, Canberra, Australian Capital Territory, 13 November 1993.
21. Interview with Peter Schuman, Perth, Western Australia, 27 March 1993.
22. Interview with Daryl Jenkin, Townsville, Queensland, 6 March 1993.
23. op cit. Interview with Jerry Taylor.
24. op cit. Interview with Kevin Byrne.
25. op cit. Interview with Warren Dowell.
26. op cit. Interview with Bob Hann.
27. op cit. Interview with Daryl Jenkin.
28. op cit. Interview with Greg Gilbert.
29. op cit. Interview with Daryl Jenkin.
30. op cit. Interview with Chris Stephens.
31. op cit. Interview with Peter Schuman.
32. op cit. Interview with Graham Spinkston.
33. op cit. Interview with Warren Dowell.
34. op cit. Interview with Kevin Byrne.

Chapter 9

1. Interview with Graham Spinkston, Canberra, Australian Capital Territory, 13 November 1993.
2. Interview with Kevin Byrne, Cairns, Queensland, 6 March 1993.
3. Interview with Jerry Taylor, Batemans Bay, New South Wales, 16 October 1993.
4. Interview with Garry Sloane, Darwin, Northern Territory, 10 September 1993.
5. Interview with Dean Cooke, Kallangur, Brisbane, Queensland, 21 March 1993.
6. Interview with Wally Burford, Glen Forest, Perth, Western Australia, 28 March 1993.
7. Interview with Peter Schuman, Perth, Western Australia, 27 March 1993.
8. ibid.
9. Interview with Jethro Hannah, Singleton. New South Wales, 12 July 1993.
10. op cit. Interview with Graham Spinkston.
11. Interview with Grahame Tooth, Bundanoon, New South Wales, 31 July 1993.
12. Interview with Mick O'Sullivan, Fremantle, Perth, Western Australia, 27 March 1993.

13. op cit. Interview with Wally Burford.
14. op cit. Interview with Kevin Byrne.
15. op cit. Interview with Jerry Taylor.
16. op cit. Interview with Peter Schuman.
17. Interview with Garry Sloane, Darwin, Northern Territory, 10 September 1993.
18. Interview with Bob Meehan, Moorebank, Sydney, New South Wales, 15 May 1993.
19. Interview with Warren Dowell, Merrimac, Queensland, 16 June 1993.
20. Interview with Kevin Benson, Ocean Grove, Victoria, 17 December 1992.
21. Interview with Tran Tan Huy, Long Dien, Dong Nai Province, Socialist Republic of Vietnam, 23 September 1993.
22. ibid.
23. ibid.
24. ibid.
25. ibid.
26. Unrecorded but witnessed interview with Nguyen Sinh at Long Phuoc, Dong Nai Province, Socialist Republic of Vietnam, 22 September 1993.
27. Dong Nai Province now encompasses Phuoc Tuy, Long Khanh, Long Binh and Bien Hoa Provinces.
28. Interview with Pham Van Canh, Vung Tau, Vung Tau Special Zone, Socialist Republic of Vietnam, 20 September 1993.
29. op cit. Interview with Tran Tan Huy.
30. ibid.
31. op cit. Interview with Pham Van Canh.
32. op cit. Interview with Nguyen Sinh.
33. Conversation with the Principal of Long Hai School, Pham Kim Luu.
34. Letter to Garry Sloane from Pham Kim Luu dated November 1992.
35. op cit. Interview with Jerry Taylor.

Chapter 10

1. Interview with Grahame Tooth, Bundanoon, New South Wales, 31 July 1993.
2. Interview with Geoffrey 'Jethro' Hannah, Singleton, New South Wales, 12 July 1993.
3. Interview with Kevin Benson, Ocean Grove, Victoria, 17 December 1992.
4. Interview with Wally Burford, Glen Forest, Perth, Western Australia, 28 March 1993.
5. Interview with Daryl Jenkin, Townsville, Queensland, 6 March 1993.

6. Interview with Peter Schuman, Perth, Western Australia, 27 March 1993.
7. Interview with Kevin Byrne, Cairns, Queensland, 6 March 1993.
8. Interview with Dean Cooke, Kallangur, Brisbane, Queensland, 21 March 1993.
9. Interview with Greg Gilbert, Windsor, Victoria, 22 May 1993.
10. Interview with Garry Sloane, Darwin, Northern Territory, 10 September 1993.
11. op cit. Interview with Geoffrey 'Jethro' Hannah.
12. Interview with Mick O'Sullivan, Fremantle, Perth, Western Australia, 27 March 1993.
13. op cit. Interview with Wally Burford.
14. op cit. Interview with Kevin Benson.
15. op cit. Interview with Grahame Tooth.
16. Interview with Bob Meehan, Moorebank, Sydney, New South Wales, 15 May 1993.
17. Interview with Kevin O'Halloran, Inverloch, Victoria, 4 January 1993.
18. op cit. Interview with Greg Gilbert.
19. op cit. Interview with Dean Cooke.
20. op cit. Interview with Peter Schuman.
21. op cit. Interview with Kevin Benson.
22. op cit. Interview with Garry Sloane.
23. op cit. Interview with Kevin Byrne.
24. op cit. Interview with Wally Burford.
25. op cit. Interview with Grahame Tooth.
26. Interview with Jerry Taylor, Batemans Bay, New South Wales, 16 October 1993.
27. ibid.
28. op cit. Interview with Grahame Tooth.
29. Interview with Warren Dowell, Merrimac, Queensland, 16 June 1993.
30. op cit. Interview with Greg Gilbert.
31. op cit. Interview with Peter Schuman.
32. op cit. Interview with Jerry Taylor.
33. ibid.

INDEX

IN GOOD COMPANY

One man's war in Vietnam

GARY MCKAY

An enthralling, accurate account of infantry soldiering in the Vietnam era. Very readable; a must for those who have never experienced combat and a vivid reminder for all veterans.

MAJOR GENERAL M.P. BLAKE AM, MC
Former CO 5th Battalion RAR

In 1968 20-year-old Gary McKay was drafted from a comfortable and carefree life of surfing and rugby football into the deadly serious preparation for war in the jungles of Vietnam. Here is his grass-roots account of the blood, sweat and tears shared by a rifle platoon in jungle warfare, a straightforward story of the fears and the camaraderie which soldiers experience in combat.

Gary McKay fashioned this account from his experience in action, leading his platoon. He wrote this story for the reader who wants to know what the soldier on the ground went through—in the fetid jungle, in battle. Anyone who wants to understand what service in south Vietnam meant to those who were there should read this book.

ILLUSTRATED

1 86448 904 9

UNCERTAIN FATE

An Australian SAS patrol in Vietnam

GRAHAM J. BRAMMER

Uncertain Fate *will stand alongside the classics written by men and women who have experienced war at first hand.*

BRIGADIER CHRIS ROBERTS

From the moment the five-man SAS patrol begins its behind-the-lines reconnaissance mission there is tension in the thick jungle air. By the time they are extracted under fire by helicopter five days later, their skills and teamwork have been tested again and again.

This is the gripping story of an Australian SAS patrol in Vietnam.

Graham J. Brammer served two operational tours of duty with the 2nd Special Air Service Squadron in Vietnam and was awarded the Order of Australia (military division) in 1990. This is his first novel.

ISBN 1 86448 793 3

200 SHOTS

Damien Parer, George Silk and the Australians at war in New Guinea

NEIL MCDONALD AND PETER BRUNE

Some of the most graphic photographs of World War II were taken in New Guinea by Damien Parer and George Silk. Peter Brune and Neil McDonald have selected the best 200 of these to tell the complete story of the Australians at war in New Guinea in as visual a way as possible. The text puts the photographs into the context of the war and combines with the captions and photographs to give a complete, comprehensive and graphic account of the Australian experience.

Neil McDonald is a film historian and the curator of *Still Action*, the first exhibition of Parer's war photography. Peter Brune is an established and successful Allen & Unwin military author.

ILLUSTRATED

ISBN 1 86448 541 8

WHERE AUSTRALIANS FOUGHT

The encyclopaedia of Australia's battles

CHRIS COULTHARD-CLARK

This work provides accounts of all the major battles fought in Australia or involving Australians overseas, giving essential facts regarding dates, places and other details. Over 300 actions are described, from battles of surprising ferocity fought between Aborigines and Europeans on Australia's frontiers and participation by colonial forces in Britain's small wars in the nineteenth century, through to the World Wars and other conflicts this century up to and including the Gulf War.

Organised chronologically, *Where Australians Fought* can be either consulted as a reference or read from start to finish as a narrative of Australian military history. It is well illustrated with contemporary drawings, photographs and explanatory maps.

Chris Coulthard-Clark, one of Australia's leading historians, has written widely in the field of Australian defence history. Among his many published titles are *Duntroon, No Australian Need Apply, Action Stations Coral Sea, The Shame of Savo, The RAAF in Vietnam, Soldiers in Politics* and *Hit My Smoke!*

ILLUSTRATED

ISBN 1 86448 611 2